FIRST PRINCIPLES

FIRST PRINCIPLES

THE CRAZY BUSINESS
OF DOING SERIOUS SCIENCE

HOWARD BURTON

KEY PORTER BOOKS

Library and Archives Canada Cataloguing in Publication

Burton, Howard, 1965–
First principles : the crazy business of doing serious
science / Howard Burton.

ISBN 978-1-55470-175-9

1. Burton, Howard, 1965–. 2. Perimeter Institute for Theoretical Physics—History. 3. Physics—Ontario—Waterloo. 4. Physics—Research—Canada. 5. Research—Ontario—Waterloo. 6. Research—Canada. 7. Physicists—Canada—Biography. I. Title.

QC16.B87A3 2009   530.092   C2008-906783-5

The publisher gratefully acknowledges the support of the Canada Council for the Arts and the Ontario Arts Council for its publishing program. We acknowledge the support of the Government of Ontario through the Ontario Media Development Corporation's Ontario Book Initiative.

We acknowledge the financial support of the Government of Canada through the Book Publishing Industry Development Program (BPIDP) for our publishing activities.

Key Porter Books Limited
Six Adelaide Street East, Tenth Floor
Toronto, Ontario
Canada M5C 1H6

www.keyporter.com

Text design: Jean Lightfoot Peters
Electronic formatting: Jean Lightfoot Peters

Printed and bound in Canada

09 10 11 12 5 4 3 2 1

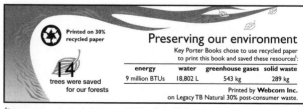

Printed on 30% recycled paper

Preserving our environment
Key Porter Books chose to use recycled paper to print this book and saved these resources[1]:

energy	water	greenhouse gases	solid waste
9 million BTUs	18,802 L	543 kg	289 kg

14 trees were saved for our forests

Printed by **Webcom Inc.** on Legacy TB Natural 30% post-consumer waste.

FSC

Mixed Sources
Product group from well-managed forests, controlled sources and recycled wood or fiber
Cert no. SW-COC-002358
www.fsc.org
© 1996 Forest Stewardship Council

[1]Estimates were made using the Environmental Defense Paper Calculator.

To Bento, who showed us the way.

CONTENTS

"Truth is its own standard"

Baruch Spinoza, *Ethics* Part II, Proposition XLI

Doctor: "Why are you depressed, Alvy?"
Alvy's Mom: "Tell Dr Flicker." *Pause.* "It's something he read."
Doctor: "Something he read?"
Alvy: "The universe is expanding."
Doctor: "The universe is expanding?"
Alvy: "Well, the universe is everything, and if it's expanding, someday it will break apart and that would be the end of everything!"
Alvy's Mom: *"What is that your business?!"*

Woody Allen, *Annie Hall*

"Physics is like sex. Sure, it may give some practical results, but that's not why we do it."

Richard Feynman

Foreword

By Roger Penrose

Who is this *Howard Burton* for whom I am writing this foreword?

Unquestionably a comic writer of exceptional talents, as the reader will readily confirm. And what a wonderfully novel idea—to invent a theoretical-physics institute, supposedly recognized around the world as a leading institution embodied by first-rank theoretical researchers engaged in probing the secrets of the universe from its smallest to largest scales!

Yet, to fantasize about resolving the mysteries of the universe is not such an unusual thing. Practically every week I receive letters or e-mails from aspiring truth seekers, each with his (yes, almost always his rather than her) exotic and unbelievable scheme for a revolutionary new theory aimed at explaining, from some seemingly outlandish perspective of swirling, twisting, spinning elementary ingredients, the entire universe (and, on their way, explaining the mysterious secrets of life and consciousness). I even have schemes of my own that, according to some colleagues and detractors, have something of a "crackpot" ring about them not dissimilar to these.

But the grandiose scheme this book describes is, in real terms, on a vastly grander scale and with a far broader perspective. What an interestingly novel idea this is for setting forth a fantasy aimed at divining the secrets of our vastly mysterious universe! Here we have a proposal to present not just one or perhaps two wild schemes, but to conjure up an entire institute aimed at probing the universe's deepest secrets, buzzing with the activities of first-class researchers: no crackpots they, but rather, each chosen with the utmost scrutiny involving impeccable recommendations from leading academic institutions around the world.

And what a clever idea it is to conjure up an almost chance encounter with Mike Lazaridis, the inventor of the ubiquitous BlackBerry—Canada's most successful worldwide electronic product—and codirector of the vast firm Research In Motion (RIM), which produces it. In a genuinely hilarious way, the author proposes to make us believe that the codirector has his own idea to initiate some such grandiose scheme—and this allows us to imagine that the necessary funding for such a research institute might be forthcoming, and that this wild idea for discovering the inner workings of the universe could be seriously supposed as coming about in reality!

So what does the author propose as the areas with which such an institute specifically concern itself? Clearly something revolutionary, in a way that befits such a genuinely twenty-first–century endeavour aimed at probing even more deeply into nature than has been done before—going beyond even the huge steps towards understanding that were achieved in the twentieth century by the great Albert Einstein and others! The magnificent physical revolutions of that century were quantum theory, telling us of the fundamentally granular nature of matter and energy, and Einstein's general theory of relativity, which tells us that space, time and gravitation are all features of an unimaginable, curved-up, four-dimensional, continuous entity.

How are we to go beyond these twentieth-century revolutions? One way may be to find an all-embracing union of the two, namely a thing referred to as "quantum gravity." This is an accepted distant goal of physicists, which has so far defeated all attempts. So what approach should our author's imagined institute adopt? The most fashionable and almost universally accepted approach in other basic physics research institutes is the famous but crazy-looking string theory. However, there are other approaches too, some looking even crazier, with philosophical standpoints completely opposed to those of string theory. So what a good idea it is to hedge bets, such that both will be taken on!

But is quantum gravity itself enough of a revolutionary idea? Perhaps we should try to improve upon one of those twentieth-century revolutions. General relativity is pretty crazy-looking, but at least it makes some kind of sense. Not so quantum mechanics! True, it has beautiful mathematics and fits all the facts; but it makes no sense at all. So our author's imagined institute proposes to put the theory to right.

I should explain that this probing of "quantum foundations" with such an end in mind is something I thoroughly approve of (as would have the quantum fathers Einstein and Erwin Schrödinger)—and I definitely believe there is a magnificent new theory waiting in the wings for some bright spark to uncover. But not many physicists would agree; so again, our author shows a canny prescience in the need for his imagined institute to balance the unfashionable with the fashionable. Accordingly, another strand to its core concerns will be the well respected field of "quantum information," which explores the mysterious subtleties and potentially extraordinary practical applications of the conventional quantum theory that has served us so well for some three-quarters of a century.

In this book, we find hilarious descriptions, through supposed encounters with numerous leading physical scientists, of how such ideas might be developed within such an institute. And all this is written with gusto and many flashes of side-splitting humour.

Yet for all this seeming improbability, there is some disturbing evidence that the Perimeter Institute might be real after all! Its name appears, for example, on an increasing number of high-quality scientific publications.

Yes, you can look it up on the Internet, and, indeed, a picture looms into view of a stunningly impressive modern building. But can we trust it? Lifelike virtual images are not so difficult to fabricate with today's technology, so we may still have serious doubts about the existence of such a place. Is this picture of "Perimeter Institute" real, or is it merely a fantastical creation—the vehicle for the author's remarkable imaginative wit?

To resolve this conundrum, you can yourself travel to the seemingly unremarkable town of Waterloo, Ontario, Canada, and make your way to 31 Caroline Street North. And lo! You will indeed find the stunningly impressive modern building you had seen on the Internet. It is, after all, no imaginary cyberspace concoction. You can thump its evidently solid concrete walls with your fist and find that they are indeed real enough. Perhaps you will overhear excited young and shabbily dressed individuals engaging in incomprehensible discussions of Planck-scale quantum geometry, of the instantaneous entanglements of quantum physics stretching over many kilometres, of quarks, strings, and super symmetry, and of the mysterious "dark matter," a completely unknown substance that comprises some 90 percent of the universe's material contents. All this in strange combinations of accents indicating participation from all around the world. You make your way to the security desk, and find that there are indeed physicists here, many of whom are distinguished worldwide in their respective fields.

But what you want is to find the mysterious Howard Burton. So you make your way to the office of the executive director. Yet there is no Howard Burton. You may mention the name, and a wistful expression will come over the face of the person you ask, as though a fleeting image has come to mind of some mythical founding deity from the distant past; but no actual human being named Howard Burton is to be found anywhere. There is no building or lecture hall named after such a person. You thump the wall again, just to check that all is not a cyberspace illusion.

So there is a mystery here. Who, indeed, is this Howard Burton who had apparently fantasized into actual existence such an impossible achievement? Perhaps, he is indeed just a comic writer—and yet, all his descriptions have a ring of truth about them, as anyone acquainted with those described herein will instantly recognize. So there is an enigma here.

And yet the enigma has an answer, and the answer is to be found in the truthful account that is this book.

Indeed, the answer to the enigma is this book!

CHAPTER ONE

Origins

Without warning, the car lurched across a lane and a half of traffic and I instinctively clutched the rear door handle in a vain attempt to steady myself. Outside the drizzle had turned to freezing rain and cars around us were slipping and sliding all across the highway, but my driver, babbling away on his wireless headset in some unknown tongue (Hindi? Swahili?), seemed oblivious to everything except his conversation, gesturing passionately to make his point to his invisible companion as we careered towards the Toronto airport.

Best not to look. I brought out my BlackBerry and tried to distract myself by reviewing recent messages, glancing at the ribbons of text as I held the rock-like gadget in my palm like some sort of secret talisman, trying to calm myself. Still, the mind wanders: What would my epitaph look like, I wondered. "Physicist dies in car crash on his way to start institute"?

It was February 2000 and I was on my way to Princeton to visit the Institute for Advanced Study and talk to some of the greatest minds alive about starting a research institute in Waterloo, Ontario. Not for the first time, I found myself wondering how on earth I had gotten myself into this situation.

The very fact that I had a job at all was a rather unexpected development. Unlike most of my acquaintances growing up in suburban Toronto, who seemed to have a fairly steady handle on how to proceed through the gates of life's unyielding algorithm—school, university, job, marriage, children, midlife crisis, reconciliation, death—I never quite got the hang of the point of it all and couldn't imagine what sort of regular employment would be sufficiently interesting and rewarding to devote the better part of one's life to. And the notion of having a boss—someone who would unhesitatingly tell you how to spend countless hours by sheer virtue of his or her position—struck me as little less than glorified slavery. Even the prestigious jobs that many in my orbit regarded as the acme of achievement, such as bank president or a brain surgeon, seemed to me rather boring and quite definitely not worth the sacrifice of time. After all, life was too short.

Of course, this is by no means a strikingly unusual view for a young man to take. The young, filled with a combination of rebelliousness, naiveté and a disproportionate sense of their own uniqueness, have been railing against the stultification of the established order for millennia; so in the overall scheme of things it is hardly shocking that someone raised in the cradle of suburbia should veer away from the twin perils of law and dentistry and direct his efforts towards less practical pursuits.

In my case, I naturally drifted towards physics. My interest in physics started in high school when I recognized that it was the only course in which one didn't have to memorize things: anyone could walk into a test with only a few general principles and derive whatever was needed to solve the problems at hand. It wasn't that I was particularly bad at memorizing, it's just that memorizing required work and I was forever looking for the easiest way out. In biology you had to learn a lot of things; in physics, on the other hand, you just had to learn a few ideas. Of course, the fact that the proto-accountants who surrounded me were continually bemoaning how difficult physics was added considerably to its appeal. There was another factor that helped too—my high-school physics teacher. Mr. Salsbury was a fairly crotchety fellow (as high-school physics teachers tend to be): an intimidating sort with a shock of white hair and a frequent scowl, who took evident delight in watching his students squirm under his steely glare. On one particular occasion we were doing an experiment to repeat Johannes Kepler's seminal work on the orbit of Mars—plotting its trajectory on paper using the same 400-year-old data of Tycho Brahe that Kepler had used. In fact, Mr. Salsbury, crafty fellow that he was, had done much more than that: determined to tangibly demonstrate to us the pitfalls of clinging too strongly to an unjustifiable theoretical framework, we were instructed to plot a circular orbit— Kepler's initial assumption, in keeping with the unquestioned consensus of his contemporary scientific colleagues. What we didn't know at the time, of course, was that this was impossible: the orbit of Mars, like all planetary orbits, isn't, in fact, circular at all, but rather, elliptical. It was Kepler, after seven painstaking years of dedicated effort, who eventually recognized this, giving birth to the modern age of astronomy and setting the stage for Newton to illustrate precisely why, under his universal law of gravitation, all such orbits would necessarily be elliptical.

Of course a circle is just a special case of an ellipse. That the ancient Greeks insisted upon circular paths for aesthetic reasons—unhesitatingly concluding that perfect circles are the only acceptable expressions of heavenly trajectories—is well known, but what is often underappreciated is that, for all the planets we can see with the naked eye, this is also a pretty darned good approximation and a clear reason why that particular bias stood up for millennia.

So when I was asked to demonstrate the circularity of the

orbit of Mars, I naturally had little difficulty in producing the desired result. Most of the points lay close enough to a circle, and with a bit of jiggling around of a few others it was not difficult to finish the task at hand. There was probably more than enough experimental error somewhere in the 400-year-old data.

When Mr. Salsbury saw my paper he swooped down upon me like a falcon on his prey, snatched the plot out of my hands and held it aloft for the entire class to see. Unbeknownst to me, I had waltzed right into his trap. Smiling mischievously, he boomed in his most stentorian voice: "BURTON! YOU'VE COOKED YOUR DATA!" My face grew flushed and I remember thinking that anyone who could spot a faker that quickly was deserving of respect. I also remember thinking that if I continued in physics, I'd better focus on theory rather than experiment. The real world had this alarming tendency not to conform to a perfectly reasonable theoretical framework.

As I moved through university, I began to appreciate that the mathematical coherence of physics that had so appealed to my high-school laziness was an essential characteristic of the field, inextricably tied to its celebrated power and elegance such that it has captivated some of the most accomplished minds of history, from the ancient Greeks to the present day. Mankind's search to understand the world around us has not only led to a stunning array of useful devices that have changed the way we live, but also stands as nothing less than one of humanity's greatest intellectual achievements, every bit as beautiful and ennobling as the most celebrated works of art or music. To understand the building blocks of matter or the structure of space and time is a truly spectacular accomplishment. That such knowledge so often ends up being of incalculable practical benefit as well only sweetens the pie.

All in all pretty heady stuff and the perfect tonic for a

young man desperate to avoid going to law school. But that was only the beginning: the wonderful thing about university is that the intellectual world seems to veritably explode before your very eyes. Soon there were countless opportunities to dip one's toes into the great rivers of knowledge and explore issues the greatest minds had wrestled with from time immemorial: What is truth? How should we structure a society? What is consciousness? What is the world made of?

The not so wonderful thing about university is that it compartmentalizes this knowledge into largely non-overlapping faculties, departments and courses—a dry, befuddling and often arbitrary process that frequently impedes a richer, more comprehensive understanding of profound issues. Of course, this is done largely for efficiency's sake: there is much to learn and only a certain number of years during which to learn the basic material. Nobody would reasonably suggest, say, replacing an undergraduate mathematics course in differential equations with one on Aristotelian ethics or Renaissance art. But it's quite another thing to suggest that aspiring physicists would concretely benefit by exposing themselves to Gottfried Leibniz and Ernst Mach, say, so as to better understand the key issues that Einstein was addressing when he developed the general theory of relativity. Unfortunately, few do.

And then there is the other direction: most non-science students are sorely ignorant of scientific accomplishments and methodology. Imagine, if you will, a university graduate from any English-speaking university who can't name at least two or three of the plays of Shakespeare: such a demonstration of ignorance would quickly result in unstinting condemnation of the student and woeful hand-wringing about falling educational standards. Now imagine a typical humanities student being asked to cite at least one of Newton's Laws of Motion, the seventeenth-century bedrock of our modern age and a rough scientific equivalent to having heard of the existence of Hamlet. In an alarmingly high number of cases, a quick apologetic shuffling of the feet followed by "I dropped physics in high school" will normally serve as ample justification of his ignorance. It is not so much the specific content, *per se*, as the methodology. Familiarity with the specifics of Newton's Laws probably won't directly impinge on one's day to day existence any more than familiarity with the any of the particular lines of Macbeth, but both provide a vital conceptual framework to comprehend the world around us. The vast majority of humanities students complete an entire advanced education without any real exposure to scientific thinking—the best that one can hope for is for the aspiring English major to stumble across the odd "science for poets" course to fulfill a stray elective. In an age when so many of our key political decisions are scientifically related (stem cell research, climate change, nuclear power), the lack of broad-based technical understanding amongst our policy makers, who almost exclusively come from the humanities or social sciences, is particularly concerning and is only further exacerbated by this widespread resonance of ignorance amongst the general public.

In my case, the core issue that set me on my personal ping-pong match between the sciences and the humanities was my encounter with quantum mechanics. Physics, you understand, is not typically a field loaded with potential for fame, fortune or even moderate social opportunities—as such, it tends to attract a category of person for whom such issues are not principal driving factors. But the one thing most physicists take considerable pride in is its no-nonsense intellectual bedrock. Chemistry, we say with a patronizing lilt, is merely applied physics, while biology is applied chemistry. When a doctor tells you that your likelihood of getting a disease is raised or lowered by some percentage as a result of some particular action, we shake our heads sadly and reflect that they only have the foggiest picture of what is really going on. In physics, you see, we know. For while a biologist's models will reduce at some level to chemistry, and a chemist's will in turn reduce to physics, a physicist should be able to give you the straight goods at the end of the day or else straightforwardly admit her current ignorance. To a physicist there is no possibility of putting off difficult questions by appealing to some other underlying model or framework—it is, quite simply, our business to find out what that framework is. In this way, physics is naturally the "queen of the sciences," occupied with providing the ultimate foundational understanding of the laws of nature and thus standing at the base of the entire scientific enterprise. The only people who dare to challenge the supremacy of the physicists in this reductionist landscape are the pure mathematicians, but with their peculiar metaphysical tendencies and perverse determination to manipulate symbols independent of the world around them, they are too far gone to recognize that much of what they do is simply irrelevant and that the only real point of mathematics is to be a tool for us physicists. Such, at any rate, is the physics culture that one is indoctrinated with, subtly and not so subtly, from the early undergraduate years onwards.

So imagine my surprise and disappointment when I finally began to study the famous theory of quantum mechanics I had heard so much about—the one that even the mighty Einstein couldn't come to terms with because of its seemingly bizarre intrinsic statistical nature ("God does not play dice" and all of that)—and was presented with nothing more than a series of curious mathematical rules to manipulate often strikingly ill-defined terms. So much for the "buck stops here/we're the reality guys" swaggering spirit I had known and loved.

Particles, I was told, had a wave-like aspect associated with them, from which we could calculate probabilities that were overwhelmingly accurate predictions of microscopic behaviour. Great. But what was this wave function really? Did it exist or was it just some sort of magical calculational device? Perhaps it just reflected how much we happened to know. If it was real, where was it? And if it wasn't real, what was going on—how did it work? And then there was the act of making a measurement itself. In the classical world, making a measurement was no big deal—you could watch something happen or not, and it either happened or didn't. In the quantum world, on the other hand, making a measurement was a very big deal: by measuring a quantum system, according to the theory, you were profoundly affecting the wave function that described the system. But how? And what did it mean to make a measurement? What constitutes a measurement, exactly? Why do only classical objects (like lab technicians) seem capable of making quantum measurements? And anyway, aren't they made up of quantum particles? How does that work, precisely? WHAT ON EARTH WAS GOING ON?

Today, these perplexing concerns are often at least tangentially addressed in the undergraduate physics curriculum, sometimes in coordination with courses devoted to the burgeoning field of quantum information theory. But in the mid-1980s, most physics departments simply weren't recognizing these issues at all, leaving the frustrated undergraduate to simply stew and become all the more frustrated. It was like a gigantic cover-up: anyone asking a professor a question about the foundations of quantum theory was likely to be stonily informed that quantum mechanics was the most tested and successful theory that ever existed and that was that. Your job as a physicist was to adeptly manipulate the symbols of this rather odd chess game. If you stubbornly persisted in your line of questioning ("Fine, but what does it all *mean*?"), you were more often than not coldly directed to the philosophy department for further inquiries. So off I went.

In the land of philosophy, things were radically different, and my first impressions were ones of unbounded delight. There I found a veritable treasure trove of activity: pointed debates on foundations of quantum theory and illuminating discussions on many substantive issues. I also had the chance to read original papers by the greats of twentieth-century physics. In a typical physics class, historical missteps, confrontations and troublesome hypotheses are airbrushed away as students are taught the finished theory as some sort of monolithic, unquestioned whole, a complete package that somehow sprung fully formed into existence, like Athena from the head of Zeus. Going back to the original sources—reading the likes of Schrödinger, Wolfgang Pauli and Werner Heisenberg—not only palpably demonstrates that this is not so (and goes a considerable way towards reassuring the anxious student who is frustrated that he cannot immediately grasp all the subtleties of the formalism), it is also one of the most effective ways to highlight the conceptual confusion and ambiguities that still beset the theory, many of which have been swept under the rug for decades.

The cultural divide between physics and philosophy was different in other ways as well. In a typical physics seminar, it is not at all uncommon for a disenchanted audience member to pop up from his chair and protest that the speaker must be dead wrong because he hasn't taken into account some issue or has forgotten about some effect. If the issue is deemed sufficiently serious, the speaker must be prepared to respond on the spot, often with detailed calculations to prove his point.

In a philosophy seminar, on the other hand, things are considerably more relaxed. At the conclusion of almost every talk there will invariably be someone who stands up and politely states: "I'm not quite sure I understand that point you were making a while back when you spoke about such and such, could you please explain it a little further?" The speaker will then think carefully for a moment and give a response that invariably uses at least a few stock philosophical words, which seems to do the trick: "When I was referring to X, I was specifically referring to X in its ontological sense rather than its epistemic effect—that is, X qua X." This will likely provoke a fair amount of thoughtful head nodding from the audience, with the result being that any further discussions on the matter will be postponed until after the formal talk. It was all far more civilized and nonconfrontational, if a little jargon-dependent.

I had great fun with my philosophical colleagues for a while: arguing subtle matters of interpretation, wading through the turbidity of Niels Bohr's prose (an experience I don't recommend to anyone, by the way, and a strong counterargument for the usefulness of consulting primary sources) and generally clarifying my specific sources of confusion. But after some time it occurred to me that I wasn't really making any genuine progress toward understanding quantum mechanics. I had a much better sense of what little I actually understood—which was useful, if vaguely depressing—and a clearer sense of what, precisely, the key issues were, but I was lacking the knowledge and tools to go any further and concretely address them.

However commendable the philosophers' determination to focus on essential problems with quantum theory, it was becoming increasingly clear to me that most of them lacked the boldness and determination to do much more than merely highlight the conceptual difficulties. It was a deeply unsatisfactory situation: physicists had grown increasingly blasé about deeply understanding their theories and stopped asking essential questions, while philosophers of science were asking the right questions but were largely unprepared and unmotivated to develop comprehensive solutions

With all of the adolescent indignation I could muster, I condemned this bizarre schism between the worlds of physics and philosophy of physics. If the theory didn't make sense somehow, a sensible way forward must be discovered. If it was working remarkably well in its nonsensical state, so much more challenging for the fixer, but that was no excuse for not trying to get out of our present conceptual muddle. In late night donut shop conversations with my fellow intellectual travelers we lamented this curious state of affairs and dreamed of a day when content would trump form, when the sociology of science would be liberated from the counter-productive labels of "physicist" or "philosopher" and smart, motivated people would be encouraged to gather to work on pivotal, difficult questions of fundamental import. This was hardly an inconceivable Utopia. After all, wasn't Schrödinger a philosopher/physicist? Wasn't Heisenberg? Wasn't Einstein? But it was becoming harder and harder to imagine turning back the clock to return to the spirit of the great Solvay conferences in the 1920s. Today's Einsteins had moved on, pursuing the likes of superstring theory with its formidable mathematical sophistication and considerably looser philosophical framework— physics had entered the world of the feasible and had long since lost its philosophical underpinnings: if a theory was somehow mathematically possible, then it could be taken seriously. Of course, this was, in many ways, quite understandable: physicists were weary of banging their heads against the wall trying to understand the foundations of quantum theory and had long since moved on, with often spectacular results: developments in particle physics, condensed matter physics and cosmology (to name but a few) had opened up rich areas of understanding and brave new worlds to explore. But one couldn't help feeling that something had been left behind, that some important old problems lay unresolved and that we were somehow moving farther and farther away from the correct means to address them. Sooner or later, at least some of these fundamental holes in our understanding that we were blithely sweeping under the rug would simply have to trip us up.

I returned to the world of physics by way of England for a change of scene, enrolling in a one-year Master's program at Imperial College in London. While I was there, I met two people of considerable significance to my own personal development: my future wife, Irena, and Chris Isham (I actually met Isham first, but I fear for my marriage if I mention them in chronological order).

In Isham I found the very essence of the consummate philosopher/physicist that I had imagined during my late night coffee klatches: a profoundly knowledgeable person with supreme pedagogical skills and a rapid fire delivery, Isham was well known to be one of Imperial's most inspiring lecturers. He was one of those rare professors whose material seems completely transparent while lecturing, but suddenly becomes opaque the moment he leaves the room. I took two courses from Chris that year—group theory and differential geometry (both of which were later turned into textbooks). In keeping with his foundational interests, the group theory course contained a diversion of two lectures on the foundations of quantum theory, and I was both surprised and appalled to find that I learned more of substance in those two classes than I had in all of my previous experiences in both philosophy and physics. Clearly going back to the rigorous bosom of theoretical physics had been the right decision.

But it was the differential geometry course that really captivated me: here was mathematics the way I had never seen it before, filled with meaning and structure and a necessary unifying force for physical theories, strikingly different from the usual "mathematics is just a tool" idiom that pervaded my physics upbringing. From the glimpses I received through Isham's intellectual peregrinations I began to consider that the world might somehow be deeply, fundamentally mathematical and that physicists, with their pragmatic tendency to pluck any mathematical device or technique from its surrounding context to develop their theoretical bouillabaisse, could be missing something truly important. Taking the mathematics really seriously, understanding the mathematical structure at its deepest level, might just enable us to pare away much of the ambiguity and confusion around our current physical theories to somehow understand what the fundamental issues really were as a necessary precursor to solving them. In short, maybe mathematics wasn't simply "a language" to best express the problem, but perhaps in some profound, mysterious way it might be something considerably more: an integral aspect of "the answer."

This mathematical epiphany was a positively radiating experience that was only slightly tainted by the fact that I hadn't the vaguest idea of what I was actually doing. Notwithstanding my newfound metaphysical scaffolding, my facility to perform earthly calculations in the subject matter was still very much opaque, resulting in me receiving a thunderous 23 percent on the final exam (and hence the course—such is the British system). Given my complete lack of practical understanding at the time, one of the most enduring mysteries of my life is how I might have amassed even 23 percent, but I certainly wasn't deterred by it: for better or worse, I have never been overwhelmingly concerned about grades per se. Inspired by Isham's luminous example, I resolved to master this fascinating material at some point.

Later that year I fell in love again, this time in the more standard way, which resulted in me spending several years in Holland to be with my Dutch fiancée, an aspiring and ambitious corporate lawyer. This suited me just fine: I fancied myself sufficiently modern and secure in my masculinity to be a "kept man," happily embracing the tantalizing prospect that she would spend her days earning the big money while I puttered around the house thinking (or at least trying to think) grand thoughts.

Unfortunately, the PhD system in Holland at the time was considerably different from that in North America or the United Kingdom, and not terribly receptive to foreigners, so it wasn't until a few years later when I returned to Canada with Irena that I had the opportunity to follow up on my determination to formally immerse myself in the world of scholarship and learn more about the intriguing concepts that had so captivated me in England. After groping around for a suitable program, I eventually settled on the University of Waterloo, where Rob Mann agreed to be my supervisor. In a fit of candour and open-mindedness sadly atypical of most academicians, Rob told me that I was welcome to pursue my geometrical agenda (which had become somewhat more refined during the intervening years) despite the fact that he was not an expert in this particular area—in other words, I could do, roughly speaking, whatever I wanted.

This freedom was essential, because at that point I had learned a thing or two about professional possibilities in theoretical physics, and the picture wasn't pretty. Despite the rhetoric one sometimes hears in the media about a future shortage of university professors, academic jobs in theoretical physics were (and still are) exceedingly difficult to come by, with even the most objectively unappealing positions being hotly contested. The standard route to academic success

involved completing one's doctorate at a sufficiently preco-
cious age at one of the world's elite institutions as the protégé
of some iconic member of the physics establishment, obtain-
ing several postdoctoral fellowships at similarly impressive
establishments (all the while publishing increasingly substantial and impressive results) before eventually settling down to
become a junior faculty member at some reasonably solid university. I had missed the boat on that route, and the
alternative—living the life of a penurious, peripatetic postdoc,
dragging one's family hither and yon while desperately apply-
ing for faculty positions at the likes of Possum Trot, Alabama,
was hardly an inspiring vision of the future. Even law school
had to be better than that.

Recognizing reality, I deliberately opted out, mentally, of a
future in physics: I would regard the PhD as a four-year hia-
tus from the "real world" and use it as a unique opportunity
to drink deeply from the cup of knowledge. This somewhat
bleakly realistic approach had, ironically, a most liberating
effect: while I watched many of my colleagues scramble to
publish largely insignificant results to buttress their CVs with
ever-rising numbers of publications or divert themselves from
their core interests to pursue more fashionable lines of
research activity, I simply focused my time and effort on learning fascinating stuff. If I was going to be self-indulgent, by
golly I would be rigorous about it.

Once enrolled in the PhD program, the first thing I did
was to pick up my old differential geometry notes from Chris
Isham's class, determined to work through them steadily to
develop an intimate knowledge of the material (in a heady
display of uncharacteristic diligence, I even noted down all
the typos, spelling mistakes and conceptual omissions in the
text and sent them to Chris for his future reference. He
replied graciously, thanking me for my efforts, doubtless

wondering to himself what sort of a pathetic creature would spend his time in such a way. Years later, when we developed a personal relationship, he was amused to discover that I was the author of such perversely meticulous notes). From there I began to build on this knowledge to explore a host of related issues in physics and higher mathematics. One area that naturally captivated my attention was the field of quantum gravity. Ever since the development of quantum theory in the 1920s, physicists have been trying to reconcile the inherent discreteness of the quantum world with the smooth continuity of Einstein's notions of space and time as outlined in his general theory of relativity. For many physicists, the unification of these two pillars of twentieth-century physics is the ultimate quest—a sort of "holy grail" of contemporary physics. Spurred on by this goal, many exciting and wondrous new developments have occurred in both mathematics and physics, but a final theory of quantum gravity remains as elusive as ever.

Given the subtleties and complexities involved in sorting through these issues, this was certainly disappointing, if not particularly surprising, but what did shock me was my growing awareness that the field was rife with dissention and sociological barriers. Superstring theorists, for example, did not interact in any meaningful scientific way with people pursuing other approaches to the problem, and vice versa. Worse still, the groups were downright hostile to one another, lobbing ad hominem and defamatory attacks across one another's bows, condemning mountains of work with a dismissive (and often ignorant) wave of the hand while trumping up the claims of their own theories well beyond any defensible level. It was simply ridiculous: here were highly educated, mathematically sophisticated people, who had dedicated their very lives to attacking one of the most profound scientific problems of our age, and they were simply refusing to engage with one another, separating off into rival sects like high-school gangs. It was not only childish, it was unproductive. The best way to make progress in any field is to be surrounded by people who rigorously question one's assumptions; and one of the more frustrating aspects of talking to these people was that, for all their evident cleverness and mathematical sophistication, they often didn't even realize what key assumptions their theories were making in the first place.

My first, albeit indirect, encounter with superstring theory was a perfect case in point. As a PhD student, I spent a good deal of time talking with Nemanja Kaloper, then a postdoctoral fellow at the University of Waterloo and now a faculty member at University of California at Santa Cruz. Actually, Nemanja did most of the talking, particularly once he discovered that I had gone over to "the dark side" by opting to spend time learning various non-superstring approaches to quantum gravity instead of his beloved superstring theory. For Nemanja, this was nothing more than a time-wasting combination of obstinacy and simple-mindedness: superstring theory simply was quantum gravity; trying to learn quantum gravity without string theory made about as much sense as writing music without notes. Nemanja, it should be stressed, was obviously an extremely able thinker and a far better physicist than I would ever be, which only made the experience all the more frustrating. The fact that he strongly disagreed with some of my (admittedly naive) conceptual difficulties with string theory (which principally centred around what theorists call the issue of "background independence") was hardly a big deal. Far more troubling was the fact that he never seemed terribly interested in understanding what they were in the first place.

The more I kept my eyes open the more I realized that Nemanja's behaviour was hardly unusual: indeed, such counterproductive squabbling and rampant dogmatism existed on all sides of the issue, making it hard to see how any genuine progress in any direction might be attained in the near future. There was an exceptional amount of preaching to the converted going on everywhere, with different approaches entrenched in rival camps that seemed determined to invoke all sorts of bizarre and specious sociological arguments to justify their cause ("We must be right because we are the most popular and therefore have objectively convinced the most people to our cause!" "We would have solved the problem years ago if these upstarts hadn't come along and nefariously sucked all of those people [and funding] towards their evil agenda!")

The Olympian heights of pure reason, when examined in more detail, turned out to be reducible to a furiously contested form of highly esoteric tribal warfare. Disappointing stuff, but there was nothing I could do about it. So with a sad shake of my head, I turned back to my studies and finished off the PhD. My four-year sabbatical from reality was ending, as I had known it would all along. It was time to move on to pay the proverbial piper.

But how? An obvious first approach to consider was mathematical finance. By the late 1990s, mathematical modelling of financial instruments was a well established route for pecuniary, if not spiritual, success for people with advanced physics and mathematics degrees; and while I had no particular interest, love or enthusiasm for the intricacies of derivative modelling, the notion of a solid, regular salary was, indeed, beginning to grow on me. During my doctorate, Irena and I had started a family, and any further thoughts of continuing a monastic existence devoted to wrestling with mathematical abstractions, however profound, was steadily losing its appeal.

In the early 1990s, it seemed that anyone with a math or physics PhD was snapped up on Wall Street as soon as they wished, but by the late 1990s things had changed and a doctorate alone was hardly sufficient to pique interest. The market was roaring and jobs were still plentiful, but "financial mathematics" courses and degree programs had sprung up across the continent and there was now an expectation that one had to have some relevant knowledge of the field in addition to a demonstrated record of mathematical competence. Still, it seemed a reasonably straightforward road to pursue and, after discussing the matter with various people (among whom was the Caltech physicist Mark Wise, whom I first met at a Toronto Starbucks through a family friend and subsequently encountered at many key times throughout the next eight years), I plowed through a few books on the subject and hustled around to land a few job interviews. After some time I procured an entry-level opportunity on Wall Street to begin in the fall of 1999.

The prospect of being in New York excited me, but nothing else did. The spectre of occupying my days with the mindless drudgery of programming financial algorithms immersed in the superficial, mercenary culture of Wall Street while physically confined in a suit and tie (invariably yellow, for some reason—I've never understood Wall Street's fascination with yellow as its colour of choice for physical constriction. Some sign of rebelliousness perhaps? A quixotic hankering for a gold standard?) was almost more than I could bear. I avoided law school for this? Quite the Pyrrhic victory.

I began to frantically rethink things. This was 1999—a time, you will recall, when alarmingly large numbers of people were getting filthy rich, often by doing nothing much at all. Unknown companies that had no product, no business plan and no real ideas were suddenly worth staggering amounts of money after a successful initial public offering, with a seemingly limitless queue of investors anxious to come aboard and drive the stock still higher. I was supposed to be a clever guy; surely there must be a better way to make a living in this climate than living in a New Jersey suburb and commuting daily to a cubicle in Manhattan.

With growing desperation, I went to the business library at the University of Toronto and began to research a few companies that seemed reasonably interesting, potentially allowing me to stave off suicide for at least another five years or so. I had no real idea what I might do there, but then, I had no real understanding of what most people did in their jobs anyway. The one thing I was sure of was that writing to human resources departments would be a complete waste of time; I could already imagine my CV fluttering into the recycling box, guided by some dutiful automaton who had quickly determined that I was not the requisite software engineer, MBA or whatever. No, what was needed was to capture the attention of someone in a more executive position, to somehow personally connect with a high-powered individual who had enough experience not to be limited by my apparent, yet obviously false, inappropriateness. The business sections of newspapers were consistently filled with senior executives lamenting the fact that they were having grave difficulty finding top talent for their organizations. Very well then, I would take the bull by the horns and write to some CEOs directly; they wanted top talent and here I was. The fact that neither of us knew of the other was just a technical detail that had to be circumvented.

After a bit of time, I found twenty or so companies to target. Most were in California, but some were in Canada and a few were quite close to Toronto. I remember being struck by the fact that one of the companies strangely possessed two CEOs. They made some sort of wireless device and were based, ironically enough, in Waterloo, but I had never heard of them before—perhaps not surprising given that I had lived in Toronto throughout the entire four years of my doctorate. Their name struck me as rather intriguing, though: Research In Motion. What to do with the problem of two CEOs? No problem: I would write to both.

CHAPTER TWO

Meeting Mike

I reflected for a day or two on what to write in my covering letter. What was needed, I concluded, was a personal touch: a display of humour, a relief from the tedium for those who must be constantly beseeched from all quarters. I'd have to find a way to stand out from the crowd. After further deliberation, I concluded that I might as well just be myself. If they wanted to meet me, they'd find out who I was sooner or later anyway.

So I wrote a covering letter explaining that I had a PhD in physics and an MA in philosophy, that I possessed all the necessary skills to be a whiz-bang employee in whatever capacity they could imagine (technical, mathematical, analytical, communicative etc.), that I had recently procured employment in the financial sector but was intrigued by their company and thought it was worth investigating career possibilities with their dynamic organization instead. I ended with the line: "Please help save me from a lucrative career on Wall Street," threw in my CV and sent it off.

I received a few lukewarm acknowledgements, but nothing terribly captivating. A week later, however, there was an email from Mike Lazaridis, one of the two CEOs of Research In Motion.

Dear Howard,
I just received your resume and am intrigued. I called
your home number but you were not in. I look forward
to speaking with you. You may be interested in what I
have to say.

Well, *that* sounded different.

I e-mailed him back immediately and we set up a time for a
phone call. It was a wide-ranging, fast-moving conversation
that touched mostly on some strange combination of science,
science fiction and prospective philanthropy. Lazaridis, it
seemed, had made up his mind to personally donate a substantial fraction of his private wealth towards some yet to be
determined scientific endeavour, and he was interested in my
opinions on the matter. Needless to say, this was hardly what I
had envisioned—and, as he had predicted, I was interested (if
still quite perplexed) by what he had to say. His principal focus,
perhaps unsurprisingly, was communications: how could we
harness our modern understanding of the physical world to one
day build a whole class of profoundly innovative, if not downright exotic, devices? What new physics or understanding might
make such a thing possible? Well, I murmured, feeling rather
taken aback by this unusual turn of events, I didn't really know.
There was quantum mechanics, of course, but the prevailing
wisdom (backed up by a few rather solid mathematical theo-
rems) was that it was nigh on impossible to exploit its nonlocal
weirdness to actually send messages in some original way that
might circumvent Einstein's special relativity. Still, my mention
of quantum theory struck a decidedly responsive chord.

"Quantum mechanics!" he enthused. "Absolutely!
Anything else?"

"Hmmm," I responded hesitantly, "I suppose you might
think of gravitational waves."

Even within the bizarre context of this most unusual conversation, such a suggestion was straining the very limits of credulity. Despite decades of heroic efforts, gravitational radiation, long predicted from Einstein's general theory of relativity, had never been directly observed. Few physicists question its existence—in fact, the 1993 Nobel Prize in Physics was awarded to two researchers who successfully calculated precise gravitational wave effects on the orbits of binary pulsars—but owing to their extreme faintness we have still not been able to even witness the things directly, let alone manipulate them. To add insult to injury, even if we somehow could use gravitational waves, they wouldn't go any faster than electromagnetic waves anyway, so it was hard to imagine the communication advantage. To suggest using gravitational waves as a basis for future communications was roughly equivalent to doing deep sky astronomy with a flash Polaroid camera—worse, probably. Still, I felt forced to say something.

The truth was, you see, that as a theoretical physicist I wasn't regularly in the habit of contemplating such things. Ask me to derive the field equations from a particular Lagrangian and I was quite confident that I would be up for the task. Query me about the mathematical structure of gauge theories and I could hold forth reasonably convincingly. I might, if pressed, even manage to say something fairly cogent about deeper conceptual issues about our current understanding of physical law. But speculate on applied technology? Ponder futuristic communication devices? You might as well question me on the finer points of Australian Rules Football.

To an outsider, such a flagrant lack of technological orientation in someone extensively trained in the physical sciences might well seem unusual, but it is, generally speaking, par for the course. Most theoretical physicists I know are not terribly adept at actually fixing or building things. While there certainly have been several cases of exceptional theorists with an interest in applied technology (Richard Feynman and John von Neumann are two celebrated examples), the vast majority of them seem to be rather in the Einsteinian mould of things—preferring to spend their time plumbing the depths of their understanding with pencil and paper rather than examining actual mechanical devices that tend to be frighteningly complicated and a far cry from the idealized models of frictionless planes, spherical symmetry and extraneous real-world effects that can be "turned off" at the wave of a hand.

Engineers, of course, are the ones who typically build things. In the hierarchy of academe, physicists invariably look down upon engineers, regarding them as a sort of practical underclass: incapable of the requisite amount of abstraction to appreciate the totality of natural law, but damned useful people to have around to build stuff and fix it when it goes awry. The standard practice of saddling physics graduate students with teaching introductory mechanics courses to intimidating hordes of vacuous, beer-swilling engineering undergraduates does much to perpetuate this negative engineering stereotype, but it may not be the only factor. By any reasonable measure, engineers tend to be considerably more social than physicists; and the consequent Brahmin-like retreat to the perspective that we are keepers of the secrets of the universe occasionally provides momentary comfort as we watch the tech billionaires zoom by in their Ferraris.

Such was the culture. But now I had somehow gained the attention of an engineer who wanted something more—an engineer who had achieved success by all the standard societal metrics, but was interested in using his wealth to go further still. But where?

A few days later we arranged to meet in person for the first time. Mike was giving a presentation to executives at Nortel

Networks and we agreed to rendezvous in the parking lot of their Brampton office.

"I drive a silver BMW and have white hair," he said.

"And I'll be driving a beige Corolla," I replied, feeling very much like I was on my way to an encounter with Deep Throat.

At the end of the call, he urged me to keep the entire conversation and our upcoming meeting strictly to myself, which I had no problem agreeing to, having not the slightest clue what we were talking about anyway.

When I arrived at the Nortel parking lot, I quickly spotted a white-haired guy chatting casually to a few other guys in suits near the entrance. I parked my Corolla and tried to sit unobtrusively in my car until they had finished their discussion. After a few minutes of this I began to get concerned: Maybe he was standing there waiting for me? Maybe I should get out of the car and introduce myself? But then, he seemed to be quite concerned about this whole confidentiality issue— it all seemed very hush-hush. I decided to compromise and get out of my car, shutting the door with appropriate force to be noticed if one was paying attention to such things, but not so hard as to necessarily draw attention to myself. Nothing. I got back in the car. A few minutes later I got back out of the car, shutting it a little bit harder and this time walking around the vehicle. Still nothing. At this point, it occurred to me that I would make a shockingly bad spy as I was behaving in the most conspicuous manner possible. I quietly got back into my car and picked up a book, peeking over the cover every so often to watch them continuing their conversation. Finally, the two suits then drifted over to the Nortel building while Mike made his way over to my car. We shook hands and decided to move out together in his car to look for an appropriate place to talk.

We settled on a dark Italian restaurant in some suburban

strip mall where we were solemnly guided to a table by a tall waiter with a funereal disposition and a green serviette draped rather forlornly over his arm. It was 2:30 in the afternoon and the restaurant was completely empty.

The strangeness continued. Mike talked feverishly, with increasing animation. "You're welcome to a job at RIM if you want," he said. "We're expanding and we're always looking for bright people, but as I told you on the phone the other day I've been doing quite a bit of thinking and I'm ready to do something quite different, something really interesting."

Well, sure, I remember thinking to myself, there are many more interesting things to do than work for a company that makes gadgets, however useful; but what, precisely, did he have in mind? The only thing he had mentioned over the phone was that he was prepared to sink a lot of money into something, but it was far from clear what.

He returned to the theme of our previous phone call and began to talk with renewed fervour about a whole host of issues, from new forms of communication to new forms of energy to the mysteries of quantum theory. As someone who had hung around physics and philosophy departments for a sizeable chunk of my life, I had been approached by my fair share of people spouting incoherent ravings about the future (more often than not citing the boundless mysteries of quantum theory and how it was related to both consciousness and the *I Ching*) and so found myself instinctively searching for the exits. But this case was different: I had contacted him. Worse still, I was looking for a job. So I listened.

And the more I listened, the more confused I became. Some of what he said struck me as naive, some of it perhaps just plain crazy. But other parts were eminently reasonable, even insightful. It was clear from his comments that he was the technical force behind the BlackBerry, and his passion and knowledge for engineering rested on a firm, practical footing of solid accomplishment.

He talked about how he laughs to himself when people tell him how "high tech" the BlackBerry is. "It's a very sophisticated piece of technology: antenna design, microprocessors, and so forth. But its fundamental principles of communication are based on nineteenth-century physics!" he cried, pounding the table. And of course he was right. But it was hardly clear what else I could do other than just to nod my head.

He continued in this vein almost nonstop for the first hour or two, periodically interrupting himself to whip out his BlackBerry and glance down at it for messages to momentarily respond to before careering off in another direction like some insatiable windup doll. It was as though it was all pouring out of him, all of this stuff inside him that had been bottled up for so long and he had decided, for whatever reason, to unload it all on me.

Why me? The letter, clearly, was the start—he had been impressed by what he had read, and perhaps his interest had been piqued by encountering a physicist. But it was more than that; throughout the weirdness of the conversation, he was making solid eye contact: Mike was reading me as he spoke, watching my face carefully to assess my reactions to what he was saying. It was a most uncomfortable situation and hardly seemed fair—he was the one with the wild speculations and I was the one being examined.

And another thing: the man had charisma; it was undeniable. While he carried on, buoyed by the passion of his convictions, he nonetheless managed to exude an honesty, a fundamental decency that pervaded all of his discourse and made him, well, likeable. If he was a nut, he was an entirely different sort of nut from those I had encountered before.

After the third hour he finally slowed down and pronounced almost wistfully: "Something big is going to happen. I can feel it."

Uh-oh, I thought, here we go. I don't have the highest regard for intuition.

"You look skeptical," he said. It was less an observation than an accusation.

"Well," I replied, choosing my words carefully, "I'm not really sure if I'm skeptical or not. The truth is I don't really know what we're talking about."

"I'm talking about doing something *big*. Something important. I'm talking about investing lots of money in *something important*. Are you interested?"

IN WHAT? I DON'T EVEN KNOW WHAT WE'RE TALKING ABOUT! I screamed to myself.

"I suppose so," I said.

He turned to the napkin in front of him and took out a pen and wrote something on it.

"Does this seem reasonable?" he asked.

What is this, now, some secret code? I wondered to myself. A combination to a safety deposit box in the Cayman Islands? Alien transcriptions from a landing strip near Roswell?

He passed the napkin to me in silence and I glanced down to see a number written on it. This was, I suddenly grasped with a flash of insight, the salary negotiation segment of this bizarre afternoon. The number was not a captivatingly high one, I must sadly confess, but seemed not inappropriate for a standard entry-level position in some company. The only difficulty was that no other evidence was pointing in that direction.

"Sure." I returned the napkin. The whole thing was completely surreal. Why spend time haggling about compensation for a position that was so completely undefined and most likely completely fictitious?

He seemed happy with this and we sat in silence for a few minutes.

"So," I cautiously ventured, "what would you actually like me to *do*?" We had been talking, as best as I could determine, about money, about physics, about the future. If he wanted research, I could give him research—reports on the return on investment in physics research, reports on the status of research and development in Canada and around the world, recommendations on best investment choices, etc. Never mind that I knew precious little about the details; I had been trained as an academic: I could write reports.

"I don't want you to *do* anything," he responded quickly. "I just want you to think. This reminds me of when I started RIM. Soon you'll have more to do than you can possibly handle and not much time to think. Now you should just spend time thinking and planning."

"Okay." I could think, after all. I had never felt comfortable with the whole job thing, but I was fairly confident of my thinking ability.

We shook hands and left the restaurant on those terms, and as I walked with him out towards his car blinking into the bright sunlight, I had the curious feeling of having somehow passed an interview for a position completely unknown to either one of us.

On the drive back home I stopped at a pay phone to call my wife to tell her the news.

"I think I have a job," I announced.

"What do you mean, you think you have a job? Is this about that banking thing in New York?" Women are such sticklers for details.

"No, no," I corrected her. "This is completely different. I met this guy, you see, and we went to a restaurant and he showed me a napkin—completely different story altogether."

"I see," she said sceptically. "A different job. And what is it that you have to do in this different job?"

"I have to think!"

"You have to think?"

"Yes. It's kind of complicated."

"I see."

But she didn't *see*, of course, and neither did I. I told her the rest of the details of my curious lunch once I got home, but it hardly seemed the sort of thing to take very seriously. After all, it had been an extremely strange experience and by the next morning the odds of any sort of repeat encounter didn't seem terribly high. Two days later, however, I received an envelope by courier. Inside was a cheque—an advance of my two weeks' salary as per our napkin agreement.

Well, well, I muttered to myself with surprise when I opened the envelope. So this whole business was actually serious after all. The pressure is on: I'd better start thinking!

CHAPTER THREE

Starting to Think

I was living in The Beaches area of Toronto at the time, which, with its copious parkland and lengthy boardwalk along the shore of Lake Ontario, happens to be a particularly good place for reflection. As soon as I received the cheque, I staggered outside to think—off to work! I ambled along the boardwalk on my customary trajectory that I had taken, unpaid, hundreds of times before, ruminating on the sudden strangeness of my world as I watched children build sandcastles and preening beach volleyballers digging for glory.

A name, I realized, was essential to move forward. As ridiculous as my situation seemed, receiving cheques from a mysterious source 100 kilometres away for daily contemplation, a name would give the project an air of solidity, a whiff of realism. Moreover, the very act of coming up with a name might give the project some clarity, some direction.

The thing should probably be an institute, I decided, because institute is one of those remarkable words that exudes both gravitas and nothing in particular at the same time: Brookings Institute, Institute for Foreign Languages, Institute for Alien Abductions, not to mention mental institute—the world was chalk full of institutes, some eminently reputable, some flagrantly prosaic, others completely flaky;

it could certainly do with one more, one way or the other.

But what kind of institute? That was the question. Typically, scientific institutes are either named after famous people (the Albert Einstein Institution, the Niels Bohr Institute, etc.) or refer stoically to their function: Institute for Advanced Study, Institute for Nuclear Theory and so forth. The name Institute for Theoretical Physics (ITP) was already taken, belonging to a prestigious centre in Santa Barbara (now renamed the Kavli Institute for Theoretical Physics), and, besides, was a little bit dry.

I walked towards the water's edge and began idly tossing some rocks into the lake. Okay, I thought to myself, let's just pretend. Pretend this is serious. Pretend someone just handed you a huge sum of money to build whatever you thought best to further the aims of physics research. No constraints. What would you do?

It wasn't as though I had never thought about the question before—as it happens, I had spent countless hours in late night doughnut shops lamenting the curious state of the field and imagining all sorts of possible ways forward. But this was different: now I was forced to somehow take it seriously, now I was, bizarrely, being paid to think of this stuff. Now it was, for all intents and purposes, real. Or at least real enough to take seriously for a little while.

So be it. Time to put my money—or at least somebody's money—where my mouth was. I began to reflect back upon all of my past frustrations with the world of physics and academeme—all of the little things I had observed as I made my way through various programs and degrees: the polarization and enmity among the different subgroups married to their own agenda, the constant willingness to shuffle vital foundational issues under the rug to be dealt with "only after getting tenure" (i.e., often never), the general deadening conservatism of academe. There was very little room for unorthodoxy; there was very little room for fun. For all their evident brilliance and intellectual sophistication, at the end of the day, these guys took themselves a bit too seriously. What they needed, to put it bluntly, was a bit of shaking up.

Then I thought of Mike. Here was a guy who obviously wasn't afraid to take a few risks, to try something new. However unusual the last week had been, however skeptical any reasonable person might be about these matters in the cold light of day, it certainly was different. Maybe we weren't such an odd match, Mike and I: if the field needed a bit of fresh air blowing through it, what better combination than a philanthropic engineer with a passion for science and an unemployed philosophical physicist who didn't give a damn about what other people thought?

Okay, then, I thought to myself, we were different, a bit on the edge, trying to challenge the limits of the establishment, of orthodoxy—indeed, hopefully, of human knowledge itself. And so naturally I began to think of related words: edge, boundary, perimeter. Hmmm, Perimeter Institute—that could be interesting, I quickly realized, on several levels:

My first thought was of a "circle of knowledge" somehow expanding outwards with our new institute at the forefront, an agent for change, pushing the boundaries. Okay, it was a bit hokey, and a little arbitrary, geometrically, to boot (why a circle or any other two-dimensional object? Why not a sphere, or a cube, or a dodecahedron? Was I still mired in a priori circular assumptions that I hadn't shed in Mr. Salsbury's physics class?). In addition, the word perimeter doesn't, of course, necessarily imply pushing anything at all—in fact it might well be interpreted in the other direction entirely, as a limit, a constraint. But still.

Acronyms, of course, are very important for such things. Whatever you call something, sooner or later somebody is going to turn it into an acronym, so you might as well think about that from the beginning to get the acronym you want. Perimeter Institute formed the acronym "PI," which easily reflects the Greek letter "PI," one of the first transcendental numbers to be discovered and a clear reference to the long and glorious history of fundamental inquiry through the ages beginning with Thales, Pythagoras and company. We may be an upstart institute, but we certainly were grounded in an impressively solid intellectual tradition.

Lastly, perimeter has, of course, RIM (Research In Motion) contained with it—the BlackBerry-making company that Mike cofounded that made, in turn, the whole venture possible. Without RIM, there is, so to speak, no Perimeter—literally and figuratively.

I e-mailed Mike later that day to tell him that I had received his cheque and had thought of a name, with the above rationale. He sent me back a quick BlackBerry response ("Sounds good") and so, just like that, Perimeter Institute was officially born. Not bad for my first afternoon's work, I thought, and retired to the local Starbucks to treat myself to a celebratory cappuccino.

Once we had a name, an institute no less, it became slightly easier to imagine the way forward. I began by sending Mike an analysis of other similar initiatives around the world, doing some rough comparisons and imagining ways that we could position ourselves differently to have the greatest impact.

I compared and contrasted physics institutes in North America with their counterparts in Europe and Asia. I looked at their different styles and structures—some were "resident-based," consisting of a permanent core group of faculty, postdoctoral fellows and visitors, while others were "program-oriented," primarily devoted to hosting conferences and workshops in a variety of subdisciplines throughout the year.

There were institutes that were little more than glorified university physics departments, undoubtedly renamed in a grandiose attempt to buttress their image and perhaps attain increased levels of government funding, others that were not institutes in the normal sense at all, but rather administrative centres dedicated to connecting like-minded researchers across a particular discipline or geographical area to enable them access to increased resources to travel, hold conferences and generally conduct their research.

All in all I looked at some twenty-five or so examples of scientific institutes around the world, examining their history, scientific mandate, budget, administration, government support, interaction with surrounding academic community and so forth. Immersed in this task, I eventually paid less and less attention to my future or the overall bizarreness of the situation, but instead just began to focus seriously on what should be done. One week after receiving that first cheque, I sent Mike a comprehensive summary, sketching out a basic framework for the structure of Perimeter Institute and a specific list of issues that needed to be accomplished to go forward.

Mike's responses to these reports were both prompt and consistently encouraging. At first, I found this mildly disconcerting: how was it that someone would entrust so much, so quickly, of the core structure of his major philanthropic initiative to a person he barely knew? Perhaps he wasn't taking it seriously. Years later, when I found myself thrust into an executive role, I came to appreciate that there wasn't much mystery at all going on: anyone who finds himself in the happy position of engaging an ambitious, hardworking individual who has the skills and determination to take ownership of a project and comprehensively move it forward to fruition recognizes that the most intelligent thing to be done is to simply encourage him and stay out of his way. As someone who built up a successful company, Mike obviously had a deep under-standing of this essential fact. Meanwhile he was also pretty busy himself, of course: the first BlackBerrys had just been launched earlier that year and an enormous amount of work was required to position both the company and the product for the considerable international success it was to have.

Looking back on things, I often think that the curious way we had met eventually made it easier for Mike and I to have a close, personal relationship—we both savour quirkiness and the unusual. From his perspective, it was as if I had just "dropped from the sky"—a straightforward young man with a physicist's training who had simply approached him with an investigatory letter, unknown to any of his circle and thus inde-pendent of any possible sense of cronyism or *quid pro quo* that he was increasingly having to fend off. I wasn't after his money and I wasn't after power; I had just wanted a job. Meanwhile, from my end, the freedom to move things forward was pre-cisely what I needed. I'm not terribly good with authority, and the notion of having a "boss" collides painfully with my stub-born character. But with Mike, the problem never materialized. Our relationship, once formed, had always taken on the form of a partnership. It helped too that I quickly grew to like him personally. He had a playful sense of humour and a keen eye for the ironic—two vital sanity-preserving traits that we both had frequent cause to rely upon as the years unfolded.

I was impressed too by the way he handled his wealth. Unlike the dot-com millionaires of the time, Mike had started RIM with two others back in 1984. The company had achieved numerous successes along the way, but had only gone public two years prior to my meeting Mike, in 1997. Now this mod-est electrical engineer, who had left the University of Waterloo towards the end of his final undergraduate year after having gained a lucrative contract for his burgeoning business that he simply couldn't turn down, found himself drenched in riches, albeit much of it on paper. Many people in his situation would flaunt their wealth and lose much of their perspective. Not Mike.

I am not a person to be terribly impressed by wealth per se, it must be said. Perhaps I had imbibed too much of Plato, with his overriding focus on the pursuit of the good life, or perhaps I had just seen far too many people squander their time away in search of ever-increasing riches, but money for the sake of money has always left me cold. Growing up in the sheltered world of upper-middle-class Toronto, I had met lots of people with far more money than brains, anxious to impress by the size of their home or make of their car—it had all struck me, and still does, as vaguely pathetic.

But Mike was different. He acted the way I imagined *I* would if I had that kind of money. He evidently thought, "Look at all this money I've got now! I don't need more than a fraction of it to live comfortably. How can I do something really interesting with it? How can I make a difference? How can I spend it on something *worthwhile*?"

Despite the fact that we were at rather different ends of the financial spectrum, our thinking on these matters was very much aligned. For him, as for me, flaunting one's wealth to impress the neighbours, or obsessing about getting rich for the sake of getting rich was little short of mindless ego-gratification.

"Imagine how much better things could be if these guys actually did something useful with their money!" he would fume, exasperated at hearing the recent *Forbes* poll or lurid details of some mega-rich star spending a small fortune on the latest craze.

This all strikes me as so reasonable as to be completely obvious, but I can't tell you the number of times people have approached me and asked incredulously, "Why on earth would Mike give all that money to a theoretical physics institute?"

Well, I feel like responding, why the hell not? Would you react that way if he bought a football team or a fleet of Ferraris or a 300-room mansion in Southern California modelled on the Taj Mahal? Why is it that that sort of outlay by the superrich goes unquestioned, but an investment of $100 million to establish a foundational physics research institute is considered as eccentric as buying the elephant man's bones? Quite frankly, what amazes me the most here is why more people don't do more of this sort of thing. Sure, I recognize that theoretical physics may not be everyone's cup of tea, but that's hardly the point. To my mind, the actions of people like Mike, Bill Gates, George Soros, Sergey Brin, Larry Page and the minority of the exceptionally wealthy who are actually using their resources to produce a substantive impact on what they believe important—be it physics or AIDS vaccines or adult literacy or global warming or saving the snowy owl or whatever—these are the reasonable people. Asking them why they are investing their resources in that particular direction is about as pointless as asking a doctor why she is wasting her time trying to improve the health of her patient. The real issue, in my view, lies in the other direction: why is it that the world seems so replete with colossally wealthy, unimaginative wankers who seem in abject denial of their mortality and whose overriding motivation seems to be directed towards some ego-drenched, self-indulgent drivel that will likely not give them any real satisfaction anyway?

Of course I don't respond that way—one must be polite. So I talk about the impact of physics and the enormous benefits to society that physics, and science in general, has brought. I ask them gently where they'd be without the laser or the semiconductor, ask them to imagine how different the world would be without electricity or the internal combustion engine or modern medicine or microwave ovens. This gets their attention, of course, and they nod their heads and go away considerably more satisfied, assured that Mike's investment will one day give them a better TV or phone. Well, it might, I suppose, but in many ways that is not really the point.

It's true, of course, that basic research has historically had a tremendous impact on society through its breakthroughs in our understanding. It's also true that if one creates a culture of intellectual excellence and innovation, if one gathers enough bright people together in one concentrated area, interesting and invariably useful things will virtually always emerge (an oft-heralded example of this is the development of the World Wide Web at the European Organization for Nuclear Research [CERN] as an incidental byproduct of efforts to build an appropriate scientific communications and database system). But this is hardly the essential issue. At some point, it is a simple question of values: one must recognize that the acquisition of knowledge, even knowledge that is not immediately or even conceivably useful, is of inherent value.

Understanding what occurred in the first few seconds of the universe is a mind-bogglingly impressive accomplishment, independent of any other consideration. Similarly, the development of a coherent quantum theory of gravity may well yield some tangible practical benefits to future generations, however unlikely that may sound today. It may give rise to an understanding of the physical world that we can harness for our own convenient ends, but then again, it may not. Yet it is well worth the time and effort all the same. In short, time spent unlocking nature's deepest secrets is not only good for us materially, it is essential to who we are or what we should aspire to as a species. Science's manifold achievements profoundly define us: they are nothing less than a testimony of the intellectual potential of humanity. To reduce these accomplishments or their motivations to the procurement of gadgetry or the immediate fractional improvement of our GDP is to miss the point no less severely than measuring a Beethoven sonata by the number of sharps or the *Mona Lisa* by the size of the canvas.

Robert Wilson, a former director of the particle physics laboratory Fermilab, perhaps said it best when asked in a congressional hearing in 1969 about the value of high-energy physics research in the support of national defense. "It has nothing to do directly with defending our country," Wilson replied, "except to make it worth defending."

There's a tendency for scientists, artists, writers and others to back away from making these sorts of pointed statements nowadays. Fearful of being branded as self-indulgent romantics in an increasingly pragmatic age (and hence sidelined in the great quest for public support), many accomplished thinkers will stress the practical benefits of their work above and beyond that of anything else, either by exaggerating the likelihood of tangible products ("We will have a quantum computer in the next five years!") or loudly appealing to positive, indirect effects of intellectual life on the economic productivity of a community ("Building an opera house will enable us to attract top management to the area!"), citing the likes of Richard Florida and others who appear to be embraced, for the moment anyway, by the ruling classes.

Practical, economic factors are, of course, important, and must be an essential criterion in any government's overall strategic plan of how best to spend taxpayers' resources; but the general unwillingness of most scientists and artists to forthrightly avow the importance of their work because of its deep resonance with core human values is both distressing and ultimately self-defeating. After all, Richard Florida notwith-standing, there are easier and more efficient ways of recruiting lawyers and engineers than building opera houses; and any argument that doesn't appeal, first and foremost, to the power, beauty and elegance of operatic music and its essential reso-nance with the human condition lacks integrity and will likely be recognized as the tactical trope that it is.

At the end of the day, the government is, of course, all of us. If opera, say, is recognized as an intrinsically essential activity for the lifeblood of the community by the greater citizenry (as it is, generally, in Europe), then it is supported by the state. Otherwise, reasonably enough, it is not. And so it should be with the likes of basic scientific research. We must make the case.

The irony is that it is overwhelmingly clear to me that the public is interested, passionately interested, in precisely these sorts of issues. In a world where Stephen Hawking's *A Brief History of Time* breaks longevity records on best-seller lists around the world, when Brian Greene's *The Elegant Universe* is a staple on the layman's bookshelves, when Roger Penrose becomes a name your average taxi driver recognizes—doesn't that tell us something? None of these people markets his books on the promise of some new technology or recruitment effectiveness that arises from our understanding of nature, but rather, simply the quest to penetrate the mysteries of the world, in all its weird and wonderful glory.

This is what we now believe to be true. This is what we don't know. Here are the fundamental questions, the unex-plained mysteries. The expansion of the universe seems to be accelerating. We don't know why. There's this thing called dark matter. We don't know what it is. We have this theory called quantum mechanics. It works wonderfully well, so far as we can tell, but in many fundamental ways we don't know what it really means, what is really going on. Some people believe that all of the particles and forces of nature are related to the vibrations of a fundamental string in multidimensional space. Some don't. Here are the intriguing successes of that approach and the present difficulties. Here is what it implies, if true. Here is how most people believe the universe started and here's why.

People *care* about these things—huge numbers of people. They may be intimidated by the mathematics; they may be skeptical of the conclusions. Most are certainly unwilling to devote their own lives to a rigorous probing of all of the details and are quite content to settle for a popular account by an acknowledged expert, but that hardly matters. The point is they care, they are interested. If we were to say to them: "Let's stop this whole business. No more Stephen Hawkings or Brian Greenes or Roger Penroses," they would rise up and shout "No! We must continue to study this. We must continue to advance, to learn, to discover. This is important!"

That much I was certain of. But there was work to be done. Despite Robert Wilson's fine sentiments, and the efforts of determined, articulate scientific spokespeople like Steven Weinberg, the American Superconducting Supercollider project was cancelled in the early 1990s to general public indifference after $2 billion had already been spent to dig a very large hole, deep in the heart of Texas. The public might be broadly supportive of basic research, but that was not at all the same thing as being informed and focused.

I began to reflect on how we might, somehow, do more—how Perimeter might not only become a unique, internationally significant research centre in its own right, but how we could go beyond the standard, aloof stereotype of an academic research institute and somehow engage in regular interaction with broad sectors of the general public. Given everything on our plate already, this was desperately, perhaps even dangerously, ambitious, but the stakes were high: success in this arena meant more than simply satisfying an idealistic sentiment; it represented an opportunity to play a meaningful role in directly and indirectly shaping public policy in an essential, long-overlooked area.

But back to reality. At this point, the only thing we had was a name, a few flowery e-mails I wrote detailing how I thought we should proceed and a promise of some future large-scale financial commitment by Mike.

By September, I had fully accepted my position as "institute-builder" and soon it seemed like the most natural thing to be doing. I was doing lots of thinking and the cheques kept coming. Trying my hand at Wall Street was now plainly out of the question: it was slowly dawning on me that I had stumbled onto quite possibly the greatest opportunity for theoretical physics since the Institute for Advanced Study (IAS) was founded in Princeton in 1930 by Abraham Flexner and the Bamberger family. I rushed out to buy a bevy of books about the IAS and Flexner, desperate to extract any information that might be relevant for my own challenge some sixty years later.

The world had changed considerably since 1930, of course: theoretical physics was now a highly competitive field with no flood of European superstar refugees to entice to our shores. But why should we try to be a clone of anyone? The world already had an Institute for Advanced Study. The whole point was to be innovative, to rigorously assess the current lay of the land and find a potentially new model that was required today, for us—something that would somehow make a difference to the field.

I thought back to my periods of frustration with so much of the contemporary physics culture: how many deep, foundational questions weren't addressed because they were considered "too hard"; how impenetrable personal barricades had been erected between several subdisciplines ostensibly engaged in answering the same fundamental questions; and so on. Quite likely I wasn't the only one who felt this way. Perhaps if I had the opportunity to travel and speak with other experienced people, I would find these frustrations resonating far beyond my own local ambit. Perhaps it really was possible to change the world, just a little bit.

I discussed these ideas with Mike and was once again pleased to discover that we were very much on the same page and I had his full support. Despite my convictions and my private swagger, the truth was that I had considerably more fear in challenging the academic orthodoxy than Mike. Who the hell was I, a lowly just-minted PhD, to even intimate that there might be room for improvement, that all might not be optimal in the upper echelons of the academic establishment? For Mike, the situation was quite different. As an entrepreneur, he was outside of academe and thus could easily shrug his shoulders at their musty criteria—and anyway, it was his money. Moreover, for him, tackling the current orthodoxy was just another day at the office. He had spent fifteen years building up a company that everyone said couldn't be built, designing a technology that everyone said couldn't compete and successfully carving out a significant market share in a global arena that everyone told him would eat him alive. He had a deep-seated contempt for the "wisdom" of the established order that was bred from long, cold experience and an unassailable conviction of his own intuition—that same intuition that had so shaken me during our first meeting at the restaurant in Brampton and was now so firmly unwavering in its support of me and my efforts.

Those first few weeks were a wonderfully intense and exciting time. I was working hard, thinking up a storm and generally having a blast. The only time I felt any anxiety was when I made the mistake of speaking to friends or family about my new job and was summarily confronted with the full force of their skepticism and disbelief. Their reaction was, of course, quite understandable—had I been in their shoes I'm sure I would have responded in the same way. But still, they didn't really know. They didn't know Mike. To them he was just a rich guy, an eccentric, a CEO. They warned me that it was all too weird, that he was probably indulging in some sort of philanthropic game and would one day lose interest and forget all about it, leaving me high and dry. Well, maybe—it was certainly quite possible and the situation was obviously unusual. But something told me that that wasn't going to happen: things were just getting too damned interesting to stop now.

For better or worse, it seemed I had begun to develop my own intuition.

CHAPTER FOUR

Getting Formal

"I think," Mike announced one day towards the end of September, "it's time to form a Board."

"Is it?" I replied. I hadn't the vaguest idea what a board was and what it might do. Moreover, I had become quite comfortable with the arrangement of dealing with just Mike on this unusual journey. I wasn't sure I could manage the dynamics of a whole group.

"Absolutely," he answered. "It's time to get more official about things."

I recalled his comment during our first meeting about how my time for simply "thinking" would be limited, and I feared for the worst. "This means that I'm going to get busier, right?"

"Yup," he replied cheerfully.

A board was duly assembled. Mike chose some people he knew well and trusted: Doug Wright, a former president of the University of Waterloo who was Director of RIM; John Reid, his next-door neighbour and a managing partner at KPMG in Waterloo; Cosimo Fiorenza, a Toronto tax lawyer who had worked for both RIM and Mike personally; Ken Cork, a Toronto-based economist also on the RIM board; and Lynn Watt, a former engineering professor (and Dean of Graduate Studies) at the University of Waterloo who had taught Mike an undergraduate introduction to quantum theory.

My job, I was told, was to bring in a physicist, someone who would be able to make a significant contribution to the institute's development, particularly at the outset.

It was an important decision. I had seen enough of the academic world to know that good character and research excellence, while by no means mutually exclusive, weren't necessarily correlated. I needed someone who would resonate strongly with the goals and mission I was developing and had significant experience in the research community, but who would be able to look objectively beyond his own research agenda and not view the institute as an exploitable vehicle for his own glorification. Selecting someone from the University of Waterloo was out of the question while it was unclear what the precise relationship between the two institutions would eventually be; it was essential that we keep some sort of objectivity on that front.

After some consideration, I knew my first choice: George Leibbrandt. George was a quantum field theorist of the old school—a serious, but unpretentious scholar who had devoted the majority of his research career to becoming a specialist in a technical aspect of the mathematics of gauge theories in particle physics. A professor at the University of Guelph with strong links to CERN and other research groups, George would also be close enough geographically to participate regularly in meetings, but removed enough to be objective. Equally important, he was also an extraordinarily decent man.

I had taken a couple of George's quantum field theory courses when I was a graduate student and had been consistently struck by both the depth of his knowledge and his measured thoughtfulness. I got into the habit of trekking over to his office in Guelph on a regular basis, equipped with a laundry list of both technical and structural questions, and George would methodically go down the list and respond to each one, sometimes answering immediately, sometimes thinking quietly for four or five minutes in complete silence before giving his typically comprehensive solution. Occasionally, however, I would manage to stump him and he would throw his arms over his head with a sigh, lean back in his chair and announce that he would have to think about the matter for a day or so. Like clockwork, a day or two later, I would have my answer.

The thought of having George on the board of Perimeter, an informed voice for sober second thought to check me while I babbled off impetuously or ignorantly in some direction or another, struck me as such an obviously good idea that I resolved to approach him immediately.

I phoned him to arrange an appointment and, he responded with remarkable enthusiasm. The truth was that I had approached him some months earlier at a personal low point, disconsolate at the prospect of selling my soul to the financial world, to see if I might pursue a postdoctoral fellowship with him. At the time, he sadly shook his head and reported that he had no funding available and could make no promises as to when he might have some. When I phoned him again, he naturally assumed I was calling to follow up on the putative postdoc. Apparently, as coincidence would have it, he had just heard that he had been awarded a sufficiently large grant to support me.

"I have great news!" he announced when I strode into the office and hurriedly took the seat he offered me.

"Me too," I said quickly, anxious to get to the point.

"I can now offer you a postdoc," he beamed.

"Great. Thanks," I said, trying not to sound unappreciative, but still not fully sensitive to the fact that not everybody's life had been turned upside down in the past two months. "But I don't think I can take it now."

"What?" he said, throwing his arms over his head and rocking back in his chair in utter confusion. "But then why did you come here?"

"I have something to offer you!" I announced theatrically. "How would you like to be on the board of a new multi-million-dollar theoretical physics institute?"

"You're joking!"

"Nope."

"You must be joking!"

"Nope."

It went on like this for quite some time. Finally, he quieted down and I told him how I met Mike and what had happened and what we were planning on doing. After I had finished, he hurled his arms over his head again with a force I had never seen before.

"Well!" he exhaled forcefully.

"Indeed," I replied, quite enjoying the moment. It was fun to have someone else experience some strangeness for a while.

"Well!" he repeated, shaking his head. "That's quite a story. I'm not really sure what to say."

"Say yes," I said. "We need you."

He paused. "I'll have to think about it. I need some time."

Good old George—nobody could rush him into anything. Ever.

"Okay," I said, "how much time?"

"I don't know. This one might take more than a few days."

One week later, George talked to Mike on the phone and another week after that he agreed to join the board of Perimeter Institute. We were now officially on our way.

Once a more formal structure of the institute began to emerge, I started to get a bit concerned. Now there was a board, but what was my official position? I had no title, no job description, nothing. When it was just Mike and me, such a preoccupation would have seemed ludicrous, but now I felt suddenly naked.

Flustered, I went to my good friend Ron for wise counsel. Ron is somewhat older than I am and greatly enjoys playing the role of guru. He likes to call himself my "personal meta-physician," which I find rather comforting, if not terribly accurate and even potentially contradictory. At any rate, it also helps that he knows a thing or two.

I had been keeping him up to date with the whole institute saga during our weekly get-togethers at a Toronto Starbucks, a tale that he evidently enjoyed for its novelty as well as the overarching irony that I, the über-rationalist, who had tried to navigate the perils of adulthood by selecting a career I had no real interest in strictly for monetary gain, had been so buffeted by fortune as to be veritably swept away by events beyond my control.

I approached him one day. "Ron, I think I need some kind of title. Things seem to be getting much more formal all of a sudden, and I have no idea what my official position should be."

"Well," he said thoughtfully, "you've got a board now, right?"

"Yeah."

"And you're officially a nonprofit, right?"

"I think so." I seemed to remember Mike's lawyer, Cosimo, talking about the mechanics of getting nonprofit status at some point.

"Then you're the executive director," he announced merrily, as if ticking off the solution to a crossword puzzle problem.

"The what?"

"The executive director. Howard the executive director—has a nice ring to it, don't you think?"

"I suppose. Whatever. But why executive director?"

"Look, it's a volunteer board for a nonprofit, right?"

"I guess."

"And you're not on the board."

"No, I don't think so."

"But you report to the board, right?"

"I don't know. I guess so." Things were suddenly getting very complicated. It was far from clear to me what "report to" actually meant anyway.

"Then you're the executive director."

"Okay," I said, unconvinced.

"You have to be the executive director," he insisted.

"Do I?" I responded. "Why?"

"Because you're the CEO. You're the guy who's in charge of getting stuff done."

"CEO? But it's a physics institute, for goodness sakes, not a car company."

"Irrelevant. It's a structural thing."

I thought more about this for a moment or two. "But isn't CEO rather over the top? I mean, I'm the only one actually doing anything. Shouldn't a CEO have underlings?"

"Doesn't matter. You're still the CEO."

"But I thought you called me the executive director."

"Same difference."

"Oh," I said. "Okay."

I peered into my coffee for a moment, trying to adjust to my title before continuing.

"Ron?"

"What?"

"What am I supposed to do, exactly, at board meetings? You said just now that I'm supposed to report to the board. Well, okay, but what does that mean, exactly?"

It was all vaguely intimidating. Up to that point, my only experience of boards and boardrooms had come from childhood recollections of Bugs Bunny cartoons, where a few fat characters in suspenders, most of them animals, spent their time smugly sitting around a big table chomping cigars with dollar signs in their eyes—hardly the most detailed or useful experience.

"Just remember, boards don't compose," he announced sagely, "they dispose."

"What does that mean?"

"You've got to give them something to do. The key is to look at them as a resource to help you get things done. But you have to recognize that most of them won't have too much time to do too much—this is a volunteer board, after all. You always have to focus on making things really concrete for them. For instance, if you want their help on something, don't just tell them you're having a problem with something; tell them you're having a problem and you'd recommend addressing it in some specific way and you'd like them to do some specific thing to help."

"Oh. Okay."

"Anyway, after all is said and done," he said calmly, taking another swig of his coffee, "a board really has only one big issue on its agenda for every meeting."

"Oh yeah?" I asked. "What's that?"

"Whether or not to fire the CEO," he declared merrily.

"Right. Thanks. I feel ever so much better now."

Meanwhile, as suspicious as I was of my new colleagues on the board, it was pretty clear that they were even more wary of me.

A few weeks after I had first been introduced to Doug Wright, he visited me at my home, ostensibly to drop off some papers, but doubtless to check me out further and get a sense of the sort of person I was. He probed me here and prodded me there—had I read this? Did I know that? Did I know who he was? And so on. It was all a pretty annoying and decidedly uncomfortable. The only thing that made me grin and bear it was my keen awareness that he was acting, however irritatingly, not unreasonably. He didn't know me from Adam and naturally felt obligated to do his due diligence to make sure I was up for the task and that Mike wasn't somehow going off his rocker.

It was Cosimo the lawyer, though, who seemed the most concerned when he first saw me, treating me with only the thinnest veneer of professional politeness that was a clear front for a mountain of contempt. He had obviously concluded that I was some kind of bizarre physics gold digger, out to prey on the generally good intentions and newfound wealth of his client.

Years later, Cosimo confided that when Mike first approached him with the notion of donating in excess of $100 million to establish a charity for theoretical physics, he had replied, "Mike, I've known you for some time and very much value our relationship, so please don't take this the wrong way when I ask you, as I feel that I'm obligated to do under these circumstances, the following question: Are you out of your bloody mind?"

Some of the board members seemed to need some time to fully embrace the merits of our new initiative, while for my part there seemed, notwithstanding my sudden U-turn from the world of finance, no way of escaping dealing with lawyers and accountants.

But that was, I quickly realized, the least of my problems.

As more people became involved in the process, rumours of a mysterious institute quietly began to spread through the local community, particularly at the University of Waterloo. As we grappled with the question of whether or not to establish Perimeter independently from UW, it seemed natural to investigate locating it on the north campus of the university: an enormous tract of farmers' fields and meadows that was almost completely empty at the time. To begin negotiations, Mike and his wife, Ophelia, invited Doug Wright, Ken Cork, David Johnston (UW's new president) and me to dinner at his place.

It was the first time I had been to Mike's house and the first time I had met Ophelia. In addition, I had never met David Johnston, aside from a perfunctory handshake at my graduation ceremony some ten months before (along with several hundred others), and it was fair to say that both Ken and Doug were highly skeptical of me at that point. I felt decidedly like a fish out of water and resolved to say not very much at all and merely observe the goings-on.

What I didn't fully appreciate at the time was that I was hardly the only person feeling vaguely uncomfortable: Doug, Ken and Mike were all naturally on very good terms with one another, and Doug, as former president of UW, knew David Johnston well enough; but Mike and David were hardly more than acquaintances and Ken had never met David at all. From his reaction and polite observations, I could tell it was the first time David had been in Mike's house and they were plainly feeling each other out: Mike seemed determined to tangibly demonstrate to David that he was a successful man to watch, while David appeared intent on exploring how Mike's wealth and inclinations might somehow be utilized by his university. My presence was hardly a concern to anyone, and soon I began to relax and observe, rather relieved to discover I was only a peripheral figure.

During the pre-dinner conversation, David took the initiative: "I hear you are interested in physics, Mike." He reached into his breast pocket and with a small flourish produced a three-page document. "You may be interested to learn that key members of our physics department are tremendously excited about the possibility of an institute for physics at the

University of Waterloo."

Mike glanced briefly at the papers and passed them over to me before holding forth in a more general way on the merits of physics and its historical impact on society throughout the ages. This went on for the better part of an hour, and as everyone nodded resolutely to Mike's enthusiasm I remember thinking what a curious situation this was: two engineers, a lawyer and an economist were sitting around a dinner table expressing bounteous appreciation for the societal importance of physics. Suffice it to say that in all my years of attending social functions, I had never encountered such a phenomenon—quite the contrary: in my experience, physics was invariably regarded as a great conversation stopper and hardly a topic for broad-based conversation, let alone untrammelled enthusiasm. Money, it occurred to me—not the first time—was truly a wonderful thing—particularly money in the right hands.

As the physics panegyrics continued, I took the opportunity to glance down at the brief proposal for UW's institute. It was a broad and unfocused document that delineated "target areas" from cosmology to biophysics, trying to encompass any conceivable direction that might be required by a prospective donor. There were even several passages on the big foundational areas of quantum gravity and superstring theory, none of which I knew were actively pursued at UW, with only Rob Mann, my former supervisor, having interest or experience in any aspects of these areas. Ironically, one of the only areas of physics that wasn't included was one that unquestionably should have been—quantum information theory.

Throughout the mid to late 1990s, a new and exciting field had slowly begun to gain traction in the theoretical physics community. A novel mixture of the information theoretic approaches of computer science and the structural bedrock of quantum theory, quantum information theory embraces the operational philosophy that "information is physical" and pushes this concept to its logical conclusion, developing a theoretical framework of information processing based on quantum mechanics rather than its classical approximation.

In the 1980s and 1990s, a few intrepid souls (Charles Bennett, Gilles Brassard, Artur Ekert, David Deutsch and so forth) began exploring how quantum theory could be used to transform concepts of cryptography and computation; but when Peter Shor developed his prime number factoring algorithm in 1994, demonstrating that a putative quantum computer could calculate some pivotal tasks far better than any classical device, interest in the field exploded. Prime number factoring, it should be mentioned, is integral to many contemporary cryptographic protocols that ensure security in everything from electronic banking to Internet shopping.

Of course, the problem was that nobody had built a quantum computer—in fact, nobody even knew if it was possible—but now it was clear that if one could somehow build it, it would be enormously useful, at least in some areas. Meanwhile, with microchip technology advancing at a rapid rate in accordance with the mysterious but strikingly consistent Moore's law (which predicted that the number of transistors on a chip would double every eighteen months or so), it was becoming increasingly evident that at some point in the not too distant future transistors would be the size of atoms and the world of technology would find itself having to grapple with the strange laws of quantum mechanics, ready or not.

In 1999, quantum information theory (often called, less exactly, simply "quantum computing") was hardly a hot area of interest in most university departments and research institutes. There were a few notable groups sprinkled around the world (California Institute of Technology, Oxford, IBM and so forth), but by and large it was a real target of opportunity for a new institution, something that had become increasingly clear to me as I investigated with some thoroughness the lay of the international physics landscape.

UW's physics department, on the other hand, anxious to find a way of diverting Mike's money towards its ambit, had missed it entirely—a situation made all the more ironic by the fact that, unknown to them, their mathematics faculty had combined with neighbouring St. Jerome's University to hire an accomplished young researcher in quantum algorithms some months previously: Michele Mosca, himself a PhD graduate from Artur Ekert's group in Oxford.

As I sat quietly at the dinner table reflecting on all this, it began to dawn on me that perhaps I was not so unsuited to this institute-building task. Almost all active researchers, however well motivated, find it necessarily difficult to look at bigger issues independent of their own personal research agendas. Ask a scientist to build an institute and the first thing she will invariably think of is designing something around her research program. This is not, of course, unreasonable; one naturally expects every scientist to believe her research program is the most exciting in the world. But such thinking is hardly the sort of objective mindset required to develop an initiative that can fully capitalize on both the strengths of the region and new targets of opportunity.

This was my first direct exposure with the notion, demonstrated repeatedly during the next seven years, that by and large universities are simply terrible at any real form of strategic thinking. Some of the difficulty lies in the nature of their internal governance process—multilayered consensus procedures of disparate, self-serving committees without any real accountability that virtually ensure the continuance of the status quo. But much of the blame rests with government, and, by extension, the general public, which never seems motivated to engage in a clear-headed analysis of what a university should actually be. In a country like Canada, where virtually all universities are state supported, the ensuing muddle is a recipe for mediocrity, for how can one achieve genuine excellence if it's not even clear what one should be striving for?

In the corporate sector, things are much clearer: the goal is simply to be profitable. Unprofitable companies eventually disappear. Thus there is enormous internal pressure to focus, carve out a niche or develop some core expertise. Given the stakes and transparent measurability of success, a clear sense of accountability develops that runs directly to the CEO—the key figure responsible for the development and implementation of a coherent strategy for the organization. The CEO is by definition the chief strategist. Bad strategy, or bad implementation, and the CEO gets fired (or should). Successful strategy and the CEO is rewarded—simple as that.

Universities, on the other hand, are considerably more muddled. They rarely, if ever, go out of business, so that pressure is considerably alleviated. But then how are they to be measured? There's the rub. For some, a university's raison d'être is centred around classic liberal values: exposing our youth to a broad-based education of arts and sciences, thereby equipping them with a combination of specific knowledge, values and critical analysis that will naturally propel society forward. For others, a university's core function is primarily economic: it is a training centre for the development of a variety of technical skills (software development, management, accountancy) that are of direct economic relevance to society: the more college graduates a society has, the better able it will be to sustain and increase its wealth. Some believe that research, not teaching, should be the focus of a successful university and that it is essential for universities to focus on basic, undirected or risky research that would generally not be pursued in the corporate sector, while others argue that our universities should be judged by the number of commercializable products they produce that are of direct relevance to society. Still others are motivated to combine teaching, research and business to conclude that it is now a primary responsibility of the university to develop entrepreneurs through select, university-based programs.

It is pretty straightforward to see that harmoniously combining all of these functions is practically impossible. In the United States, this issue is dealt with by combining private philanthropy, government support and market forces, resulting in a plethora of different postsecondary institutions with manifestly different functions—small, liberal arts universities, elite research universities, solid state schools and low-level junior colleges. In strictly state-supported environments in Europe and elsewhere, the issue is often dealt with more subtly, with a reliance on history and tradition ensuring that denizens of Oxford, Cambridge and the Grandes Écoles, say, are recognized as the cream of the crop.

In Canada, however, there is typically no clear way forward at all, resulting in the rather curious situation where university presidents will flexibly adopt whatever raison d'être for their institutions they feel maximizes the momentary likelihood of procuring additional government resources for their cause—indeed they are presumably chosen for the role with precisely this sort of dialectical dexterity in mind in the first place. And so we naturally come to the point where the president of the University of Waterloo, hearing that a prospective philanthropist in his neck of the woods is interested in physics, immediately sets upon the task of convincing the would-be donor that his institution would make the ideal spot for such an enterprise. Tomorrow, of course, there may be another philanthropist who is passionate about Bollywood films or Babylonian architecture or bioinformatics, and one can rest assured that the president will unhesitatingly spring into action to argue the overwhelming resonance of his university with those endeavours as well. It is, in the end, his job.

But even David Johnston must have been unprepared for what happened next at Mike's house that unusual evening. After dinner we all trekked downstairs to the basement to see Mike's home theatre. Unlike most home theatres, Mike's really felt like a small cinema, with two rows of luxurious tiered seats and an enormous, high-resolution screen dominating the wall. Working with a local contractor, he had designed essential aspects of the acoustical properties of the room himself, and spent considerable time telling David about the challenges he faced and the materials he used. We sat down in the cushy chairs, oohing and aahing appropriately as Mike slipped out of the room to load a DVD.

"Listen to this," Mike announced proudly as he forwarded the DVD to a particularly loud moment, the seats rocking to the resonant vibrations of the events on the screen. We were watching *Armageddon*, a film rife with explosions and screaming layered over a dominating soundtrack. Even in this artificial setting, determined as he was to impress the president of the nearby university with his accomplishments and professional profile during their first intimate meeting on his turf, Mike couldn't help but be sidetracked by the science, by the technical achievements of the room. I began to like him more and more.

He reset the DVD at the beginning and we watched the opening scenes as I glanced at my watch and wondered how much more of this I would have to endure. For all my appreciation of the larger than life acoustics, the movie struck me as both incredibly loud and not a little silly, with the inveterate Bruce

Willis cast in the all too familiar role of humanity's last macho hope, selected to save our planet from an approaching killer asteroid.

After half an hour or so, it began to dawn on me that, much to my horror, we were going to watch the entire movie. To this day, I'm not entirely sure why we did this; perhaps Mike had run out of things to talk about or perhaps he was trying to send David a not so subtle message that science was the key to saving civilization. Or then again, maybe he was just getting into the picture. Whatever the reason, we all stayed rooted in our comfy seats, buffeted by the monsoon of special effects for the full two and a half hours.

As I staggered out to my car after midnight to begin the drive back to Toronto I phoned Irena and reported proudly:

"You'll never guess what I did this evening."

"Ummph," she responded vaguely, evidently not terribly impressed that I had awoken her to play late-night twenty questions.

"I just watched *Armageddon* with the president of the University of Waterloo at Mike's house."

"That's nice," she replied with a yawn. "When are you coming home?"

While the unusualness of this situation seemed lost on my sleepy and indifferent wife, for me, on the other hand, it was a welcome reassurance from the recent activity surrounding boards and money and men in suits. As long as things still contained an element of the bizarre, I felt, I would be okay.

CHAPTER FIVE

Moving Forward

Back in the boardroom, things were settling down into some sort of a routine. Taking my friend Ron's advice to heart, I created detailed reports for every meeting, highlighting progress that had been made on a number of different fronts, together with specific areas of concern and concrete recommendations. With remarkably intense activity for a volunteer board (a notion that was completely lost on me at the time), we met regularly every six weeks or so and I quickly became quite comfortable in this new dynamic. Meanwhile, the initial skepticism between the board members and myself began to fade. I rented out an office in Ken Cork's office complex in downtown Toronto and took advantage of the opportunity to drop in on him frequently to chat and ask his advice on a wide range of issues. After a few months of detached observation, Doug Wright began warming to me as well, spontaneously offering me a number of helpful articles and papers, including F. M. Cornford's *Microcosmographia Academica*, a highly amusing and frighteningly useful text on how to navigate the perils of professional academe ("Being a Guide," as it is subtitled, "for the Young Academic Politician"). Somehow I had passed the threshold and been deemed suitably capable to take seriously.

A principal issue of concern to us during those first few months was that of confidentiality. With the intense media scrutiny of the tech sector during the bubble of the late 1990s, we were naturally worried that any large-scale personal donation by Mike of RIM stock might be misconstrued as a lack of confidence in the company or, perhaps worse still, some delusional attempt by one of the CEOs to create a research and development arm for e-mail pagers based on quantum gravity.

An official launch of the institute was planned for October 2000, but before that point much work needed to be done towards establishing our precise structure and mandate, and the last thing we wanted was to be blindsided by unfounded media reports and a consequent run on RIM stock.

We hired a Toronto PR firm to help us organize our official public launch and to handle damage control should word somehow leak out in advance. It was my first experience with the world of consultants and would be a bitter harbinger of all similar forays: regardless of their willingness to assist, the amount of work required to educate them on the details of theoretical physics and the uniqueness of our situation resulted in my spending a large amount of time and trouble handholding. In addition, I was forever fighting an uphill battle to tone down their hyperbole:

"Now, for the launch," they said to me excitedly, "let's hold a huge press conference with a visually stunning PowerPoint demonstration to show clearly that this is the best institute in the world."

"No," I replied curtly.

"Why not?"

"Because it isn't the best institute in the world, yet. It isn't even the worst institute in the world—it isn't really an institute at all yet!"

"But you want to be the best in the world, right? Why don't we say: 'Perimeter Institute is determined to be the best in the world in three years.'"

"No."

"Three years is a long time, Howard."

"Not for a physics institute."

"Five years?"

"No."

"Can we say we'll be the best in Canada, at least?" they asked plaintively, determined to say something impressive.

"No," I said again firmly, imagining the furious faces of those at the Canadian Institute for Advanced Research or the Canadian Institute for Theoretical Astrophysics scanning through the paper the next day. "I'm really not sure what you're trying to achieve by all of this."

"Well what can we say?"

"Say that Perimeter Institute is a bold new initiative that represents the cutting edge of an exciting new breed of philanthropy. Say we are determined one day to be a leading international centre for foundational physics inquiry."

"That's not very sexy," they replied, sadly shaking their heads. "I don't see why we can't at least say we're the best in Canada."

Our frequent clashes were not terribly surprising, of course, given the radically different mindsets: in marketing, the whole object of the game is to shout something new and exciting as loudly as one can, muscling one's way into the public eye. Scientists, on the other hand, are deeply skeptical of hype and superficial, inflated claims. Their entire culture, from peer-reviewed journals to coolly presented seminars, is based on a belief structure that is focused on substance rather than style. Of course, this is something of an idealization: many scientists have been justifiably accused of overinflating the scope of their own research or field, but most of the time the general response to these claims is to quietly take a wait-and-see approach until the facts are in. Those who do rush things and circumvent the usual rigours of science, such as Stanley Pons and Martin Fleischman with their infamous cold fusion press conference,[1] become the objects of widespread contempt not only for their transgressions, but also because of their general sullying of the entire process of science.

In addition to marketing plans those first few months involved considerable effort given to financial mechanics. Mike was keen to donate the $100 million in one chunk and get it over with, but there was a significant logistical hurdle involving our charitable status. From the beginning we were motivated to establish the institute as a registered public charity. The fact that this would naturally result in a personal tax credit for Mike's donation on par with donating to a hospital or university was precisely the point: we were determined to structure matters to establish PI as equivalent to any other research or educational institution for future fundraising.

But this gave rise to additional complications. In an otherwise reasonable determination to crack down on fraudulent personal charities, the Canadian government then held the policy that no one individual could contribute more than 50 percent of the funding towards a registered public charity. We knew this regulation might well be in the process of changing (it subsequently has), but at the time it represented a rather

[1] In March, 1989, two chemists, Martin Fleischman of Southampton University and Stanley Pons of the University of Utah, held a press conference to announce that they had discovered tabletop "cold fusion" from the electrolysis of heavy water with a palladium cathode. While their findings were immediately publicized around the world as a breakthrough in the production of cheap, safe energy, their scientific findings were never successfully replicated to any significant degree.

significant constraint. The only way Mike could donate the full $100 million in one shot was if we could somehow find another person or group to donate an additional $100 million. Even for the frenetic financial climate of the late twentieth century, this seemed a bit too much to ask. But we did find a way to settle for something only a little bit smaller.

At one point in the middle of a board meeting when we were hashing through the details of this issue, Mike excused himself. Such things were not entirely uncommon—we had all grown used to him glancing down at his BlackBerry with fairly regular frequency (particularly during the more boring parts of the meeting) and had naturally assumed that some urgent RIM business had arisen. Five minutes later he came back and proclaimed with a smile:

"Doug's in for ten."

Doug Fregin, a cofounder of RIM and a friend of Mike's since his school days in Windsor, had just agreed to give $10 million to PI.

Later, Jim Balsillie, the other co-CEO of RIM, donated a further $10 million to PI based on an understanding that Mike would return the favour when Jim's initiative (the Centre for International Governance Innovation) would be launched at some point in the future.

So equipped, we started planning a formal launch for the fall of 2000, announcing a private donation of $40 million in hand ($20 million from Doug and Jim and $20 million from Mike) together with a commitment for a further $80 million from Mike in the years ahead.

By the time of our first Christmas dinner in 1999, we had made some significant progress on a number of different issues, from structure to finances to communications, while discussions were underway with UW officials to investigate possible land for the new building. Fall 2001 was targeted as a possible start-up time for research in a temporary facility to be determined. Given that the board had only been in operation for a few months, and that Mike and I had only met for the first time that August, an impressive amount of groundwork had been accomplished in a relatively short time.

Working with our PR firm, we had even come up with a logo for PI, the one we're still using. There had been considerable debate around the boardroom table whether to just use a version of the letter Π, or to anglicize it by explicitly incorporating the P along with it. After a long discussion, we decided that leaving off the P would make us seem a bit pretentious and inaccessible and so we resolved to leave it in. The marketing guys added the little triangular hat, which I was told was a stylistic reference to the residence-based notion of the institute, but I'm convinced they put it in just because they thought it looked cool—which is, of course, just fine. The logo reminded me of the mathematical symbol for the canonical momentum operator, which struck me as a good thing. One can never have enough momentum.

In fact, from where I stood, things were still going terribly slowly. I had had enough of speculating in boardrooms about logos and unlikely stock runs: I was determined to get out and talk to people at different institutes around the world to get some realistic feedback on what they thought might be possible. Travelling to other institutions would also, I thought, be a low-level form of advertising. The theoretical physics community is not that large, and the sooner an unknown like myself started making contact with the influential movers and shakers, the better.

As I bided my time, I gave the other board members copies of the initial reports of other physics institutes I had made for Mike some months earlier, detailing where I wanted to go and why. I bought copies of a history of the Institute for Advanced

Study (*Who Got Einstein's Office?* by Ed Regis) for every director, and wrote additional commentaries to help them pierce the jargon and become acquainted with basic aspects of theoretical physics. While several of the board members had extensive academic experience, the majority did not—and in any event, George was the only one who had any deep understanding of the world of theoretical physics.

By the end of January 2000, we had a communications plan in place to deal with any leaks that could be traced back to Mike and RIM and I could finally begin my travels. At some point someone suggested that I get some business cards to take with me. I had never had business cards before. Did they matter? Perhaps they did. No scientist I knew actually cared about business cards, but I supposed administrators might, and I was now an administrative guy. I was executive director—that was pretty damned impressive. I probably did need a business card. Maybe I wouldn't be taken seriously unless I had a business card. Yes, I should definitely get business cards. But where?

I now know that there are shops devoted, more or less, to the procurement of business cards. Somewhere, there are likely business card consultants who make a reasonable living designing the optimal business card for their clients' needs. But at the time, the only thing I knew about business cards was that I didn't have any and you could make your own at one of those self-serve machines that could be found in shopping malls.

So I went to the nearest mall and printed off fifty or so flimsy business cards that simply displayed "Perimeter Institute for Theoretical Physics" with my title, name and e-mail address centred on a plain white background—no phone number, no street address, nothing else. I had discussed the issue earlier with Mike and we had agreed that this was the best approach—in addition to safeguarding our confidentiality from prying eyes desperate to connect the dots from Perimeter to RIM, the palpable lack of information on the card had a certain appeal to both of us, conveying a sort of whimsical mystery.

So equipped, I was ready to roll. My first stop: Princeton's fabled Institute for Advanced Study.

CHAPTER SIX

Moving and Shaking

The first person I was intent on seeing at the Institute for Advanced Study at Princeton was Freeman Dyson. Of course all the physics faculty at the institute were tremendously impressive and intimidating, but Dyson was somehow special: an enormously wide-ranging and penetrating thinker (many believe his work in quantum electrodynamics was sufficiently significant that he ought to have been a corecipient of the 1965 Nobel Prize that went to Richard Feynman, Julian Schwinger and Sin-Itiro Tomonaga), throughout the course of his long, productive life, he had tackled issues as diverse as the origin of life and fusion-propelled interstellar spacecraft, in addition to writing fairly widely on ethics and religion. Dyson came to the institute in the late 1940s and was thus also a link back to the glory days when Einstein would be strolling across the fields with Kurt Gödel while John von Neumann was building his computer and throwing wild parties.

I went to the IAS website and looked up Dyson's number, going so far as to pick up the phone, and ready my fingers to punch the appropriate buttons. Suddenly, I felt completely overwhelmed. What in God's name was I thinking, strolling down to Princeton to pepper Freeman Dyson with questions of building a physics institute in Waterloo, Canada? Didn't the man have better things to do with his time than put up with the likes of me? Who the hell did I think I was? I put the phone down for some moments and stared at it dully. How, I berated myself heavily, could I ever have overlooked this one, vital aspect of the entire venture: the whole thing was completely crazy! It was one thing to write reports and fill a boardroom with smug, sanctimonious phrases, it was quite another to confront eminent people directly, badgering them for responses to my silly suggestions.

Still, what choice did I have now? I had talked myself into this situation, even going as far as expressing frustration at the delay in making these ridiculous trips—I had nobody else to blame but myself. There was no going back now: I had to either continue along this path or admit defeat, resign my position and lurch back towards the spectre of a soul-destroying life in finance, this time with the haunted memories of my cowardice ringing in my ears for many years to come. I unhooked the phone again, took a deep breath and punched the numbers.

"Hello?" a voice on the other line responded after a ring or two.

"Prof-professor Dy-Dyson?" I stammered.

"Yes," he replied patiently.

This was, somewhat bizarrely, not what I had expected. You don't phone the president of the United States and expect the commander-in-chief to respond "Hello?" directly after a few rings, and I had expected nothing less from Dr. Dyson. Surely, I had thought, there was a secretary of some sort, a firewall of intellectual security to penetrate.

"You have reached the office of Freeman Dyson, thinker extraordinaire. If you are a bona fide colleague of his and are collaborating with him on a paper, press 1. If you are a member of the press searching for a pithy quote, press 2. If you are a member of the general public and would like his comments on your pet scientific theory, please stay on the line and you will be passed to our wackos department where someone will be pleased to assist you."

That was the sort of thing that I had imagined. But now the clock was ticking, and I was keeping the good professor waiting.

"Professor Dyson," I repeated again after vainly searching for a worthier title—Lord High Professor? Grand Poo-bah? "My name is Howard Burton and I am conducting investigations for the formation of a new Canadian institute for physics. I will be in Princeton next week and was wondering if I might have the chance to talk to you."

"Sure," he replied warmly. "I'll be around. When would be good for you?"

It was as simple as that. I put the phone down and bounded over to Ken's office:

"Ken," I exclaimed breathlessly, feeling like I was six years old at Christmas. "I just spoke to Freeman Dyson!" This was hardly the height of professionalism, and might well have gone some way towards unravelling the growing confidence some board members were beginning to show in me, but I really couldn't help myself. I mean, Freeman Dyson! Wow.

"That's nice, Howard," replied Ken, looking up from his papers with a kind smile. "I'm happy for you."

It was sometimes quite comforting to have more experienced, nonjudgemental types around.

Soon I had lined up interviews with a number of others at the institute: faculty members Nathan Seiberg, Stephen Adler, Frank Wilczek, John Bahcall, Director Phillip Griffiths and Treasurer Allan Rowe. The only relevant person I didn't see was Ed Witten: he was visiting California at the time, which struck me as just as well. I was quite pleased with myself for taking the bull by the horns and engaging the mighty directly, but Witten, near universally regarded as the brightest scientist alive, might have been slightly beyond the pale.

In spite of my cab driver's profound lack of interest in my personal welfare (or his, for that matter), I made it to the airport on time and a few hours later found myself in Princeton, sipping a coffee on Nassau Street, mentally preparing for my meetings. I understood well that despite how accommodating the institute's scientists had been in arranging to see me, I still faced an uphill battle: theoretical physicists are quite used to flaky and downright mad people enjoining them to tap into their hidden force field or check out the perpetual motion machine in their basement. I would be on an understandably short fuse: a few missteps and I would find myself, justifiably, out on my ear.

I saw Seiberg first. In my geometrical wanderings as a graduate student I had come across Seiberg-Witten theory only tangentially and had resolved, like many other areas, to read about it more, but never got around to it. A great pity and yet further proof of the unpredictable practical benefits of a theoretical physics education.

Regarding me coolly, Professor Seiberg politely motioned me to take a seat and I began telling my tale. I started off by relating that a group of businessmen (group, specifically, to dispel any undue speculation about Mike personally or RIM), from Waterloo, Ontario, were interested in starting up a theoretical physics institute. I said that I had been tasked with making preliminary investigations into a whole host of issues and was specifically soliciting his views on matters structural, operational and so on, as well as any specific recommendations he might have for people worth considering at this early stage, either for the first recruits or for the institute's Scientific

Advisory Committee (SAC). I was pretty nervous and spoke too much, too quickly and probably didn't listen as much as I should have. This was a shame, as Seiberg was one of the four "cluster hire" superstring theorists that Rutgers simultaneously recruited in 1989 in a bold and successful determination to build a world-class group (along with Steve Shenker, Tom Banks and Dan Friedan), and he was most candid and forthcoming about his positive and negative experiences in that situation, as well as his assessments of the strengths and weaknesses of his more recent position at the IAS.

Dyson was next, one door down. He was working quietly at his desk when I saw him, forcing me to disturb him by knocking lightly on his open door. With a warm smile he too motioned me to sit down and I began repeating the same introduction I gave one hour earlier to Seiberg, trying to smooth out the rough spots his questioning had highlighted. Dyson listened quietly and then remarked wonderingly and without a hint of sarcasm:

"It sounds like you are on quite an exciting adventure."

"Yes, indeed," I remarked quietly, all the while trying desperately to ignore the little voice in my head frantically shouting: "You are having a conversation with Freeman Dyson. Don't say anything stupid!" The truth was I was a bit of a wreck. Seiberg had been very civil, but I couldn't help sensing that he had quickly concluded that I was, if not a crank, at least rather significantly out of my depth, and I couldn't help but concur. Here I was wandering around the hallowed halls of the Institute for Advanced Study, treading the very same ground that Einstein, von Neumann, Oppenheimer, Yang and, yes, Witten, had graced, all the while feeling very much like a used-car salesman with my bizarre patter of a new Canadian institute. I didn't want to talk to Freeman bloody Dyson. I wanted a good stiff drink.

And then I noticed his ears. Dyson has, in the grand British tradition, rather protuberant ears, to which, in my heightened state of nervousness, I found myself inexorably drawn. This was, of course, simply idiotic. I screamed at myself to forget about his ears and focus on the obvious pearls of wisdom I could glean from this brilliant, original and dynamic fellow who had experienced life so richly; but of course it was little use. Like the psychology test case who is told not to think of the colour red, I found myself drawn, irrevocably, to his ears.

Meanwhile Dyson, in his own modest, wonderful way, carried on, seemingly oblivious to the basket case seated in front of him. "So you're here for some advice?" he asked.

"Absolutely," I replied quickly, trying desperately to get back on track.

He paused again.

"I'm trying to think of something suitably meaningful to say," he said with a laugh. "Probably the best advice I can tell you is to keep things fresh. They probably should have kicked me out of here long ago, but my family was happy in Princeton and it's really a very pleasant environment, you know."

We chatted pleasantly for a while longer on a number of issues and he was quite forthcoming with his views, but at the end he cautioned me to ignore everything he told me as the musings of an old man.

"Don't listen to old people," he said. "They think they know all the answers because they've seen it all. And don't listen to young ones either," he added with another laugh. "They think they know all the answers because they haven't."

I felt like I had just had a conversation with Yoda. And the ears didn't help.

I went through the rest of my appointments that day in rapid succession, bouncing from office to office throughout the institute. The discussions quickly began to fall into a certain routine and I learned to develop a keen appreciation for how it must sound from the perspective of the scientist opposite me.

During those initial investigatory trips I gave my speech more than a hundred times and got so that I could do it while focusing on the facial expressions of my interlocutors in mid-delivery so as to best assess their reactions. However overwhelmingly bored I was from repeating the whole story time after time to every person I met, I had to keep reminding myself that he hadn't heard it before and it was essential that no corners were cut so that each of them could draw the most comprehensive background picture of what we were trying to accomplish. Every so often I would try to increase my efficiency by talking with more than one person at a time, but I would invariably find this much less useful: talking privately with people is a completely different dynamic from speaking with them in groups, particularly groups of their colleagues, where they tend to be far less candid and forthcoming (a lesson I put to good use later on when managing our scientific staff). Invariably, I would find myself reverting back to individual conversations.

Looking back on it now, I would have to say that those trips were probably the hardest things I have ever done, particularly the initial ones. I would typically have between eight and ten hour-long meetings a day, each beginning with me in the uncomfortable position of needing to demonstrate my sanity to a highly knowledgeable and illustrious scientist. After a time, I began to see the telltale signs of, if not persuasion, at least the significant diminishment of skepticism. "Well," they seemed to say to themselves, "this guy does seem to know a thing or two about the field. He has made a few careful studies of other places and we are living in an age of instant millionaires, many of whom have struck it rich through technology. It is possible, after all." Inevitably, that was right about the time in the conversation when they would ask, "So who is this 'group,' exactly, you say is funding your institute?" At that point I would have to sadly inform them that, for reasons of confidentiality, I wasn't presently allowed to disclose the name of the donors. Poof! There went whatever little credibility I was able to slowly build up during the meeting.

Still, I was, quite frankly, amazed at how welcoming and forthcoming most people were. I had expected coldness and arrogance at every turn. After all, if I were some big-shot faculty member of the IAS or CERN, I likely wouldn't give myself the time of day. But surprisingly, that wasn't the general reaction at all.

Frank Wilczek, who was just then grappling with the notion of giving up his post at the institute and moving to MIT (he subsequently did move, and received the Nobel Prize while on faculty there a few years later), was most candid and helpful in his assessment of the strengths and weaknesses of the institute over lunch. Like Richard Feynman, who declined a position at the IAS long ago in favour of Cornell and Caltech, Wilczek seemed to feel much more comfortable in a university environment with the more earthly mixture of students and courses than in the austere, Platonic world of the IAS, where, as Feynman reported with exasperation, "there was nothing to do but think," resulting in many people folding under the pressure. Wilczek was also known to be somewhat frustrated by the recent dominance of more formal, mathematical approaches to theoretical physics, such as superstring theory, and with Seiberg and Witten (and later Juan Maldacena), the IAS was veering very much in that direction. Given many aspects of the structural similarities between PI and IAS, my time with Frank was particularly important. I shamelessly rewarded his graciousness and approachability by inveigling him to sit on our SAC years later. No good deed, as the saying goes, ever goes unpunished.

Like Frank, Stephen Adler was also exceptionally warm, welcoming and candid. Phillip Griffiths, the then-director, was particularly accommodating, spending considerable time with me in his office and strongly recommending that we establish ourselves as an independent institute to safeguard our flexibility, but that we "find a way to ensure that things stay dynamic" at PI, an oblique reference to the concerns of stagnation and rigidity that sometimes plague aspects of the IAS. Allen Rowe, then IAS treasurer, forthrightly gave me an overview of relevant financial issues, highlighting various areas I might want to consider as the institute evolved.

The general spirit of helpfulness I experienced on that first visit was very much appreciated indeed, and put to rest a good deal of my initial unease. The whole thing was almost an unqualified success. The only person who reacted with the sort of disdainful skepticism that I had initially feared was John Bahcall, the renowned astrophysicist. After I had finished my introduction, Bahcall fixed me with a stony glare and asked me, point blank, how I came to be qualified to even investigate such a question as how best to build a new physics institute. It was, of course, not an unreasonable query in the overall scheme of things (and one that I asked myself on an hourly basis), but it still struck me as not terribly productive, particularly given that he had agreed to make the appointment to see me in the first place. Moreover, for a physicist to gratuitously offend someone who is allegedly fronting a multimillion dollar effort towards physics research is not merely unhelpful, it is actually fairly shortsighted, regardless of how deluded or under-qualified you may feel the person in question is. Don't bite the hand that may feed you, and all that.

In a strange way, though, I actually took comfort in Bahcall's treatment, because I was expecting it at some point and it is always good to have the worst happen and realize it's not so bad, and also because it was gratifying to gain first-hand evidence that, even in the realm of all these monster minds, some of them could still occasionally act in a way that wasn't very astute. If it came to a confrontation, I might still stand a chance, as long as I chose my battleground carefully.

While at Princeton I also visited Scott Tremaine, a planetary astrophysicist and the driving force behind the formation of the Canadian Institute for Theoretical Astrophysics during his years on faculty at the University of Toronto. Scott reacted quite differently from his colleague Bahcall, despite the fact that I strongly suspect his internal sentiments and suspicions were virtually identical. Unfailingly polite and a good listener, equipped with a wealth of specific knowledge together with a sizeable amount of common sense, Scott is one of those rare individuals who is both a highly accomplished scientist and an enormously capable administrator—for this, unsurprisingly, he inevitably finds himself punished by being saddled with as many administrative functions as he can handle. I naturally did my part to add to his burden: during the course of our initial meeting I promptly asked him to serve on our Scientific Advisory Committee. In due course, Scott ended up being the chair of the SAC for the first three years, adeptly steering both the SAC and the institute through the first few pivotal years of our existence. Following Bahcall's death in 2006, Scott has since been appointed chair at the IAS.

From Princeton I went to Washington, where I spoke with various people at the American Institute of Physics, including John Rigden, then Director of Physics Programs. John, a talented scholar with a diverse record of accomplishment in science, history of science and education, was most excited to

hear of my interest in developing a spectrum of outreach programs, and we had an engaging and productive discussion of
future possibilities as he strongly encouraged me to do everything I could to make this an essential part of our mandate.
For his passionate urgings he was justly rewarded: several
years later, we invited John to Waterloo to kick off
EinsteinFest, our three-week public festival to honour the cen-
tenary of Einstein's miraculous year of 1905, by giving no less
than four separate lectures on Einstein's 1905 accomplishments on the opening weekend, thereby giving John the largest
possible audience to put his money where his mouth was. He
rose splendidly to the occasion.

From the AIP I visited the University of Maryland at
College Park, where I met with relativists Charles Misner,
Dieter Brill and Ted Jacobson. Just as at Princeton, their
names were familiar to me through their books and research
papers. Jacobson, in particular, I had always admired: he
undeniably marched to his own drummer. His papers were
sometimes quite removed from the mainstream, tackling
difficult conceptual problems in unusual and thought-
provoking ways, and I was therefore looking forward to
hearing what he had to say. He certainly did not disappoint,
but he did surprise, strongly recommending that I highlight
quantum computing as an area of focus, and pointing me
towards Artur Ekert's Oxford group. As previously mentioned, quantum computing had been on my radar from
earlier investigations, but the fact that Ted Jacobson, a relativist who had spent much of his career occupied with
quantum gravity investigations, was suggesting it as a focus
was a rather interesting surprise. But that was Ted.
"Quantum computing is pretty hot," he said simply. "Lots of
bright young people are going into it. Check out those guys
in Oxford."

I did go to Oxford, but first travelled through many other scientific institutes and departments, some physics-oriented and some not, throughout many countries in Western Europe. As my presentation became increasingly streamlined, I began to develop more confidence and my line of questioning became more comprehensive. Depending on whom I was speaking with, I would address a wide range of issues, spanning research orientation, recruitment, management, governance, finance, government support, interaction with the surrounding academic community, community outreach and even architecture. I asked general questions about what was and wasn't working at each person's respective institutions, what they would specifically recommend to do or not do and inevitably conclude with: "What would you do differently if you could somehow rebuild your institution over again?"

I visited the Institut des Hautes Études Scientifiques just outside of Paris—France's home for advanced research in mathematics and theoretical physics, which was created in the late 1950s as an explicit European counterpart to Princeton's IAS. There I discovered many things—including, unsurprisingly, given the location, the importance of good food and relaxed surroundings in creating a desirable atmosphere to attract and retain faculty and visitors. The bistro at PI owes much to my initial lunchtime experience at IHES. I visited the theory group at CERN outside Geneva and witnessed the Schrödinger Institute in Vienna. Given my wider structural remit, I also occasionally dropped by institutions that weren't explicitly physics-related: an institute for molecular pathology as well as the Vienna Institute for Applied Systems Analysis. I paid particular attention to those places that seemed a bit past their prime and tried to get a good sense of why.

In Trieste, I visited the Italian Institute for Advanced Study as well as the International Centre for Theoretical Physics, where I met with the director, Miguel Virasoro, a renowned mathematical physicist, in what was surely one of my more depressing discussions. He glumly informed me that in his view there was no future in theoretical physics and advised me to focus on mathematical finance instead, a recommendation I found curiously ironic given the story of PI and my own personal flirtations with Wall Street. Perhaps unsurprisingly, he was replaced as director shortly after I met with him.

I travelled to the small town of Golm, Germany, just outside of Potsdam, to visit the Max Planck Institute for Gravitational Physics (otherwise known as the Albert Einstein Institute), where I spoke with two of their three directors, Bernard Schutz and Hermann Nicolai. Nicolai was cool but rigorously polite, while Schutz was considerably more engaging.

While in Golm, I also met with Lee Smolin, who was visiting Fotini Markopoulou-Kalamara, a promising young quantum gravity postdoc at Max Planck to whom he was then married. During my time as a graduate student, I became quite familiar with Lee's work: one of the pioneers (with Abhay Ashtekar, Carlo Rovelli, Ted Jacobson and others) of a geometric approach to quantum gravity now commonly referred to as loop quantum gravity, Lee was regarded by many to be a deep, if somewhat iconoclastic, thinker. On the train to meet him, I plowed through his popular book *Life of the Cosmos*, which I was surprised to discover was hardly the usual sort of layman's guide to science stuffed with pedagogically friendly reviews of existing scientific dogma, but rather was structured around an intriguing new hypothesis describing how the universe's "fine-tuning problem" (why the fundamental constants of nature are seemingly arbitrarily fine-tuned to support stable chemical compounds and, in turn, life) is fundamentally related to the existence of black holes. I didn't appreciate it at the time, but the book was Lee in a nutshell: strikingly original, thought provoking and a clear and passionate articulation of a bold new idea, but not terribly rigorous. While stereotypes are always dangerous and it is possible to find people who resolutely defy any type of categorization, theoretical physics, too, has its groupings: meticulous calculators who will not announce the slightest result unless it is checked six ways from Sunday, and wild speculators who indulge themselves by sketching out crazy theories. When someone from the first group announces a result, you can be sure it's right, but not at all certain it will be interesting. When someone from the second group announces a result, you can be certain it will be interesting, but not at all sure it will be right. It takes all kinds to build an institute, and Lee is very much of the second kind. For the sort of place we had in mind, he was an obvious person to consider.

Lee, Fotini and I went out to dinner that night in Potsdam. They were extremely receptive to my story and displayed immediate interest themselves in being associated with the development of a new institute with the explicit motivation to positively affect the prevailing culture. Fotini, in particular, consistently expressed frustration with the notion that postdocs had no real influence or say in the goings on of most research institutions.

"I can understand that they don't want us in charge," she mused. "But it would be nice to at least be asked, occasionally, what we think. I've spent many years in advanced university training, write my own papers, go to conferences and participate fully in the research culture, and I can't even choose what bloody coffee to use in the machines!" This was hardly the first time I had heard these types of comments and I was most sympathetic. Contrast the academic culture with that of modern business, where energetic, capable entrepreneurs can emerge in leading roles of their companies at a precociously young age: in physics, despite the fact that the majority of breakthroughs have historically been made by scientists who were in their twenties and early thirties, the culture has remained largely unchanged over the centuries. Years ago, when the alternative to a research career meant slogging away for thirty years up some corporate pecking order, perhaps the system was still sufficiently stable. But today there is a real risk that the entire field may suffer as many of the best and brightest reluctantly abandon the anachronistic academic orthodoxy out of frustration and vault instead to start the next Microsoft or Google.

As for Lee, he was in transition at the time: formally on faculty at Penn State, he was spending a sabbatical year visiting Chris Isham's group at Imperial College and exploring some possibilities there as well. Increasingly, academics tend to find themselves personally attracted to, by disposition or circumstances, other academics, resulting in a logistical struggle of significant proportions as both partners search for professorial jobs in the same geographical area, often at the same university and sometimes in the same department. Ask any academic administrator what her greatest impediment to recruitment is and I would be willing to bet that the infamous "two body problem" would be close to the top of the list. Most universities have now reacted by developing a separate policy for spousal hires, given that it is typically unlikely that there are open positions for both candidates or, more problematically, that both of them are considered equally desirable by their respective groups of colleagues.

Lee was in a somewhat unusual state for an academic as he possessed a significant grant from a private foundation that gave him the means to have additional research freedom, which had, in turn, led him to do quite a bit of thinking on how best to structure the ideal scientific institute. We began talking a good deal about these ideas over the next few months as it became clear that he was genuinely interested and enthusiastic. Characteristically, I soon grew to appreciate the fact that he would say many different things at many different moments: some naive and questionable, others bold and insightful. Throughout all of our discussions, however, he was unfailingly positive and committed to the development of the venture. He seemed very excited about the prospect of being associated with a new institute; and in a sure sign of engagement that I was beginning to recognize as a cornerstone to recruitment, had begun to take a real sense of ownership in its development.

A few days later I left Germany for England, where I crossed paths with him again. He invited me to drop by Chris Isham's house for a regular meeting of an informal discussion group on foundations of quantum theory. This was, I must confess, a rather unappetizing prospect. I had long given up on trying to comprehend quantum theory and the last thing I wanted to do was hang around Chris Isham, for goodness sake, this time in his home, and exhibit my ignorance. Besides, I had travelled throughout a good portion of Western Europe in the last week doing my dog and pony institute-building show to countless scientific experts and was feeling pretty drained. Still, it was difficult to say no under the circumstances. So I bought a bottle of wine and trudged reluctantly to Chris's flat to join the foundations party. Once more into the breach.

There I found Chris holding forth with his customary machine-gun delivery, firing this way and that on all kinds of issues, from physics to psychology to philosophy. He didn't recognize me, of course, but he was very much as I had remembered him, other than the fact that he walked with a decided limp, dragging one leg across the room as he moved about distributing the wine. He was, I soon learned, suffering from a mysterious neurological disorder that caused him severe discomfort, making it terribly difficult to continue with his teaching and research duties. Chris being Chris, however, he plowed on resolutely regardless.

Fay Dowker, a physicist then at Queen Mary College, was in attendance that night, as was Jeremy Butterfield, a philosopher from Oxford. The conversation was lively, though not, truth be told, terribly different from the sort of thing I remembered from years past: there were discussions of the measurement problem, hidden variables and so forth. I remember at one point Fay becoming very animated and exclaiming that she was desperate for quantum mechanics to be "fixed," but that she couldn't for the life of her see how. Jeremy, who was a very knowledgeable and insightful person (I had read several of his review papers on quantum gravity that he'd coauthored with Chris) and the kindest fellow you're ever likely to meet, had this rather annoying tendency to start all his comments with "I'm just a philosopher, of course, but I think..." which struck me as rather counterproductive and not at all according to the rules of the game: I mean, say something or don't say something, but don't try to lowball matters by introducing sociological irrelevancies like which faculty you are a member of into the proceedings. Lee, meanwhile, did his customarily effective job of synthesizing the arguments and isolating the crux of the matter, but from there we could get, unsurprisingly, no further. For my part, I regarded the whole scene quietly, pretending to observe but really just feeling bored, frustrated and tired. I didn't want to be in Chris Isham's house. I didn't want to be listening to a discussion on foundations of quantum theory and I certainly didn't want to feel obligated to say something meaningful on a subject about which there was so little to say in front of all of these people who had thought about the issues far longer and deeper than I had. So I simply said nothing at all, and reflected quietly to myself on how the great physicist Paul Dirac, famous for his laconic tendencies, once found himself forced to endure a long presentation by two physicists who had enthusiastically cornered him after he had given a talk at their university. According to the tale, Dirac listened patiently for more than an hour until the pair had run out of steam, then asked pointedly, "Where is the post office?" and duly strode off in the designated direction. Not such a bad role model, all things considered. And then, of course, there's the Dirac equation.

Chris glanced over at me a few times during the course of this evening, trying to suss out who I was and what Lee's motivations were, but I didn't give him very much to go on, I'm afraid. There would be time enough later on, however, for us to have many frank conversations.

I spent the next few days back in my routine, talking with people at Cambridge and Oxford. At Oxford I had the opportunity to meet Roger Penrose for the first time, yet another highlight. Roger had always been one of my heroes—a quiet, demure man armed with a steely intellect and quintessential British resolve behind an exceptionally polite and courteous exterior, he had pioneered a number of hugely profound insights in mathematics and theoretical physics. From singularity theory to mathematical tiling to twistor theory, Roger resolutely went his own way, following his profound mathematical instincts to develop deep insights and connections between subdisciplines. Lately, with efforts such as *The Emperor's New Mind, Shadows of the Mind* and, most recently, *The Road to Reality*, he had also become a bestselling author and a household name only slightly less recognized than Stephen Hawking. In a display of characteristic iconoclasm among his peers, Roger doesn't believe that quantum mechanics in its present form can be the final story, even suggesting that a full resolution of its mysteries might well be tied to a coherent theory of consciousness. Typical for Roger, he has come up with an intriguing way to test his hypothesis, by developing an experiment where gravitational effects can play a leading role in forcing the "collapse" of a quantum object and thus directly shedding light on the mysterious measurement process of quantum mechanics.

When I went to talk to him about the institute, it was this that we ended up talking about after a few minutes, his eyes shining brightly as he excitedly described the experiment being developed by colleagues in California. This, too, I later learned, was fairly typical for Roger: he vastly preferred talking about science to sociology and made a habit of not talking very much about matters on which he was non-expert. When it came to a general discussion about what we might do at PI, Roger was typically forthright.

"I dare say," he told me simply, "that much can be improved upon in the current model. Too many people are doing physics without thinking about it very much and we are not, by and large, doing a tremendously good job of training them to do it properly or encouraging them to tackle the really hard problems. But then," he sighed, "there is really so frightfully much to know nowadays and the hard problems are really very hard indeed and one wants to make some sort of progress—it's all quite problematic."

He paused a moment before continuing: "I am all for the creation of a different sort of place and I'm quite delighted that your benefactors seem to have the presence of mind to fund something along those lines, but that's about all I can say, really." He looked at me and gave a little laugh, shrugging his shoulders. "I'm afraid I haven't been terribly much help."

On the contrary. This must be, I thought with a smile, one of the very few occasions where the great Roger Penrose was dead wrong. His heartfelt, cogent response might have been significantly short on operational detail, but it drove right to the heart of the matter and encapsulated the spirit of Perimeter Institute far better than most of the comments that have been said about it before or since. For that, and a good deal more besides, I promptly asked him to sit on our Scientific Advisory Committee.

In keeping with Ted Jacobson's recommendation, I also met Artur Ekert and his quantum information group when I visited Oxford. Artur is one of those eminently likeable, unpretentious people with remarkably good social instincts who makes one immediately feel at ease. Just off the plane from somewhere or other (Artur is always just getting off the plane from somewhere or other, I later discovered, and he is always fit and never jet-lagged—a veritable inspiration to world travellers everywhere), he invited me to lunch at Keble College, where we proceeded to have a long, enjoyable chat about quantum information science and the potential of the field. I was not surprised to hear that he was pleased we were considering including quantum information theory in the ambit of the institute, but was interested to note that he, too, welcomed a wider mandate incorporating other related aspects of the foundations of quantum theory (judiciously chosen), perhaps evidence of his earlier experiences as a graduate student of David Deutsch. No stranger to group building, Artur was the leader of Oxford's efforts at quantum computing and a world renowned researcher who pioneered various seminal developments in quantum cryptography in the 1990s.

The remarkable thing about talking with Artur was the ease and clarity that pervaded the conversation. I had spent countless hours discussing multiple scenarios and complex aspects of convoluted structural issues with dozens of eminent scientists and administrators, but after half an hour with Artur we were already on our way in a far more practical and beneficial direction: imagining people to recruit, contemplating specific strategies. As someone who actually spent considerable time and effort in hiring people himself, Artur knew well that the details of their research agenda were often secondary to overriding issues like perspicacity, intellectual horsepower and character. What sort of person would work best in the environment? Who was the liveliest young mind available? Who might conceivably be induced to come and under what circumstances? Those were the key questions. Exegetical analysis of how one might construct the ideal research environment in a perfect world was deliberately eschewed, rightly recognized as the modern day equivalent to pondering how many angels might fit on the head of a pin. Artur, needless to say, is also on our SAC. In fact, I'm seriously considering giving him a life appointment.

I also met with various other members of Artur's Oxford group, including Lucien Hardy, a serious looking fellow with wild flowing hair who spoke in high-speed, occasionally inaudible prose as he described his ambitious agenda of reinterpreting quantum mechanics in a rigorous axiomatic framework motivated by his operational views of quantum information theory. At least that's what I think he was saying, as I missed every second or third word when it dipped below my auditory threshold. Much later, after having recruited Lucien to PI, I discovered that he has one of the keenest senses of humour anywhere and I've often wondered if he wasn't mumbling utter nonsense just to gauge my reaction. It would hardly have been out of character.

CHAPTER SEVEN

Moving and Shaking Some More

By March of 2000, Irena and I were close to narrowing down our selection of a home in Waterloo. It was clear that commuting to Waterloo from Toronto could not continue indefinitely. In addition to the manifold irritations of the drive itself, I had discovered that all the local officials in Waterloo I was now dealing with took me much less seriously when I told them I lived in Toronto. If there was a profound perceptual difference between the adjacent municipalities of Kitchener and Waterloo (and there definitely is, believe it or not), as a Torontonian, I might as well have been from Mars. Of course, my initial attitude didn't exactly make things easier for myself either: I didn't really like Waterloo. Well, it wasn't really Waterloo, but rather the fact that it was a small town and I didn't fancy myself a small town kind of guy. In fact, even though I was born and raised there, I wasn't terribly impressed by Toronto either; it struck me as rather insular and parochial, merrily repeating Peter Ustinov's glib categorization of itself as "New York run by the Swiss" to anyone within earshot, while untrammelled condo developers destroyed the waterfront and the urban infrastructure crumbled.

I had always imagined ending up somewhere somehow more substantial—London or New York or Paris—somewhere interesting. But everything is relative. The experience of attending university in Waterloo during my PhD gave me a newfound appreciation for my hometown. Towards the end of my degree, I only had to go to Waterloo every week or two to talk to my supervisor or hand back papers I was grading as a teaching assistant. I came to refer to those occasions as my "Toronto Appreciation Days." Driving back along the Gardiner Expressway into the bright lights of the big city after the small-town dullness of Waterloo, I thought to myself, "You know, Toronto is really not so bad." Every single time.

So it naturally took a while to get my head around the notion of buying a house in Waterloo, but eventually we became convinced it was necessary. The fact that my commute would be shaved to under ten minutes was an obvious bonus, and it certainly helped that the Waterloo housing market was considerably more reasonable than its counterpart in Toronto, where dilapidated, semidetached fixer-uppers with "charm" significantly out-priced spacious Waterloo family dwellings bordering parkland, but all in all I found the stress of buying a house surprisingly overwhelming. Somehow even more than getting married or starting a family, purchasing a home seemed so terrifyingly adult, and once denial was no longer an option, I naturally approached the whole process with a mix of fear and dread.

And so it was that late one night in mid-April 2000, I found myself signing papers to purchase our first home in Waterloo, Ontario. Early the following morning, I hopped aboard a flight to Los Angeles to visit physicists in California, trying not to think too hard about how old I would be when the mortgage would be paid off or how long I might remain a Waterlooian (Waterlooer? Waterloser?).

The Institute for Theoretical Physics (ITP) at Santa Barbara (now the Kavli Institute for Theoretical Physics—KITP) is one of the premier fundamental research centres in the world. Established as a partnership between the National Science Foundation and the University of California system with an explicit mandate to serve as a focal point for advanced conferences and workshops in theoretical physics throughout the United States and beyond, the KITP also has a small number of exceptional faculty and postdoctoral fellows. The explicit partnership the institute created by its association with UC Santa Barbara is a revealing example of how an otherwise unremarkable university can transform itself into a specialized powerhouse by a consistent and targeted effort: UCSB's faculty alone, even independent of the neighbouring KITP, is now extremely impressive. The fact that the institute is located in a compelling natural setting—adjacent to a beach in a consistently temperate climate—further contributes to its appeal as a conference destination. Clever people, those scientists.

While the IAS was regarded by some to be somewhat staid and oppressive, simultaneously benefitting from and circumscribed by its past glories, the ITP was hip and Californian, where things were at. Even the mighty Witten, it was rumoured, was contemplating leaving Princeton for the sunnier climes of California at a new string theory centre jointly funded by Caltech and USC, a little ways down the road from Santa Barbara in Los Angeles (he didn't go, as it happened).

As usual, I had procured quite a few appointments in advance involving faculty members at both the institute and UCSB. I also arranged to see Amanda Peet, a postdoc there who had just accepted a faculty job at the University of Toronto and with whom I was naturally anxious to interact.

David Gross, the director, had not responded to my request for a meeting, which didn't strike me as particularly out of character given everything I had heard about him (he has a rather severe reputation for being, well, rather severe). An extremely accomplished scientist who shared the 2004 Nobel Prize with Frank Wilczek for their contributions to understanding the strong nuclear force, Gross has, by all accounts, done an admirable job as director of KITP, maintaining the highest academic standards through fully utilizing their unique combination of dynamic programs and top quality faculty and postdocs. Still, it's always curious to me when people of influence choose not to investigate a few possible gift horses heading their way. A few years after I passed through, the philanthropist Fred Kavli had transformed the ITP to the KITP after donating $5 million dollars to the cause—an obviously remarkable amount, but not quite of the order we had come up with.

Although Gross was otherwise engaged, I did see Deputy Director Dan Hone, but when I knocked on his office door, I sensed that something odd was happening. Hone was completely preoccupied with his computer screen, occasionally muttering expletives. This, in itself, was nothing terribly unusual—physicists will often mutter to themselves when staring at a computer screen—but when I looked closer, it was clear that he wasn't looking at e-mail or a calculation, but rather the website for the NASDAQ. The stock market, it appeared, was melting down.

I went through my standard story of Perimeter, but it was obvious that he wasn't paying a great deal of attention, raising his eyes periodically to peer at the latest market update. When I got to the point in my story describing the money committed by the group of entrepreneurs, Hone turned to me and said pointedly:

"I hope they invested it wisely."

"Oh sure," I said airily, waving my hand through the air. "No problem."

But there was, of course, a problem. A big problem. Not only had the pledged funds not been invested widely throughout the market in a variety of stocks and bonds, they hadn't even been officially committed yet: no public announcement of intentions, no official mention of an institute, and, for that matter, no mention of Mike at all.

All the money we were counting on was wrapped up in the value of Mike's RIM shares, which were falling like stones with each passing hour. I carried out my meetings that day on autopilot, mouthing words I had said countless times, but I was otherwise preoccupied with concerns I could neither affect nor reveal.

What if that was it? I couldn't help thinking to myself frantically. What if my grand adventure had been suddenly wiped out in one mad dash, erased by a capricious stock market crash of tech stocks? What if Mike turned to all of us at the start of the next board meeting and sadly reported, "Sorry guys. I had wanted to do this, but now it's impossible. Maybe next year." What on earth was I going to do then? And here I was, miles away in California, having just bought a house in Waterloo yesterday!

I met with Jim Hartle and Gary Horowitz, two scientists for whom I have enormous respect, but was just mindlessly going through the motions and have no recollection what either of them told me that day. Things were going from bad to worse: I left the campus and tried to get a grip on myself. I decided to send Mike an e-mail to steady my nerves, but knew I needed to act carefully. Whatever kind of day I was having, he was doubtless having a worse one and he certainly didn't need me pestering him with worries about his resolve.

I decided to take a much more positive approach, describing how impressed people were in California at what we were planning on doing (not entirely true) and how optimistic everything was looking (even less true). I fired off the e-mail from my BlackBerry and waited anxiously for the response. Nothing.

Mike was typically extremely fast at responding to messages, particularly those of an optimistic sort, and I was expecting just one or two lines in acknowledgement, but this time I received nothing. I morosely dragged myself out for a burger, idly wondering if there was any point in returning at all.

The next morning I awoke to find the bleeding unchecked. NASDAQ was spiralling ever downwards and I still hadn't had a response to my e-mail. Maybe, I thought hopefully, he had been distracted by other things and hadn't seen it. I sent him another one. Still nothing. Things were looking very bad indeed. Worse still, I wasn't in a position to let anything on: here I was in California, I'd better go about my business as if all was fine with the world. So I continued. I met with Joe Polchinski, Tony Zee and Amanda Peet before driving down the highway to check out the Salk Institute in La Jolla, a renowned locale for medical research that had been recommended by several people as a place worth visiting. The people at the Salk Institute were particularly hospitable, proudly showing me around their highly impressive facility while I trailed behind like some zombie from *Night of the Living Dead*, privately fixated on the cruel turn my life seemed to have taken.

By the end of the week, the market seemed to have bottomed out, with RIM stock, for some curious reason, getting hit particularly hard. I kept sending e-mails to Mike once or twice a day, but continued to hear nothing back at all and now did it more out of some nervous habit than any real expectation of a response.

By Friday afternoon, I was a wreck. I had meetings in Santa Fe on the Monday and was due to leave San Diego on Sunday afternoon, but decided to switch my schedule and go to New Mexico a day earlier instead. I had always enjoyed the desert, with its serene, quiet beauty and peaceful rhythms.

The best thing for me to do now, I decided, is relax, take a breath, and sit by a pool somewhere staring at cacti. By Sunday afternoon I felt myself calming down, resolving with all the intensity of a man desperate to believe good news that I was probably exaggerating and things weren't nearly as bad as they might seem on the surface. Indeed, I had nearly mastered my skittish emotions when I casually opened up the Sunday *New York Times* and was suddenly confronted, on the front page of the business section, with an in-depth story on the collapse of RIM stock and the effect it was having on the little town of Waterloo, Ontario, with an explicit reference to its hitherto overinflated real estate market. Well, I don't mind admitting that I lost it for a second there. If the bloody *New York Times* was also part of this growing conspiracy to turn my world upside down, what possible hope did I have of emerging victorious?

Suddenly, like a storm breaking, I realized the ridiculousness of the situation and started to laugh. What was the worst that could possibly happen? The institute would die or be temporarily shelved and I would have had an interesting experience for the better part of a year; I had met Freeman Dyson and Roger Penrose, among many others—events I couldn't possibly have imagined happening in the normal course. Houses can always be sold again if need be, or I might find myself staying there and working at RIM or another company in the area. Worst case scenario, there was always financial mathematics. Stop taking yourself so seriously, I chided myself. When all is said and done, it's only a physics institute, for goodness sake—it's not like anybody's dying or anything. Do the best you can and stop worrying about things you can't control.

For perhaps the first time since the whole business began I was forced to put things in their proper perspective and fully appreciate the unique opportunity I had somehow been given to do something genuinely interesting. From despair I turned quickly to a swaggering John Wayne type of optimism (aided, perhaps, by being in the southwest). This ship may be going down, I thought to myself, but I'm certainly not leaving it without a fight. I'm having far too good a time.

That moment in New Mexico, cut off from all contact with Mike and forced, through a bizarre combination of the NASDAQ, skeptical physicists and the *New York Times* to rigorously assess my situation, was a personal turning point and I've often drawn upon its core message whenever I've felt myself starting to lose perspective. (Later, I found out that Mike had never received any of my increasingly distraught messages. We had fallen into the habit of sending messages directly to each other's BlackBerrys by PIN instead of through general e-mail, and he had moved on to a more advanced device with a different PIN so nothing was getting through. "I was wondering why I hadn't heard from you in a while," he responded absentmindedly when we got together shortly after I returned. It was all I could do to restrain myself from slapping him.)

The next morning, fully re-energized, I met with people from the Santa Fe Institute. Created from the passion and sheer force of dynamism of a few charismatic scientists, among them the legendary physicist Murray Gell-Mann, the Santa Fe Institute had received mixed reviews from the scientific establishment. Some thought its bold mission to devote itself to the new science of complexity placed it firmly on the scientific cutting edge, while others disdainfully regarded it as a one trick pony, a solution in search of a problem that was based on the woolly and misguided premise that if you throw a physicist, biologist and economist together in a room interesting things will necessarily happen. The fact that some of the institute's founders had contributed strongly to the significant hype surrounding the sfi in its early days (many a glowing self-promoting piece was written detailing how the sfi was "redefining science") doubtless didn't exactly help its cause among the wider scientific community once it ran into its inevitable growing pains.

Perched atop a mesa with spectacular views of the surrounding countryside, the sfi is serenely self-contained, geographically and culturally distinct from any surrounding academic institutions. The original idea was to create a dynamic environment of consistent intellectual ferment that would challenge the established orthodoxy. Faculty were not tenured, but rather on five year contracts, with the explicit understanding that that would create a spirit of vitality and turnover. The problem, then-president Ellen Goldberg explained to me ruefully, was that not much actually seemed to be changing.

"People came to us and said, 'You've got the exact same people here you started with fifteen years ago. You guys aren't dynamic at all—you're the exact opposite.' So we knew we had to change something. It wasn't change for the sake of change, of course, more of a recognition that we had to do something to get back to our original mandate."

So a purge was effected—many of the old guard were dismissed and several new faculty hired. "It wasn't pretty," Goldberg told me, "but it had to be done." I asked her how.

"Ah," she replied, "that's when our advisory committee earned their stripes. You see, an advisory committee can sometimes be a royal pain. Most of them have rampaging egos and are convinced they should make all the decisions, but that would be a huge mistake: they're all brilliant, of course, but brilliant at science, not management, which is something rather different indeed. You can't let them run the place—it would go down the tubes in a heartbeat. But one of the vital things they can do is to provide real objective oversight and point you candidly in the direction that you need to go for your overall organizational health. In our case it was our advisory committee that brought matters to a head and made us fully recognize that some fairly drastic changes needed to occur."

I hadn't seen the SFI before the recent management crisis so I was in no shape to make any sort of comparison, but I still couldn't help thinking that the place had a subdued, almost forlorn air about it when I visited. Perhaps I had arrived too soon after the recent battle and things would take off again shortly afterwards, but it was certainly cause for concern and left a strong impression on me that this balance between dynamism and stability was one that would have to be handled very carefully indeed.

From Santa Fe I travelled across the desert to Los Alamos to have lunch with Raymond Laflamme. Ray's was a name I had been coming across frequently in my travels: originally a relativist who completed his PhD in quantum gravity with Stephen Hawking in Cambridge, Ray later switched to the emerging field of quantum information theory, achieving significant new understanding in how a quantum computer could handle errors as it computed. This was a highly valuable result: any calculating machine must have sufficiently robust "error correction" algorithms to enable it to consistently and accurately calculate in the midst of a real world filled with random extraneous noise, and there was much concern in the early years that a putative quantum computer would be waylaid by any natural errors or noise introduced into the system. Recently, Ray had switched his core field yet again, this time expanding on his theoretical activities to incorporate experimental ones, with his current work at Los Alamos National Laboratories centred on building an early stage quantum computer with nuclear magnetic resonance (NMR). Anyone who could successfully change orientations twice—first across disciplines and then, even more impressively, across the theory-experimentalist chasm—was worth looking at seriously. Moreover, Raymond, with his perfect mix of interests and experience in quantum gravity and quantum computing, two areas Perimeter was motivated to develop a presence in, would be an obvious person to consider.

I arranged to meet Ray for lunch at a local Los Alamos café, unwittingly causing him grave concern in the process. I had offered several times to meet him at his office at Los Alamos, but he had consistently and politely refused. Typically when arranging meetings with scientists I didn't know, my default was to come to their office in an attempt to be as respectful as possible and cause them the least amount of inconvenience. I also recognized that from a psychological perspective this was generally much preferable to them—they'd be on their home turf and if I started frothing at the mouth or something, they could just boot me out of the office and return to their normal routine. So when Ray suggested we meet for lunch, I assured him that I was fine with that of course, but reiterated my willingness to drop by his lab instead if that would be more convenient.

Of course, what I didn't fully appreciate at the time was that I couldn't just "drop by" Los Alamos National Laboratories, owing to the miasma of national security regulations any unknown visitor (let alone a foreign national) must face when visiting. My knowledge of Los Alamos largely consisted of stories of Richard Feynman running around cracking safes during the days of the Manhattan Project. Unquestionably there was much I had not fully appreciated.

Ray being the polite and respectful person he is didn't say "Are you out of your mind?!" or words to that effect, which might have made me realize I couldn't possibly obtain the upper security clearance required to enter an American weapons establishment. Instead he rather gracefully tried to steer the meeting towards neutral ground, all the while silently assuming I was probably a spy. As it happens, the laboratory was in the midst of a huge public spy scandal, and such concerns hardly seemed paranoid (one of their scientists, Taiwanese-born American Wen Ho Lee, was formally indicted by a federal grand jury in December 1999 for mishandling classified nuclear information, and rumours were swirling about a possible Chinese infiltration of key American security establishments).

Not surprisingly under the circumstances, I found Ray somewhat cool and distant at first, but he quickly warmed up and we eventually had quite a lively conversation. I knew he was Canadian, and hence the prospect of luring him north of the border towards somewhat less temperate climes might be more feasible than with most, and I was gratified to see that he seemed genuinely intrigued by my story. I was interested to hear that, coincidentally, the University of Waterloo had offered him a faculty job some years ago in their physics department, but he had declined because both the salary and research resources were considerably less than his current situation at Los Alamos.

This was a most interesting development, because as keen as I was to explore the possibilities of recruiting Ray, I wasn't at all sure what I could recruit him for. We were a theory institute, and it must be admitted that, despite the fact that he was an accomplished theorist with a background perfectly suited for Perimeter, he was indeed spending much of his time being an experimentalist. But if the University of Waterloo could be cajoled into making a complementary investment in quantum computing, particularly involving a spectrum of experimental avenues, then we not only might be able to jointly recruit Raymond, but could also go on to develop Waterloo, through the combined efforts of PI and UW, as a truly formidable international focal point for both experimental and theoretical quantum information science research. To become a genuinely global force in this new, emerging field would require more than just theoretical physicists and computer scientists; we needed to create an environment where theorists and experimentalists could naturally and productively interact on a regular basis. If we could somehow induce UW to devote significant resources to this area, then it might be possible to create a meaningful partnership that would be naturally centred around a joint vision of global excellence in quantum information science.

From our perspective, this would not only increase the critical mass of top scientists in the region, we would also have a necessary tie-in to the experimental realm through interaction with the University of Waterloo—a helpful way of positively affecting the culture of our rather abstract theoretical research institute. It wouldn't hurt to regularly remind some of our researchers of the real world as they built their sophisticated models of spin networks and compactified extra dimensions of space-time.

I knew well from my many discussions with Mike that he was enormously excited by the prospect of a complementary initiative in quantum information science at UW, and he began once again mooting the possibility of additional personal philanthropy to make it possible. The immediate focus, though, was on recruiting Raymond, who we imagined would be the director of such a project. Shortly after I returned to Waterloo, I began discussions with Jim Lepock, the chair of physics at UW and a thoroughly reasonable and straightforward fellow, about how PI and UW could best combine forces to recruit

Raymond. I suggested giving him special status as a part-time member of PI, while UW agreed to offer him one of their new senior Canada Research Chairs. In the meantime, we hoped the prospect of becoming the director of a new, well-funded institute presented a large incentive for Ray, while at the same time enabling the University of Waterloo to focus around a timely initiative that would naturally allow it to leverage its existing strengths in math, computer science and engineering.

For my part, with Lee and Ray I had found two strong possibilities for creative, foundational thinkers in two different areas of the institute's purview: quantum gravity and quantum information theory. I knew it was essential to find someone of exceptional stature in superstring theory, not only because it was the dominant area of foundational physics research (and as a new institute dedicated to fundamental physics, we couldn't possibly not have people doing string theory at the highest levels), but equally because it was important to send a message to the physics community that PI was determined to do things differently, with active high-level research programs in string and non-string approaches simultaneously. I was intent on establishing that we would neither be the second incarnation of Penn State (the quantum gravity centre led by Abhay Ashtekar where Lee, Carlo Rovelli and others had done much of their pioneering work) nor simply a bastion of string theory, but rather a place where, in the absence of experimental evidence, competing ideas could be debated forthrightly in a spirited, rigorous and potentially iconoclastic manner. But to successfully create that atmosphere, it was vitally important that we recruit high-quality string theorists, and those were mighty hard to come by, given that virtually all of them had already been wooed away to top American research universities and had settled comfortably in a climate of ample resources and brilliant colleagues. A common lament heard during my travels outside North America at the time was that most European research centres had simply given up trying to build successful string theory groups because competing with the United States for talent had become virtually impossible.

Fortunately, there was one string theorist of sufficiently impressive stature whom I suspected might be a real possibility to lure to PI: Rob Myers. During my investigatory trips, Rob was recommended as an obvious first choice by a significant number of highly illustrious scientists of various persuasions, who were all impressed by his unique combination of scientific excellence and quiet, unassuming character. Despite the respect he had obviously garnered throughout the community, many considered him still somewhat underappreciated—precisely, it was generally felt, because he wasn't the sort to go around loudly beating his own drum. Others cautioned that despite his relatively low profile, things were likely to change soon: there was considerable speculation that he was already fielding offers from prestigious American schools, determined to recruit him away from his current position at McGill.

Shortly after I returned from California, I travelled to Montreal and went out to lunch with Rob, fellow McGill faculty member Cliff Burgess and visiting scientist Maxim Pospelov. I talked to them about Perimeter, and cautiously explored their level of interest. I welcomed the opportunity to meet Burgess, as well, as he was widely regarded as a first-class researcher with an exceptionally large scientific breadth that ironically resulted in him sometimes being underappreciated within science's often narrow zones of judgement. Pospelov, a dynamic young particle physicist, I hadn't yet heard of.

As it happened, I had met Rob several years earlier when I was determined to return to physics to do my doctorate; I had approached him both to ask his advice and investigate if he would be available to supervise me. He respectfully declined taking me on, citing too many current students and responsibilities, but recommended Rob Mann at Waterloo instead, where I eventually settled. I was pretty sure Rob wouldn't remember the encounter, which I found vaguely embarrassing, highlighting as it did my relative inexperience in the field, and was somewhat relieved that he showed no sign of recognition when I gave the three of them my standard PI spiel over lunch that day. But of course, I was wrong: years later I found out that Rob had remembered, he just didn't see the point in mentioning it, sensing it might be impolite and realizing, in any event, that it was irrelevant to the issue at hand.

At any rate, all three seemed suitably intrigued by the story; Rob, I was gratified to see, showed definite interest in exploring the situation further and I resolved to follow up with him as soon as possible. Seven years later, all three of our summer luncheon party are significantly involved in PI: Rob as a founding faculty member and Cliff and Maxim as associate members, splitting their time between PI and McMaster and University of Victoria respectively.

But all that was still to come. By August 2000, I had completed my initial investigations. Throughout all my travels, I had been writing reports back to the board, highlighting my findings and recommending consequent action. It was now time to firm up what and how we wanted the institute to be: on October 23, 2000, we were going public.

CHAPTER EIGHT

Going Public

Aside from eventually prodding me towards some much-needed perspective in the middle of the New Mexico desert, the stock market meltdown of early 2000 also provided a tangible demonstration of Mike's commitment to the enterprise. The first board meeting we had after the stock had collapsed was a somewhat jittery one as several people were quietly wondering if things were going forward at all. The stock had fallen from $250 to twenty dollars per share, and all of a sudden $120 million seemed like a good deal more money than it had at the previous board meeting. Mike, however, carried on as breezily as before. At one point he felt compelled to announce, silencing the unspoken murmurs: "I had made up my mind to do this when the stock was at fifteen dollars and I'm not about to change it now."

And that was that. Over the next few years, I'd casually follow RIM stock and watch it go through several iterations of remarkable highs and lows, often seemingly untethered to real world events, but I never again let it bother me. It simply wasn't my concern. Mike had to worry about RIM. My job was to build a physics institute.

And so I turned my attention to the task at hand. Throughout my travels I received a rather wide variety of comments and advice. Much of it tended to cancel itself out in the overall scheme of things: some thought we should be broader in focus, others narrower. Some recommended a large number of permanent faculty with a matching contingent of postdocs; others believed the number of postdocs should be far more numerous than the faculty. While most people, after some reflection, believed theoretical physics was ruled too strictly by sociological forces and that many meritorious avenues of research were going unsupported, there was a considerable divergence in opinion as to what, precisely, should be given more support, with most people, unsurprisingly, recommending some area they had been involved with at some time or another.

The central point almost everyone seemed to agree on, however, was that we should remain structurally independent of any surrounding university to safeguard our flexibility. Independence would give us a real competitive advantage to move quickly and boldly to recruit top research staff and set up ambitious programs, but it was recognized that it also had a downside—that we had to find a way to incorporate dynamism within the structure itself so as not to become unduly entrenched. There are many examples of independent scientific institutes that go great guns for the first ten or fifteen years and then gradually begin to diminish in productivity as their initial faculty age. Of course, the single greatest tool towards ensuring a dynamic environment is youth: we already had a strong commitment to building a healthy complement of postdoctoral fellows, but it would be better still if we could also create some mechanism for incorporating graduate students within the core of the institute.

Back in the boardroom, the notion of building an independent institute with a dynamic, youth-friendly atmosphere was something everyone was quite receptive to: but how, precisely, to achieve it? How could we remain independent of a university and still foster strong, regular links with graduate students unless we became a degree-granting institution ourselves? This issue was naturally linked to how, precisely, we could and should interact with the surrounding academic community to ensure the institute acted as a catalyst to create a heightened reputation for high-level research activity in theoretical physics throughout the entire region.

After much deliberation, we elected to try a hybrid model where we wouldn't give tenure directly to our faculty, but would instead offer them renewable contracts at the institute while simultaneously trying to arrange for a tenured or tenure-track appointment at a neighbouring university. For those who elected to take up this cross appointment, there would be a corresponding commitment of light teaching duties at the university as well as an expectation of supervising graduate students, many of whom would then be in resident for some period at PI.

Of course, "try" is the operative word here and is worth stressing. Throughout the years I have often been struck by the fundamental difference in attitude between the board members and research community. To a researcher used to living in the strict milieu of the academic canon established in medieval times (if not, indeed, before), academic policies of tenure and titles are fixed points of light in the heavenly firmament, never to be questioned, only to be dutifully passed on from generation to generation. The board members, on the other hand, understood the institute to be a great experiment and recognized that things would most likely have to be adapted as we went along. The cross appointments appeared to be an effective way of fostering real interaction with the surrounding universities while developing a mechanism to incorporate graduate students within the institute. It seemed like a reasonable plan, but might not work as well as hoped, or only up to a point—in which case, we would have to revisit the issue and likely change something. This pragmatic "wait and see" attitude, seemingly innocuous and replete with common sense, has an amusing ability to drive many an academic, desperate for the certainties of an inviolable world, completely around the bend. In time, it became abundantly obvious to me that, whatever one might think of the merits of tenure, Perimeter's decision not to give tenure to our senior researchers was proving a significant impediment in our ability to attract and retain the highest quality faculty. This was, correspondingly, changed in 2007.

Once we had decided to be independent, it was natural to begin investigating more seriously where to actually build the place. The City of Waterloo showed considerable enthusiasm at the prospect of a physics institute after it was made clear to them that we were a theoretical scientific enterprise and thus wouldn't be occupied with any nasty experiments involving hazardous materials. When we confidentially disclosed to them the magnitude of the monies that had been committed to the institute as well as our determination to be involved in public outreach, they were overwhelmed and immediately offered to donate a site, giving us a choice of four prime properties. Three of the four sites were typical spots for research institutes: attractive wooded areas bordering conservation sites and well off the beaten track. The last option was located in the heart of Waterloo, adjacent to a large pond (named Silver Lake, despite the fact that it's neither silver nor a lake) and currently the home of an old, dilapidated hockey arena that was slated for demolition. As soon as Mike and I saw it, we knew this was it: an easy stroll to the shops and restaurants, walking distance to both the University of Waterloo and Wilfrid Laurier University and yet still in a parkland setting. Even more important, this was a space with a presence—a spot that would galvanize attention from the surrounding community. For two people intent on demonstrating to society at large that theoretical physics was important, simply no other site would do. It was perfect.

Well, it was almost perfect. It still had a hockey rink on it, and while the arena's days were over, saying that and knocking it down were two rather different matters. By the time the city offered us the site, the arena's life had already been prolonged for several seasons by distraught hockey fans. Worse still, the arena was associated with something altogether different again: war veterans. Shortly after the Second World War, many Canadian towns built community recreation centres officially dedicated to the fallen. So it was that the hockey rink we were intent on demolishing was named Memorial Arena; and even though only the façade from the 1947 structure remained, listing to one side, and the roof had been replaced fifteen years earlier with a shoddy, inflatable bubble, it was fondly regarded as one of the cornerstones of our community. Suddenly, building a physics institute on our perfect site was tantamount to an assault on Canadian values, sullying the memory of those who had made the ultimate sacrifice to free the world from the tyranny of fascism.

When I told Mike of our looming public relations concerns, he was simply beside himself.

"What does a hockey rink have to do with the war?" he exclaimed.

Mike, you must understand, is one of the few Canadians I have ever met who is positively anti-hockey. Every now and then one encounters a few people who are brave enough to express steadfast indifference when informed of the latest NHL trade or playoff result, but I had seldom encountered someone who regarded the game with such passionate disdain. This made it easy to provoke him, which I greatly enjoyed doing, despite my fundamental sympathy to the cause. When I really got him going, he would lapse into his thesis that hockey, like most organized sports, was a massive diversion perpetrated on witless humans by aliens determined to ensure that we would never achieve our full intellectual potential and expand out of the solar system where we might become a nuisance to more advanced civilizations. For Mike, the only thing worse than hockey was golf, a peril that he had seen many of his fellow executives fall victim to and for him represented nothing less than the acme of inanity.

"Have you every seen a hockey game?" I asked. "It's actually a lot like war."

"Unbelievable," he muttered to himself, ignoring my blithe taunt. "We're building an institution of scholarship, of learning, of science!" he cried, pronouncing the last word with an almost religious awe. "And they are upset because we are knocking down a collapsing, condemned hockey rink!"

He turned to me, suddenly, eyes flashing. "Howard, are we doing the right thing? Do these people deserve a physics institute?"

That was Mike in a nutshell. How many people, I thought fondly, could look at the world that way—regarding a scientific research institute as a treasure to be cherished by society, earned as the collective fruits of some sort of good behaviour.

"I don't know if they deserve one," I replied. "I'm not even sure I know what that means. But they're going to get one. And they're going to like it."

From this belligerent, knee-jerk reaction I was brought once more to reflect on what might be possible to raise the image of science in the public consciousness. Why couldn't we create a society where a physics institute would be as warmly welcomed as a sports complex? Sure, it was a long shot, but it was certainly a valiant goal.

Furthermore, I thought to myself, this was a wonderful chance to go considerably beyond physics and include a whole tapestry of exciting, high-level activities—from continuing education courses in the history of science to lectures on art to top quality musical performances. Instead of merely crying into my late-night doughnut-shop coffee about the false dichotomy of art and science together with the public's shameful ignorance of both, here was a concrete opportunity to actually lead by example. I began to imagine top quality musical performances in the intimate confines of our lecture theatre, internationally renowned recording artists playing chamber music surrounded by blackboards filled with physics equations to an appreciative public and enthusiastic research staff.

Of course, such an effort would be very valuable for community relations and raising the public profile of the institute; and any successful effort in this vein would go a considerable distance to making the area more attractive and culturally diverse, which in turn would assist in our recruitment effort. But the principal reason I became so excited about the prospect was the simple joy of opportunity: here was a chance to do something extraordinary, to foster an environment of high-level science and art and create a culture of excellence for activities I truly believed in. The only limits would be my imagination, energy and creativity. If I build it, I thought to myself, maybe they really will come.

Back in the mundane world of hockey rinks, however, things were grinding along. The city had sensibly elected to rename its new recreation centre across the street the Waterloo Memorial Recreation Centre, complete with an official rededication ceremony and procession from the old arena to the new complex—so that took care of the veterans' sensitivities. The hockey-playing public, on the other hand, while never pleased at the prospect of the loss of one of their ice surfaces, was largely distracted by the prospect of a brand new complex opening in the east of the city that promised no less than four ice rinks.

This situation, too, was not without its share of ironies. En route to the local airport one day to fly off to meet a federal politician, Mike spent the whole drive relaying to me how the city had run out of money to build its new recreation complex and, in desperation, had turned to RIM to help: "They begged us for donations," he complained, "and told us that it was vital for the community. So what could we do?" Then he turned to me with a look of utter exasperation: "Do you know what they're going to use it for?" he demanded. "Hockey and golf! Unbelievable! They've got my company saving the day for hockey and golf!"

A significant number of RIM employees did eventually step up and donate a considerable sum of money in the form of shares to ensure the facility could be completed. What Mike didn't tell me at the time, quite possibly because he wasn't aware, was that in a last-ditch effort to drum up the necessary resources, the city had frantically gone back to the local corporate sector and promised they would rename the facility after whoever became the largest donor. So it was that the fancy new Waterloo sports complex became known as RIM Park, much to the chagrin of many angry residents who regarded this as an abdication of their public ownership and yet another shameful example of aggressive corporate marketing. The story took a still further turn towards the ironic when it was discovered that the public financing of the entire project was fundamentally flawed, resulting in higher taxes, an irate public, a new council and considerable distaste for the entire venture. The day the story broke, Mike came running to me waving a front-page headline of the local paper that screamed "RIM's Financing Flawed!"—ambiguously conflating the recreation complex with his company. "You see!" he screamed to me. "You see what happens when you get involved with hockey and golf!"

Meanwhile, we held a press conference officially announcing the existence of Perimeter Institute on October 23, 2000. Thankfully, none of our fears of inflated rumours and runs on the stock had materialized and the announcement proved a complete surprise to the world at large. I said a few words and introduced Mike, who spoke generally about his motivations and passion for science. It was not a particularly large press conference, but representatives were there from the major national papers, TV and radio, and the next day the story was front-page news. Mike was, of course, quite familiar with press conferences at RIM, but it was my first and I was struck by the condensed nature of the media experience. For one brief shining moment we were "news" and the hordes descended furiously, forcing me to reiterate my prepared lines as I answered the same questions over and over: "Why was Mike doing this?" "How does this help RIM?" "Are there any other institutes like this in the world?" "How much money do you have now?" "Are you getting government support?" I did TV, radio and newspaper interviews all day long for one or two days. Then nothing. Finished. Yesterday's news. The transition was breathtakingly abrupt.

While Mike was used to the press experience, it was nonetheless different for him: there would be no unveiling of new products or announcement of business partnerships. This time it was strictly personal: his money, his philanthropy, his commitment. In those days, it's worth recalling, Mike was almost completely unknown outside the tech community. Most people hadn't heard of RIM and even those who had would typically confuse it with a dot-com company. Mention "BlackBerry" to the average man on the street back then and he would naturally assume you were referring to the fruit. Today, it is a rather different story.

Still, a press conference was a press conference.

"Keep it simple," Mike urged me, sensitive to my tendency to lapse into convoluted, prolix sentences in a desperate attempt not to trivialize. "Stay on message. Don't confuse people."

"What if they're already confused?" I countered.

"Keep it simple," he repeated, ignoring me. "The most important thing is that people realize that this is a good thing."

My concern, however, lay in the other direction. My experience with our communication consultants had alerted me to the hyperbolic tendencies of the media and I was determined not to antagonize the entire national and international scientific community by emitting hubris-laden phrases on how we were going to do things differently, bigger, better, etc. Better no announcement at all than that happening.

On the whole, I think, we were fairly successful. The basic message got out—philanthropy, physics, $120 million, new institute—while the hype was kept to a relatively dull roar. There was, of course, a fair amount of ambiguity: the association with RIM proved difficult to shake and even today there are many who regard Perimeter Institute as "that RIM thing," convinced that we are somehow a research and development arm of Research In Motion. There were also the inevitable mistakes regarding our independence. Despite our explicit clarifications, many viewed PI as part of University of Waterloo, a confusion that proved particularly troubling with neighbouring academics and administrators.

The surrounding academic community reacted to the announcement with frigid politeness, which, all things considered, was both understandable and expected. Here was a mammoth donation by a new breed of entrepreneur specifically targeted towards basic research, surely an event that would resonate deeply with the fundamental values of a university, but directed instead at an independent institute with an unknown structure led by an unknown person. "It's a wonderful opportunity," was the standard sort of quote one would hear, a grudging admission of potential with the tacit addendum, "And they'll probably screw it up."

Of course, there was a good dollop of envy and jealousy. One could just imagine the thundering voices of local university presidents collectively haranguing their respective fundraising staff: "How could you have missed $120 million!" Perhaps the most frustrated of them all was David Johnston. Here was the largest philanthropic donation in Canadian history by a local entrepreneur to establish a new research institute, and it was down the road from David's well-established technical university, but clearly (and provocatively) independent of it. David had understandably tried to convince Mike to put PI inside UW (and suffered the slings and arrows of *Armageddon* in the process), but the board (including, it is worth mentioning, a former president of UW) had wisely concluded that we would be better off this way.

A less savvy person might well have let things slide at this point. But David took a strikingly opposite approach despite what must have been a clear disappointment: he engaged as never before. He tried to understand why PI elected to become independent of any university and what sort of special relationship we might be able to form with UW to our mutual advantage. He helped smooth out the relationships between PI and UW, worked diligently with me to recruit cross-appointed faculty to the area and supporting the institute at key times during our efforts to procure funding from the federal and provincial governments. And rather than becoming frustrated by Mike's large-scale funding of a new, independent academic initiative, he redoubled his efforts to integrate Mike into the UW fold, awarding him an honorary doctorate for his community leadership and technical accomplishments with RIM and selecting him as Chancellor of the University.

Such actions might seem obvious, given that he was dealing with a philanthropically inclined billionaire with a passion for science, but one should never underestimate the academic propensity for veering away from the obvious and doing something petty and counterproductive. Not for David, however; and his continued persistence was rewarded some years later, as we had planned, with the full-blown development of UW's Institute for Quantum Computing.

By opting for pursuing a policy of steady engagement with PI, David chose the eminently rational—indeed, scientific—approach. Not bad for a lawyer.

CHAPTER NINE

On the Edge

By the end of 2000, Lee Smolin, Rob Myers and Fotini Markopoulou were ready to make the leap to come to PI the following fall, and we began advertising for our first three-year postdoctoral fellowships. Tenured academics typically have the contractual opportunity to take a year's unpaid leave from their current position, a provision that both Rob and Lee capitalized on from McGill and Penn State respectively. While to an outsider their keeping a foot in both camps might signify a lack of commitment to our cause, that would be a gross misreading of the situation: coming to a fledgling physics institute in Waterloo that existed only in name was a significant career risk—to even consider such a move was risky. To needlessly give up one's preciously earned post while doing so would be little less than sheer lunacy.

All three were interested in investigating cross-appointment possibilities with UW, resulting in long, drawn-out negotiations with university officials as we tried to work out just what, precisely, such agreements would entail. The university was naturally determined to avoid being a mere "tenure backstop," only encountering PI researchers once they were cast out of the institute for being washed up, while I was agog that they would consistently regard the top quality researchers we were attracting solely as "career risks." Still, their reticence was quite understandable: here was a new, unproven institute that was asking them to make long-term commitments to faculty in an area of research they were not currently focused on, whom they effectively hadn't selected, and for whom this new institute wasn't prepared to accept as long-term risks in the standard academic tradition while their institution was struggling to make ends meet on declining government support. All of this while still smarting from the rebuff of not placing PI within UW to begin with; to a skeptical UW official it doubtless smacked of trying to have one's cake and eat it, too.

It helped that the Institute for Quantum Computing (IQC) was moving ahead, albeit painfully slowly. In early 2001, David Johnston held a dinner at his farmhouse for Mike, all relevant members of the upper administration—all six deans, provost, vice president of research, past president and so forth—and me. This was the opportunity Mike and I had repeatedly discussed and been waiting for: the chance to impress upon all relevant parties the opportunity to collectively seize the day on quantum computing. At the time, Raymond Laflamme had not officially signed on to UW and PI and was being actively wooed by a number of other institutions.

Mike held forth enthusiastically on the prospect of a quantum computing institute at UW and the potential for PI and UW to develop the critical mass to make Waterloo a pre-eminent global destination for quantum information science. Then he dropped the carefully prepared bombshell: a commitment in principle to another overwhelming amount of personal scientific philanthropy, but this time to UW's incipient IQC, and only on condition that they successfully work with me to recruit Raymond as well as find ways to match fifty percent of his donation. This matching stipulation was borne of Mike's understandable frustration that he was turning into a one-man granting council. It was also a sign of our growing awareness of the way things worked in the world of research funding: in a climate where both the Canadian and Ontario governments were taking increasingly active and productive roles in research support, it should hardly be impossible for a determined university to find a way of matching large, third-party grants towards cutting-edge science, which government should arguably be investing in anyway. And unlike, say, superstring theory, quantum information science held the promise of much more tangible accomplishments in the relatively near future.

We knew we'd get everyone's attention: a properly constructed IQC would involve a wide spectrum of research expertise through an interdisciplinary approach that would hold something tangible for virtually every dean sitting around that table. Mike's announcement was met with the usual paeans to his unbridled generosity and vision, but the matching condition was an immediate and obvious concern. "How can we possibly find that sort of match?" they asked him earnestly. "What would you suggest, Mike?"

It was hardly the most proactive and enthusiastic response imaginable and did much to confirm the necessity of imposing such a constraint in the first place. Still, we left the dinner amidst determined avowals to jointly move the case along and take over the quantum computing world. Afterwards, Mike and I drove to a nearby Tim Hortons for a post mortem. I got there first and was reflectively sipping my coffee when Mike bounded in several minutes later like a kid at Christmas, bouncing up and down in his chair: "I think they're finally going to do it!" he exclaimed. "I think this is finally going to happen!" Not for the first time it struck me as somewhat ironic that the guy who was actually donating his money should be brimming with excitement, while the potential recipients were hunkered down glumly somewhere, wondering how they might ever find a way of satisfying the conditions of the gift.

Meanwhile, back at PI, we were gearing up for our first Scientific Advisory Committee (SAC) meeting. From the very beginning the SAC was a rather contentious topic: there were some on the board who were opposed to its creation on principle, feeling that its very existence would represent a kowtowing to the court of established scientific opinion that would naturally limit the institute's rebellious potential. George and I, however, were adamant that a SAC was essential: I knew we would have a difficult enough time establishing the credibility of PI within the scientific establishment given our unusual beginnings, but without a SAC it would be virtually impossible. Once labelled by the establishment as a wacky place, the institute would never garner the respect it needed to attract candidates of the highest order. On the other hand, it was indeed a tricky balancing act: the forces of conservatism were very strong and an overriding preoccupation with one's credibility would inevitably lead to PI becoming virtually indistinguishable from any other institute.

The issue of the SAC cut right to the heart of what we wanted PI to be: we didn't want to be different for the sake of being different—such an attitude is hardly mature or productive. After significant reflection, we recognized that the natural conservatism of academe combined with various socioeconomic factors (lack of funding for basic research, lack of academic positions) had led to a situation where many bright, creative people were streamed, sometimes unthinkingly, into rigid ideological positions; where conceptual risk-taking, either rethinking issues from first principles or tackling old conundrums long ago swept under the rug, was considered "too dangerous" to be undertaken by younger, untenured researchers who were often in their prime; and where all too often in a theoretical physics climate removed from the vital counterweight of data, mutually exclusive sects had developed, much to the detriment of the entire scientific enterprise.

That was how we wanted to "make a difference" as the saying goes. But the devil truly was in the details. It is all very well to talk about "mutually exclusive sects," and there is indeed much to be lamented about the way fashionable research avenues are often dogmatically trumpeted by some influential people to the exclusion of other approaches, but on the other hand one must be very careful: listening exclusively to those outside the mainstream is just as dangerous, if not more so, as blindly following it, and I had no intention of having Perimeter labelled an institute for lost causes. Popular approaches are often popular for a very good reason: they can be the most promising way to solve the problem at hand. Ignoring the mainstream not only runs a grave sociological risk, alienating wide swathes of the scientific populace and eliminating access to many of the brightest young minds, it is usually a pretty dumb thing to do scientifically as well.

As Roger Penrose summarizes in *The Road to Reality*, "To some extent the popularity of a theory provides a measure of its scientific plausibility—but only to some extent." Achieving the right balance between orthodox and unorthodox would not only be difficult, it would require constant vigilance and reassessment. In the end, of course, as for most things, it comes down to people: you can churn out propaganda and mission statements all day long, but if you don't have people who can carry the ball forward, it is all just, well, a theoretical exercise.

Considering how best to achieve the difficult balance of broad-mindedness and excellence often made me reflect on the unique scientific culture of the UK, which mysteriously seemed able to produce provocative, independent thinkers, such as Oliver Heaviside, David Deutsch and Julian Barbour, to name but a few, virtually every generation. Prestigious American universities are remarkably impressive in their ability to suck up top talent, of course, but there is something uniquely wonderful about the British, with their propensity for somehow fostering quiet iconoclasm, which should be scrutinized by anyone interested in rigorously considering best practices in such matters. A sometimes forgotten story is that of string theory pioneer John Schwarz, whom many suspect would never have lasted long enough in the scientific mainstream without the consistent support of Murray Gell-Mann and other Caltech colleagues who stubbornly encouraged him to hoe his own row. Without their constant support, it is questionable whether string theory would have flowered into anything like it is today. It's safe to say that the climate in top American institutions has not become any more welcoming to unorthodoxy since those pioneering days of Schwarz (rather ironically, given that it is the string theorists who now have the upper hand), while the UK still seems to maintain a considerable tolerance of scientific diversity, perhaps borne of a longer experience in witnessing revolutionary thinking arising from the unlikeliest of places.

For my part, I began to think there might be a sort of historico-geographical opportunity here. As a Canadian institution, perhaps we could credibly position ourselves as a mélange of the best of the American and British academic worlds: the rigours of Stanford with a twist of British eccentricity thrown in for good measure.

At any rate, I knew that moving forward with Rob and Lee together would definitely raise some eyebrows and be a concrete demonstration of our scientific and cultural intent, while recruiting the likes of Raymond Laflamme to build up a presence in quantum information science was one of the more obvious things to do, given the combination of his character and unique scientific pedigree.

Choosing the original SAC members, however, was equally important. I knew I needed a collection of people with impeccable scientific qualifications, but also with some sympathy to the spirit of the venture. People such as Roger Penrose, Jim Hartle and Chris Isham were obvious choices in this respect. Artur Ekert could not only give helpful advice on how to build up a successful group in quantum information theory, he could also add a refreshing dose of common sense. Scott Tremaine's principal scientific expertise lay outside of the core research mandate of PI, but that didn't strike me as necessarily a bad thing, as he could lend objectivity to the proceedings, particularly in light of his administrative expertise. Ian Affleck was an expert in condensed matter theory who had begun his career in particle theory, and I felt his views would be particularly salient as we developed. The question of whether or not to have a condensed matter theory group at PI has been a hotly debated topic since I started my first conversations about the institute with members of the academic community, and it seemed important to have a representative from that perspective as well. (Ian certainly didn't disappoint, and was a passionate, although doubtless often frustrated, advocate for a strong condensed matter presence at PI throughout his tenure on the SAC.) Cecilia Jarlskog, a particle physicist from CERN and Lund University in Sweden, had a unique combination of high-level scientific and administrative experience in addition to a broader perspective as a successful woman in a male-dominated field, while Joe Polchinski, a renowned string theorist from Santa Barbara, would be able to assist directly in building up that pivotal area we all knew would likely represent one of our biggest challenges.

When I first met Joe on my way through Santa Barbara in the midst of the stock market meltdown and other consequent preoccupations, he expressed some sympathy for what we were trying to accomplish but confided that he was not really "the committee type." I told him that was exactly the sort of person I was looking for. Six months later, he reluctantly agreed to serve a three-year term—largely, I suspect, out of respect for Rob Myers, who had by then joined PI.

I contacted each SAC member personally to ask if they would be willing to serve and followed up with an official engagement letter in November 2000. In the letter, I thanked them for their participation, described their intended roles and gave them some brief background of the institute: a list of board members, our research mandate and a list of the individuals we were presently recruiting (Lee, Rob and Fotini). The letter met with a resounding silence, which I naively assumed to be approbation, but I later realized only reflected the business of term time when most nonessential correspondence goes unread. A month or two later, someone twigged to what had happened and I saw the full extent of the firestorm I had touched off when I was inadvertently copied on an internal SAC e-mail:

"Do you know what he's done?" cried one indignant scientist to another. "He's gone ahead and made some offers already!"

We were off to a somewhat fractious start. From the SAC's perspective, such unilateral action represented the height of insolence; and the fact that I had forthrightly announced it in the engagement letter none of them had bothered to read made it even worse.

One could see their point. Serving on academic committees is hardly the most enjoyable task, and no reasonable person is going to invest the time and trouble of sitting on an advisory committee if those in charge are going to plow ahead regardless of what you say. Worse still, any action that smacks of trying to leverage the goodwill and scientific reputation of an advisory committee to justify actions they didn't recommend or formally approve of will necessarily backfire in the worst possible way, leading to massive resignations and a torpedoing of any credibility that might have been gained by appointing the committee to begin with.

I hadn't, of course, tried to do this, as was evident by the transparency of my engagement letter to them. The problem instead was cultural. The standard way to start up a scientific institute is for a collection of famous scientists to be appointed by a governmental agency, which then delegates all significant start-up decisions to this body. In our case, things were quite different: we had the money and a sense of what we wanted to do and we wanted to get going. We recognized that a SAC would be most helpful for a number of reasons, but we were anxious to move forward and strike a course and were excited at the targets of opportunity we had already found—many of whom had been identified after widespread, albeit informal, consultation with the likes of people on the SAC (and some of them personally).

It also didn't escape me that with all the grumbling and rumbling from some SAC members as we moved towards our first meeting, despite the frequent skepticism and innuendo of incompetence, nobody on the SAC ever questioned our judgement in selecting them. The fact that the same apparent bumblers who had structured the institute and engaged initial researchers had also simultaneously chosen them for the SAC didn't seem to assuage their fears of our poor judgement—it was as if that particular selection (and only that) were somehow divinely inspired.

The first full SAC meeting was set for March 2001, but a month or two before then I had arranged for an investigatory meeting to discuss prospective candidates for foundations of quantum theory and quantum information theory at Roger Penrose's house in Oxford, with Chris Isham and Artur Ekert. Jim Hartle joined us by phone.

Outwardly I tried to project an image of competence and cool objectivity, but inside I was more nervous than I had ever been in my entire life. I had met Roger only once before at his office in Oxford where I spent the vast majority of the conversation completely unable to concentrate on what was being said, suffused with feelings of accomplishment just for having somehow arranged to be in the same room with him. Artur Ekert was a world leader in quantum information science. Jim Hartle was one of the deepest thinkers there was, while Chris Isham had been nothing less than my inspiration, the primary reason I went back into physics and thus in some way responsible for the whole business. It was as though I had suddenly found myself promoted from toiling in Little League to managing the New York Yankees. The 1927 New York Yankees.

My nerves weren't exactly helped by the fact that Chris spent the entire trip up from London in his car browbeating me about the institute, emphatically informing me that everything I had done (aside from, of course, the selection of SAC members) was dead wrong. The one positive effect of all this was that by the time I stumbled out of the car at Roger's place, I was far too beaten down to be overwhelmed by the grandeur of the personalities. As we passed through Roger's study, I remember watching Artur and Roger animatedly discussing some subtle point of quantum theory in front of a blackboard. I wanted to go home. Alone.

But then, in my very nadir of insecurity, when visions of Starbucks barristahood started dancing seductively in my head, I was saved, yet again, by comedy. The time had come to call Jim in California to begin the meeting, but Roger couldn't find the phone. This was not a wireless phone, you understand, but an old-fashioned, beige British Telecom phone at least twenty-five years old that had doubtless never left the study, but it seemed to have escaped somehow. Where was Vanessa, Roger's wife? She could find the phone. But Vanessa was nowhere to be found—out taking Max, their young son, for a stroll in the pram. But wait! Here was the phone—hidden under a mass of paper and books. Victory! Despair quickly followed when we realized it was unplugged with no obvious outlet in site. It went on like this for quite some time: repeated technological hurdles arising, frantic searches for Vanessa, long detailed discussions about possible approaches to the problem, partial solutions. We finally managed to get through to Jim and couldn't hear him. We phoned him back and he couldn't hear us. It was like a Monty Python skit. Here I was, having a meeting with four of the smartest people on the planet about a physics institute that had been launched on the success of a wireless technology company and we were stymied by the prospect of operating a telephone.

I started to relax and enjoy the moment. I'm no Roger Penrose, but in my house, at least, the phone is regularly plugged in, and calling overseas is generally not regarded as logistically equal to launching the space shuttle.

When the conversation finally got going, with all four of us huddled over the phone on the floor in Roger's study like lions after the kill, I relaxed some more. It was clear that many were finding the prospect of identifying ideal candidates trickier than they first thought. It was one thing to talk about what sort of people might be appropriate in an ideal world and quite another to start talking turkey about who, when and how.

"Well there's so and so," one would start. "He'd be great. But his wife is an anthropologist and they'd never relocate.

Then there's such and such. But I can't ever see him leaving California for Waterloo." And so it went. In the end, we produced a list of desirable suspects with an acknowledgement that we would likely be unsuccessful.

"It is absolutely essential," averred Chris stentoriously on the way home, "that you get the best people." It was not the first time I had heard this sage advice directed my way and I was never quite sure what to make of it. As a general rule, I make a point of not arguing with tautologies and this seemed like a doozy. What did he think I was trying to do, get the worst people? Get mediocre people? Get any people I could find? And anyway, best at what? For a fledging institute with rather unique and ambitious goals, one might indeed want to deliberately recruit combinations of people that are somewhat nonstandard.

I had learned from my travels that more often than not "the best people" was a phrase that people trotted out when they really meant themselves or their friends. Of course there were the Ed Wittens of the world, those very few of such obvious intellectual dexterity and accomplishment that they transgressed any petty rivalries or cliques, but after that matters tended to get very muddy very quickly, with one man's superstar belonging firmly in someone else's "academy of the overrated." With Chris, the paradigmatic honour-bound English gentleman, I was quite certain his version of "the best people" didn't involve any sort of cronyism, but rather referred to some abstract Platonic form of Great Scientist I was far from certain existed.

Once I returned to Waterloo, local matters quickly returned to prominence. As previously mentioned, our rather ambitious plan from the beginning was to do more than just create an exciting new independent research centre, but also to galvanize the surrounding academic community so that the entire region became a dynamic centre of theoretical physics inquiry. Our original idea was that in time, each university would partner with PI to further develop its own subspecialty of excellence in a particular field—quantum computing, for example, would naturally be at the University of Waterloo, while cosmology, say, might be a focus at the University of Toronto, with its strong reputation as the home of the Canadian Institute for Theoretical Astrophysics. Integrating with the surrounding universities, however, was always a very dangerous game, as university officials tended to be almost schizophrenically leery of PI—oscillating between fears that we would interfere with their autonomy and "dictate an agenda to them" and concerns that we would simply ignore them as we raced ahead.

In an attempt to move forward in good faith and build appropriate bridges, we introduced the notion of a PI Associate Membership—someone who is jointly recruited to both PI and a neighbouring university with the expectation that she would meaningfully contribute to the development of both, concretely integrating students, postdocs, faculty and others from both places. As expected, some universities were more determined to proactively capitalize on this opportunity than others, resulting in a situation where, to this day, PI has considerably closer and more productive links with some universities than others.

For our part, there was the worry that surrounding universities would regard us as simply a bank or granting council—a misunderstanding that is of constant concern. The fact that a well-funded behemoth with determinations of international excellence had suddenly popped up in their midst would naturally roil the surrounding atmosphere, both in terms of money and attitude.

This was, of course, completely natural and had nothing

whatsoever to do with physics. Imagine, if you will, that you happily find yourself in possession of plentiful financial resources and are determined to establish a world-class centre for, say, tropical medicine in Nottingham or Nantucket or Novosibirsk. Now, none of these places (I think, anyway) is currently synonymous with outstanding levels of international excellence in this area, but doubtless the establishment of such an effort would meet with not inconsiderable resistance. There would be those who are fairly knowledgeable about aspects of tropical medicine who would take offense at the notion that they hadn't been involved with this new initiative in their own backyard; there would be numerous others who would loudly express frustration that such a centre was focused on such an esoteric topic as tropical medicine instead of core areas of acknowledged local expertise (i.e. typically their own); and there would also be the odd specialist who for whatever reason found herself nearby and with whom it would be beneficial to interact.

The obvious challenge is to find constructive ways of involving these select local experts, while forthrightly building a centre of the highest international standards, all the while somehow engaging the others who might feel resentful for all of this new money being directed to something not immediately relevant to them. It is a rather tricky business.

When I set the first PI postdoc salaries back in 2001, I turned unhesitatingly to the premier American research institutions as points of comparison, recognizing that however difficult it would be to attract top postdoctoral candidates to a new place, it would be frankly impossible to do so without at the very least being financially competitive. This meant that our initial postdoc salaries needed to be effectively double those at surrounding Canadian institutions—a fact that, needless to say, caused considerable consternation among the local officialdom.

"Don't you see what you're doing?" they cried in anguish.

"You're introducing tremendous inflationary pressures into the system!"

"Precisely," I replied. "How on earth are we going to attract the best postdoctoral fellows if we don't at least pay them enough to match other offers?"

It wasn't that I was unsympathetic to their financial pressures, of course, but the status quo wasn't going to get us to where we needed to go. Moreover, there was hope that by firmly facing up to this fact, we might be able to induce influential people in government that something more significant than incremental patchwork efforts needed to be done for us to become a serious option for top international researchers.

Still, first things first. In March of 2001 we held the first full meeting of our Scientific Advisory Committee in a hotel just outside Waterloo. First meetings are always difficult, but given the uniqueness of the institute and the miscommunication that had already transpired with my introductory letter, I was particularly concerned. The board was anxious to involve the SAC, but was equally anxious to ensure they wouldn't take over and veer towards micromanagement. I met with George, Doug and Lynn, the board academics, who agreed that I should say as little as possible during the meeting, a role that suited me just fine.

In the tension of the moment, even the smallest things took on disproportionate importance. When looking at the draft agenda that Scott Tremaine sent me for my comments, I remember George fuming:

"Why all these in camera meetings? If they want to spend so much time meeting by themselves, why do we have to fly them all the way here to do it?" I had a rather different take on things: from my perspective, any meeting that didn't involve my presence was a good idea. They could have done the whole bloody thing in camera if it had been up to me.

The evening they arrived we held a small ice breaker for the SAC and board members. Most of the scientists spent their time prodding Mike to see what his intentions really were, while I passed the night in guarded conversations with SAC members, frantically trying to eavesdrop on their conversations with Mike. Everybody was feeling each other out and from what I could see not much ice got broken.

The next day the formal part of the meeting began with Doug speaking candidly about the project. He explained that while we very much counted upon the SAC's advice and looked forward to increased interaction with them as the institute developed, the board was quite pleased with the way things had progressed and was determined to continue moving dynamically along, hopefully with their assistance. No stranger to academic politics, Doug had a clear understanding of the natural sense of entitlement many of the scientists would be feeling and recognized the importance of navigating the fine line between engagement and control.

The rest of the day went surprising smoothly. We discussed several possible new hires along with general strategic issues and approaches. I had arranged a more formal dinner that night with both administrative and scientific representatives of the surrounding universities, which seemed to go off quite well. When the meal had ended and some SAC members stood up to toast the promise of our new institute, I thought we were one big happy family.

Wrong. Never confuse, I was to learn, friendly off the cuff toasts by relaxed academics with their core business. When the meeting resumed the next day there were several heated exchanges and any trace of the previous evening's bonhomie was replaced by a cold, austere judgement that a great deal could be improved upon. To make matters worse, the entire meeting was plagued by serious technical problems: neither Chris nor Roger could attend that first meeting and for some reason the teleconference facilities didn't work well at all. It was only slightly better than my experience at Roger's house a few months back, and hardly the sort of thing to inspire confidence in our professionalism.

As soon as everyone had left, I was keen to sit down with George to analyze what had happened and plan our next steps. We had grown quite close over the past year and a half, discussing everything from academic strategy to details of the new building, and I was most anxious to hear his views. It was then end of term, however, and we had to delay our debriefing session a week so that he could turn his attention back to his seasonal duties of exam setting and managing distraught students. That first SAC meeting would be the last time I would see him: four days later, George had a massive heart attack and died.

Suddenly, academic politics no longer seemed so important.

CHAPTER TEN

I'm a Lumberjack and I'm Okay

George Leibbrandt's sudden death was a considerable blow in all directions: the institute lost one of its staunchest advocates, while I lost both a friend and one of my strongest supporters just as we began to venture forth into the increasingly turbulent seas of scientific public opinion.

It was clear to me from the very beginning that if Perimeter ever gained traction, I would be its Achilles heel. I knew it would be extremely difficult for the external community to countenance an institute led by some unknown upstart, whatever his initial role. Mike, of course, would be tolerated as the donor, brought out for awards and recognition of his largesse, but in time pressure would mount to shunt him off to some titular position out of harm's way as the scientific experts fought to exert greater and greater control. The knives for me, on the other hand, would come out immediately.

I told Mike this quite candidly, right at the very beginning. He understood my point, but it never seemed to bother him terribly much—in fact, I always had the feeling he felt a perverse thrill at poking his finger in the eye of the establishment, something he had been forced to do at RIM for some time. And anyway, it was his money.

But for me it was a considerable burden. I am naturally a fairly confident person with a rather robust opinion of myself and my abilities, but acting as executive director of an international physics institute was just about the most uncomfortable thing I could possibly do. The culture in academe for such things is awfully strict: it is the groundbreaking researcher who ends up the big cheese—Nobel laureates abound in such positions of authority. I knew a thing or two about physics, sure, but wasn't at the same level of scientific expertise as the people I was recruiting. Moreover, the thought of acting as a poseur, putting on airs and pretending I was a peer of the likes of a David Gross or Jim Hartle, was deeply offensive to me. I was caught in a Groucho Marxian nightmare of creating a club that I shouldn't even be a member of, let alone lead.

Others, I recognized all too well, either through jealousy or frustration at a perceived missed opportunity, would pounce on this to discredit the institute. "You don't go into the woods to find a lumberjack to run a scientific institute," Bill Unruh was reported to have harrumphed at an international gathering a short time after Perimeter's unveiling. While this remark belied his confusion about how the institute came into being, it was, I had to appreciate, not an entirely unreasonable reaction.

If I were Bill Unruh, sitting in my office in Vancouver having achieved considerable international renown during a life dedicated to the pursuit of foundational physics and one day discovered that huge amounts of money had been invested by some guy halfway across the country to start an institute centred around many of my interests led by some unheard of fellow, I'd likely be pretty miffed too.

On the other hand, I probably wouldn't start publicly frothing at the mouth, recognizing that such comments, however understandable in the wider scheme of things, have no possible upside and might just make their way back to their target, complete with full attribution. In short, it's a decidedly unproductive thing to say and a clear example of a curious nugget about academic administration that I had stumbled onto: leadership and administrative expertise is largely unrelated to research excellence. In fact, in many cases there is a strong argument that it is inversely related: most great scientists are positively lousy administrators. For an established university or institute with a clear organizational structure and corresponding delineation of duties, an administratively-challenged director may well represent a setback of sorts, but for a fledgling independent institute such as ours that needed to invent everything from scratch, the result would be little less than catastrophic.

I began to think more rigorously about what someone in my position actually does, and the more I thought about it the more it dawned on me how strange the standard academic solution really was. Creating an institute, I came to appreciate, required breadth, verve, guts, tremendous dollops of energy and a corresponding sense of ownership to see things through to their conclusion. It was essential to have a sharp nose for bullshit, an understanding of the prevailing political mindset, an ability to strategize and put oneself in other people's shoes and a willingness to rethink things from first principles to see what might be done differently. One had to write clearly and effectively, believe deeply in the cause and be willing to invest significant amounts of time and effort attending to tasks others might reflexively look to delegate, such as grant writing or communications.

There is, of course, recruitment. Arguments are often made that it is necessary to be a scientific expert to recruit exceptional candidates. While I certainly don't question the advantage of having specialized knowledge, it is important to recognize that identification of suitable candidates is hardly done in a vacuum and, when all is said and done, is not usually all that difficult: getting a sense of the top ten or twenty people in some scientific subdiscipline can usually be ascertained fairly quickly by asking a bevy of acknowledged experts around the world their candid views. One could, I expect, do the same for the top ten or twenty symphony conductors or high jumpers—the essential thing is to develop a good network of experts and utilize sound judgement regarding issues of character. In any case, it is inconceivable that any one person would be an expert at everything and could, or should, do such a task independently. Finding out which people would fit best in the culture we've established is harder, of course, and requires careful discussions with everyone concerned. But most of the time, there is a self-selection process at work: if someone is excited by what we are doing here, and by the unique atmosphere and possibilities that exist at PI, then they will be very interested. If they are uncomfortable with what we're doing they won't be persuaded. In my experience a far harder task than identifying suitable candidates is triggering their interest in the institute in the first place and disabusing them of any false impressions they might have about what it is and why it was created. While it is doubtless true that having an eminent super-brain as executive director of the institute would in itself be a tremendous draw that would directly assist recruitment, it is by no means a panacea: many institutes have just such a structure and there is no place that is successful in attracting everyone they want (not to mention the fact that most of the world's top scientists simply don't want to be a director of anything, vastly preferring the opportunity to occupy themselves with doing science). Often there are additional factors at play—spousal employment, cultural factors, and climate. Frequently, there is the appealing attraction, or conversely unappealing responsibility, of building up a significant group of faculty and postdocs. Sometimes the prospect of coming to a place that doesn't have an *éminence grise* in firm control is in itself an appeal. One just never knows.

In my experience, one of the most important aspects of recruiting is developing a sense of personal trust and respect with each candidate—trying to get a clear sense of the world from her perspective. Coming to a new institute may represent an opportunity, but it also likely represents a certain amount of fear and uncertainty. Overcoming the latter invariably boils down to trust—the candidate must have the confidence that you are resolutely determined to create an environment where she has every opportunity to achieve her full research potential. On our side, we must have the confidence that new recruits will embrace our unique culture and work well with the existing faculty—one or two rotten eggs at an early stage of development would significantly jeopardize the entire enterprise.

The closer I looked, the more starting an institute resembled starting a business; and as time went on I began to realize, quite shockingly, that I had quite an entrepreneurial temperament. By this I don't mean, of course, that I thought business standards—return on investment, revenue generation and so forth—should be applied to a theoretical physics institute, but rather that it was essential to fix firmly on a goal one believed in and then work like hell to get there.

It's always interesting to see what people will sweep under the rug when it's convenient to them. The precedents for building independent, endowed theoretical physics institutes dedicated to fundamental research aren't many but there is one notable example: Abraham Flexner, the architect of Princeton's famed Institute for Advanced Study and its first director, wasn't a physicist or a mathematician at all, but rather an educator and idealist who had established a reputation by critically researching medical schools throughout the United States and forthrightly exposing the many fraudulent ones. When the opportunity came, through the largesse of Louis Bamberger and Catherine Fuld Bamberger, to do something different and original, to create an environment resonating, unsurprisingly, with Flexner's Platonic ideals and beliefs, he jumped all over it, determined to capitalize on his good fortune and create something truly unique.

I, too, was captivated, as any entrepreneur would be, by the opportunity to dream big and live by my wits to achieve. From innovative research to an innovative building, from public lectures to musical performances, from government support to private fundraising, I had a blank slate to achieve something interesting and substantial. My only constraints, largely self-imposed, were that I had to ensure that all programs were at the highest international level and that I found a responsible way to pay for them all—a significant challenge if one is determined to grow the endowment throughout.

I often confuse visiting scientists who see me. Ushered into my office in the tried and true bureaucratic fashion, they invariably feel obliged to proffer comments on how wonderfully well we're doing: how nice the building is, how impressive the researchers are and so forth. "That's nice to hear," I'll respond politely, "but what I'd really like to know is what you think we're doing wrong and what can be improved. That's ever so much more interesting."

There is nobody more keenly aware than myself that Perimeter Institute was hardly inevitable and every day I naturally measure the institute's success by comparing it to what we might possibly achieve: Has the international physics world been substantially and positively affected by our existence? Have we inspired and informed students, teachers and the general public? Is our community significantly enhanced by our presence? Is science better appreciated? How, in short, are we making a difference and making it in the best possible way? Why are we here? What would happen if we disappeared?

Academic administrators, I learned quickly, typically have a rather different perspective. From chairs to deans, vps to presidents, the existence of their institution is a given: it was there well before they came along and will continue long after them. Personal ambition is a driving factor, and while many are, of course, motivated to make a positive contribution, they are primarily fulfilling a role, a position, a title, a notch on their belt, a line in their cv. There's nothing wrong with that, of course, but it does tend to give one a different view of things and affect the entire spirit of the enterprise.

As Cornford's *Microcosmographia Academica* elegantly warns:

My heart is full of pity for you, O young academic politician. If you will be a politician you have a painful path to follow, even though it be a short one, before you nestle down into a modest incompetence. While you are young you will be oppressed, and angry, and increasingly disagreeable. When you reach middle age, you will become complacent and, in your turn, an oppressor; those whom you oppress will find you still disagreeable; and so will all the people whose toes you trod upon in youth. If you persist to the threshold of old age you will be a powerful person yourself, with an accretion of peculiarities which other people will have to study to square you. The toes you will have trodden on by this time will be as the sands on the seashore; and from far below you will mount the roar of a ruthless multitude of young men in a hurry. You may perhaps grow to be aware what they are in a hurry to do. They are in a hurry to get you out of the way.

I must confess that I have always looked upon academic politicians with the same sort of profound bemusement that I regard skydivers, alligator wrestlers or dentists: I simply don't understand why they're doing what they're doing. An academic career doesn't come without sacrifices: the pay is generally mediocre, many of the daily tasks are routine and uninspiring and the pressure to consistently perform in the community of one's often highly immature and backbiting colleagues can be particularly taxing. Yet the perks of the trade—the freedom to do research, the opportunity to pursue one's own path towards knowledge while simultaneously training and being challenged by enthusiastic, like-minded youth—these are the priceless consolations of an honourable tradition and a refuge from the generally inane hurly-burly of existence that most people unthinkingly slog through their entire lives. To then give all that up for the sake of some grossly diluted form of political ambition—not the real kind, you understand, where one is in charge of billions of dollars and can develop policy that would affect millions of lives, but a pathetically myopic version where one has to mediate between petulant professors to establish where to put the faculty coffee machine—well, that I have never been able to understand. It would be one thing if academics were drafted into administration, like military service or jury duty, but the notion that there are those who relish the thought of climbing the greasy pole of university hierarchy, who spend their days and nights plotting and scheming at how to outfox their opponents and move up the next rung of the administrative ladder, quite frankly that leaves me, as my British friends would say, completely gobsmacked.

In many ways, it is as if the system were deliberately designed by the devil himself: the very sort who is desperately angling for (and will thus likely ultimately attain) an academic administrative position is the very sort who should, generally speaking, be as far away from that decision-making power as possible. Academics are notoriously selfish, socially malad-justed and narrow. Most have no strategic sense whatsoever as, blinded by their own self-importance, they are incapable of imagining what others are striving for. They naturally tend to be decidedly reactionary and incapable of looking objectively at the strengths and weaknesses of either their institutions or the system in general. Of course there are mavericks within any university (and typically the better the institution, the more mavericks), but they would never countenance giving up their fun-loving role of the straight-talking outsider to join the establishment, and they would never be accepted by the majority even should they wish to.

So university administrations tend to be replete with peo-ple who are often reasonably accomplished in their own narrow line of research but generally lack any sense of strate-gic or tactical sense, boldness, objectivity, candour, breadth, judgement, management skills, political instinct, financial awareness or, quite frankly, personality. Worse still, they are invariably ambitious, meaning that they are desperately deter-mined to cling to their hard-earned titles and eventually swap them for something shinier and more prestigious.

It is this last characteristic that is perhaps most dangerous. Academics, with their natural conservatism and innate hier-archical sympathies, have a particular reverence for titles and once one has achieved a particular administrative distinction it is as if the slate is wiped clean from previous experience. So it is that I would repeatedly find myself at round-table meetings of influential experts with a wealth of academic administrative experience sententiously discussing issues and policies surrounding, say, funding for scientific research, before suddenly realizing that many of these people were specialists in Elizabethan poetry or Marxist interpretations of Tolstoy and couldn't solve the simplest undergraduate mathematical equation, let alone empathize in any serious way with the research community. Curious that.

The instinctive determination among academic administrators to cling to their positions has given rise to a naturally craven culture among the elites as they resolutely avoid saying anything controversial about pressing sociological issues. This, too, is a worrying trend.

When federal budgets are unveiled that minimize research and education, the reaction from most leading academic administrators is invariably lukewarm, ever fearful that a strong, coherent expression of concern might result in a further diminishment of their funding. When the governments of the day, madly groping through their scientific illiteracy to formulate an effective national research policy, unthinkingly suggest the problems with universities lie in commercialization and encourage them to be more like a business, do our academic leaders give a thoughtful, measured response? Do they boldly proclaim that the risks in trying to corporatize the university are not only culturally severe—a diminishment in the value of non-directed research and unfettered intellectual inquiry that universities have vitally fulfilled for a millennium—but also largely unproductive? Do they publicly question the naive view that universities are chockful of wonderful practical ideas that are lying buried under mounds of paper waiting for bureaucrats and administrators to direct businesses to commercialize them? Do they loudly trumpet, instead, the pivotal role that a university plays in our society by training people to think—an immeasurable cultural, social and economic good? Do they engage the public directly with the question of what the role of a university should be, whether or not our system has been successful and how it might be improved?

No, they do none of those things. These are, you see, dangerous things to say: one's funding could be cut; one could lose one's job. If these guys want commercialization, we'll give them commercialization. The next guys will want something else and we'll find something for them too. Our job is to keep the taps flowing.

Of course I understand this—funding is important. But for what? That is the key question. If universities become little more than a publicly paid apprenticeship for the likes of Microsoft, shouldn't taxpayers be paying less and Microsoft more? Perhaps we have little choice in where things are headed, but shouldn't it at least be broadly discussed? If universities continue to increase their focus on the lucrative areas of management and business rather than concerning themselves with advanced research and exposing our youth to provocative ideas of science, history, mathematics, economics, philosophy, political theory and the like, won't society suffer culturally, socially and, eventually, economically? Most people, I imagine, would think so. Yet many of those who should be publicly indignant remain silent, fearful of losing a title or position they have devoted a lifetime to attaining. Who speaks for the university?

This is hardly just a Canadian issue.

When Larry Summers resigned his position as president of Harvard, many unhesitatingly concluded it was a direct consequence of the incendiary comments he made a year earlier concerning possible explanations for long-standing female underrepresentation in the mathematical sciences.

Doubtless the truth was considerably more complicated than that—it seems there had been several points of conflict between Summers and the Harvard Faculty of Arts and Science over the years—but the interesting thing about this case is that it underscores a much larger issue: a fundamental ambiguity in the role of a university president and, by implication, the role of a university in our society.

Summers was evidently under the impression that his job should be that of intellectual leader. He considered himself, as he said, "someone who wanted to lead the institution to new places and to challenge it and change it." While many supported him throughout, there were many who objected to his presidency not so much because they disagreed with what he was specifically doing (although there was doubtless a good share of that as well), but more because he had the presumptuousness to put himself in that situation in the first place.

It is one thing to dump a leader because there is a general loss of confidence in where he is taking the institution and another entirely to dump him because he has the temerity to lead rather than merely act as a conciliator and chief fundraiser for the status quo. It will be interesting to see how his successor deals with the situation and how much genuine leadership and influence she will be able to invoke.

My situation, on the other hand, was quite different from all of that. Obviously the scope of our narrowly focused institute was orders of magnitude smaller than a university, but there was a fundamental difference in kind as well: I was flagrantly indifferent to titles, status and all that. For me, the whole experiment was naturally all about the institute, about creating something worthwhile and seizing an opportunity, rather than my career. I had never, quite frankly, seen the point of a career anyway, never deliberately aspired to running a physics institute (or anything at all for that matter) and could imagine myself quite happily existing doing a number of completely different things in strikingly different circumstances. But here I was doing something I believed in, and passionately thought was right, was necessary, was important. Might as well enjoy it.

This is a wonderfully liberating perspective. There is simply no point in worrying about failure: the only thing to be done is to honestly try to achieve the goals one sets and see what happens. There is no point, either, in worrying about the board, or getting fired, or whatever: if the board was not fully supportive of me or my approach, then why should I want to stay around anyway? The moment I become fearful of doing the right thing, the moment I begin to let issues of pragmatic self-interest colour my perspective and judgement, is precisely the moment I should step down, because then it becomes about me and not the institute.

The algorithm was remarkably easy: all I had to do was be true to my beliefs and try to implement them in the most constructive way I could. I wouldn't for a moment pretend to be something I'm not, but would steadfastly shrug off the inevitable deluge of knee-jerk skepticism I knew would bombard me from all sides. And anyway, I told myself, don't take things so seriously. George W. Bush was far less qualified for his job than you are for yours and *that's* a real issue. The worst I could do would be not to build the best possible theoretical physics institute, which would hardly be a crisis of global significance.

In other words, relax, have fun and be yourself—words any reasonable lumberjack could happily live by.

CHAPTER ELEVEN

The Trouble with Physicists

In the fall of 2001, well before construction on the new building started, we began research operations in a temporary facility. Finding the right space had been a struggle—Waterloo is not a large town and there was almost nowhere for a rapidly expanding research institute in the small core of the city. After spurning multiple offers from real estate agents for space in one of the high-tech low-rises in outlying areas, I finally managed to get a floor in a featureless office complex downtown. It was far too corporate and generally uninspiring, but at least the location was good. A few days before we were set to move in, Colleen Brickman, now our director of human resources whom I had hired in 2000 as my first administrative support staff and general all-purpose assistant, was over in the office measuring space for furniture when it became clear that there was a rather pressing problem: it seemed that one of the offices we had understood was ours had in fact been earmarked for someone else. A few phone calls later proved that the situation was quite intractable. In desperation, we contacted another real estate agent to see if anything else could be arranged at the last minute. Coincidentally, a restaurant across the road unfortunately had gone broke a day or two before and their space was now available.

It took some imagination to consider what I saw the next day as a future theoretical physics institute. Dirty dishes and cutlery lay abandoned on square tables still forlornly bedecked with checkered tablecloths. A large industrial kitchen dominated the back of the room, complete with broken plates and more dirty dishes piled high in the sink. A blackened kitchen fan was humming overhead and the lights were flickering. Upstairs, the bar area was a potpourri of cigarette butts and half-filled beer glasses perched on pool tables. There was a hole in the wall and the whole place stank like an ashtray. It looked about as appropriate for a house of scholarship as a trailer park.

Still, there was no denying its potential. A nineteenth-century clock-tower building that had originally been the town post office, it had lots of space and not a little charm. The former bar upstairs could serve as a meeting area, while the pool room could be easily converted into a seminar room. And if the physics institute thing didn't work out, we could always open a restaurant. I took it.

Colleen and I set to the somewhat daunting task of quickly renovating the space, anxious to make the move from a *theoretical* theoretical physics institute to an actual theoretical physics institute. Soon all we needed were actual physicists.

Be careful, as the saying goes, what you ask for.

The whole concept of management has always been a mystery to me. I don't primarily mean how it should be done, but rather why it should be necessary at all.

The way I look at it, humans are incredible, almost miraculous creatures. The product of billions of years of a painstakingly statistical process, we represent the culmination of a heroic odyssey that began with single-celled organisms mired in primordial slime and evolved through increasingly complex stages of amphibians, mammals and primates to become the conscious, dynamic beings we are today. Through our remarkably penetrating intellects we have come to dominate the planet, mastering not only our essential survival needs of food and shelter, but going ever so much further: creating art, music and literature, discovering the fundamental laws of nature, developing tangible rules for human behaviour and erecting wondrous cities in which to successfully apply them. By any objective standard, what Homo sapiens has accomplished from decidedly inauspicious beginnings has been nothing short of breathtaking.

We are the species of Shakespeare and Rembrandt, of Schubert and Balzac, of Gödel and Hume. We have peered into the human genome and precisely analyzed the cosmic microwave background. We have built space shuttles and skyscrapers; we have explored the furthest reaches of our globe and the very structure of our thoughts. Man is a remarkable, breathtaking creature whose potential and creativity are virtually unbounded.

Surely, in light of all of this, the very concept of human beings needing to be "managed"—to be guided, supervised and generally led towards their daily or weekly goals like some mindless herd of cattle—is not just inappropriate, it's an insult to the very core of what it means to be human—a dire castigation of the entire species. It is, as the great physicist Wolfgang Pauli once put it so disdainfully, "not even wrong."

Except that there actually seems to be quite a lot to it.

We all tend to fall back on our own experiences and proclivities as a natural baseline to interpret the world around us. From my earliest memories, I seemed incapable of doing anything without questioning the established hierarchy I was confronted with. It wasn't so much that I was rebellious— although I was that, too, later on—but rather that I found the entire notion of taking things on faith deeply abhorrent and was fundamentally unwilling to accept anything I couldn't somehow justify. The standard carrot and stick approach that seemed to have such an effect on so many of my schoolmates has never worked for me: a stern remonstrance for challenging an obviously insecure or delusional teacher was only to be expected given his flawed perspective; and anyway, what did I care about receiving a poor grade if I rejected the entire evaluation procedure? Of course, this was in many ways a severely limiting attitude: just because I couldn't fully appreciate the point of something hardly meant it was deserving of contempt or indifference, it might simply mean I had missed something somewhere. But such a possibility rarely crossed my stubborn mind; I was the sole arbiter of my fate and if I couldn't be persuaded something was worth doing then the hell with it.

According to my perspective, then, little can be more unappetizing than the prospect of being saddled with a boss. Fortunately, I managed to avoid this unpalatable fate by the curious circumstances that resulted in me becoming an institute builder. Unfortunately, however, these very same circumstances conspired to place me, ironically, in a position of authority myself. As Einstein so succinctly put it many years ago in what sadly appears to be the only clear resonance between myself and the great man: "To punish me for my contempt for authority, fate made me an authority myself."

I reacted to this curious state of affairs by denying the problem—invoking simplistic, high-minded, evolutionary arguments like the one above. Perhaps, I concluded hopefully, all this business about management theory was simply wrong—little more than a scam projected on an unwitting populace by management hucksters out to reap their fortunes by convincing the great unwashed of their false need to be told what to do in a structured environment. Maybe I could do much more than just establish a physics institute; perhaps I could confront the entire field of management theory with its inherent superfluousness and thereby force it to commit a collective form of *supuku*, liberating jargon-downtrodden masses the world over!

Much of this, it must be admitted, was a rather grandiose way of justifying my overwhelming distaste at the prospect of telling people what to do. I had no interest in creating organizational flowcharts, setting task lists or giving people performance reviews. But why should I? Our institute would contain a combination of scientists and administrative staff. The scientists, of course, being rational, independent people, would naturally have no need for such silliness; while the administrative staff would be specifically selected and groomed for independence, the front line of the new army against vacuous management types.

I was somewhat taken aback by the reaction these sentiments evoked. My wife, for example, who was usually willing to indulge my speculative theories, was particularly harsh. I distinctly remember her looking up from her newspaper after I had just finished explaining how I was going to create a non-hierarchical environment and calling me a damned fool. "People need to be led," she interrupted abruptly, before disdainfully turning back to her paper. "You might not like it, but that's just the way it is. Human nature."

Chris Isham, who had developed this mysterious and annoying ability to engage in some sort of long-distance, tag-team chastisement game with my wife, was equally negative. "At the end of the day," he declared, "someone has to be accountable for the decisions. Someone has to lead. Somebody has to manage the others."

I soon learned how right they both were, but, as always, I had to learn the hard way. Perhaps I would have management difficulties with the administrative staff, I thought, but not

174 · FIRST PRINCIPLES

with the researchers. These were eminently rational people, all rigorously trained to solve problems in a logical, coherent framework. How hard could it be?

Soon after we started up research operations in the old post office building in the fall of 2001, I started to hold weekly administrative meetings. There were only ten of us at the time (Rob Myers, Fotini Markopoulou, Lee Smolin, Raymond Laflamme, Mike Mosca and four postdocs: John Brodie, Olaf Dreyer, Constantinos Savvidis and Oliver Winkler), and in those days virtually everyone participated regularly. At first we informally discussed items of interest on a variety of topics. It was warm and convivial, but after a couple of months it began to dawn on me that not much was actually getting done. There was a great deal of talk, but nothing of substance was happening—no decisions were made, no practical policies implemented. Lee, in particular, was a great one for this sort of thing. While I certainly applauded his dedication to the cause, it was clear that his efforts weren't always maximally efficient. One of his favourite activities was to try to convince us all to formally commit ourselves to some policy of fairness or innovation or something or other, based upon some bizarre amalgamation of the founding documents of Oxbridge Colleges, economic portfolio theory, Thomas Jefferson and virtual reality. Fifteen minutes before the meeting was to start he would e-mail all of us a convoluted thirty-page manifesto upon which he was prepared to expound at length throughout the course of the meeting. After a while attendance started to decline and it became evident that things ought to be restructured a bit.

I started creating agendas for the meetings, sending them out a couple of days beforehand. I also began increasingly to assume the role as chair, leading the discussion and cutting people off when they strayed too far off topic, which happened with alarming frequency. After recognizing that the meetings seemed to mysteriously expand to fit whatever time was available, I made them biweekly and set an upper limit of 1.5 hours for each one. I established a committee structure for research seminars and postdoc selection, and crafted policies for researcher travel and visitors. The more I did, the more it became obvious to me that this made the research staff happier. It was an odd situation: here I was concerned about coming across as a heavy-handed tyrant unilaterally setting policy, and most of them simply didn't care. They really didn't want to be involved in making the rules; they just wanted to know what they were.

This was, all things considered, quite fortunate because most of them were just plain lousy at making rules. The first time I was starkly confronted with this was when we were developing our visitor program.

A vital aspect of any scientific institute is its visitor program. A steady flux of visitors is essential for providing a lively and stimulating environment—visitors not only bring with them different insights, they also serve as conduits of influence, taking away developments happening here. Of course, our researchers also travel widely, giving seminars and interacting with scientists from across the globe as well as actively collaborating through e-mail and phone calls with other far-flung scientists; but face-to-face interaction in an informal setting is key. It was obvious to me that one of the easiest ways for PI to quickly develop a strong international reputation while producing the best quality science was to ramp up our visitor program as quickly and coherently as possible. As a result, there would be, I announced, no budget per se for the seminar series: speakers should be chosen strictly on the basis of quality and it made no difference whether they came from Minneapolis or Malaysia. This provoked some general consternation.

"No budget?" I was assailed. "Why can't we have a budget?"

I was taken aback. "You want a budget?" I asked, stupefied.

"We've always had budgets before."

"Maybe you don't understand," I began slowly. "Not having a budget in this case doesn't mean that you can't do something—quite the opposite."

"So we should spend more money?"

"No, not necessarily." This was proving surprisingly difficult. "It just means that you shouldn't let any financial concerns be a factor in the selection of speakers. Just pick the ones you think would be the best scientifically."

"Wouldn't it just be easier to have a budget?"

Then things got stranger. After a number of seminar series became established, I began hearing other complaints.

"We have too many seminars."

"Pardon me?"

"Too many talks. If I go to all the talks, then I can't get any research done."

"Well..." I began, as if talking to a very small child, "then don't go to all the talks. Nobody's forcing you to go to each one."

"But they look interesting. And I don't want to be rude."

"So let me get this straight: instead of just not attending some talks, you'd like to declare an official institute policy limiting the number of talks, even if some people want more talks."

"That's right."

Then it got even weirder still. People began complaining that in light of the frenetic pace of our seminar series, it was sometimes difficult to find a free slot to invite people for a few days and work on a paper together. I pointed out that working on a paper was often logically independent from giv-

ing a talk and therefore created a new category of visitors—
"collaborators." Henceforth, I declared with a flourish, all PI
researchers, including postdocs, would be eligible to invite a
certain number of collaborators per term. These visitors
would be invited by each individual researcher and would
not, generally speaking, be expected to give a seminar. I was
expecting, I must confess, some form of emphatic appreciation for such a move. Here I was, demonstrably responsive to
the needs of my research staff, determined to structure matters to provide the best possible experience. This was the sort
of place I hoped PI could be: responsive, non-bureaucratic
and efficient.

Instead, a few weeks later, there was just more anxiety.

"I've just invited a collaborator here and some people want
her to give a talk."

"So?"

"She can't give a talk. There are no slots available."

"And anyway," someone else perked up, "she shouldn't
give a talk: she's a collaborator. Collaborators don't give
talks."

"Look," I began, slipping into my now timeworn talking-
to-researchers-about-administrative-matters lilt, "just because
someone is classified as a collaborator doesn't mean they can't
give a talk. It just means they don't have to. It would be a bit
odd to learn that someone visiting here is somehow being
forcibly prevented from giving a talk."

"But what if they want to give a talk and there are no
slots?"

"Then they can go out to the bar area and give a talk," I
mooted. "We can start a whole new seminar series called
'Impromptu Talks.'"

"But who's going to organize those?" came back the plain-
tive response.

The stereotype of an academic is someone who is brilliant, self-absorbed and detached. Like any stereotype it is a broad simplification that often doesn't apply (few are brilliant, for example), but usually manages to capture essential aspects of a real phenomenon. University professors lead a life of the mind in relatively cosseted circumstances, removed from many of the pressing details of everyday life and expected to focus their efforts on teaching and research. They are generally not phenomenally well paid, but have instead willfully and knowingly sacrificed the prospect of strong financial gain to instead spend the majority of time immersed in intellectual pursuits.

While there are, one hears, some people who live for their work and would remain in their present employment even if suddenly presented with untold riches, most of us are forced to grapple with finding our own solution to the time-money problem: how best to manage the trade-off between finding the time to do what one truly wants and the resources to live comfortably. There are those who are willing to sacrifice years of their life in the financial sector in the hopes of one day reaping all the freedom independent wealth can bring, while others would prefer to live a quasi-monastic life of poverty so as not to sacrifice any of their time to "the man." While hardly monastic, most academics adhere to the latter philosophy: garnering an unspectacular wage in exchange for the privilege of being relieved of many of the pressing concerns of everyday life, safe in the knowledge that an essential part of their job description is to lead a life of the mind.

Such a perspective has a natural tendency to lead to insularity—not just because academics are cosseted from the harsh realities of the real world with its cutthroat competitiveness and financial scheming, but primarily because the very nature of scholarship drives one in that direction.

Any academic, be she a physicist, economist or historian, is naturally expected to take the view that her research is the most interesting and engaging thing going. In the world of academic freedom, it is folly to pursue research for any other reason than a perception of its own intrinsic promise. True, there are those, particularly younger, researchers without permanent positions who sometimes feel pressure to incorporate aspects of whatever is currently fashionable in their work to curry favour with the "establishment," but by and large active researchers are committed to the value of their own research. The whole business of academic scholarship involves an attempt at convincing one's colleagues of the merits of one's efforts.

Yet there is a problem. This passion and self-confidence, so intrinsically related to individual research excellence, can prove rather disastrous when applied to the business of building institutes of scholarship. It is not just that the vast majority of academics will naturally assume the ideal environment should contain a disproportionate number of people working on their particular research agenda (although that is certainly the case as well), but they will also unthinkingly conclude that all successful researchers should be of their temperament. They will, in short, always be trying to clone themselves.

Theoretical physicists come in many flavours, but there are nonetheless a few ways to broadly characterize the practitioners of the field. There are the more conceptual thinkers—the big-picture types who are prone to questioning our key assumptions and making groundbreaking leaps in our understanding; there are the calculators whose work is primarily oriented towards an emphasis on detailed, often very technical, calculations. There are those who thrive on interaction with their colleagues, spending untold hours in animated discussions; and others who prefer to spend the majority of their time in quiet contemplation. Of course, these are generalizations which can never be rigorously upheld: even the most interactive of scientists needs to submit himself to long periods of quiet contemplation and calculation to actually come up with any concrete result, while simplistically dividing the field into those who come up with the ideas and those who calculate is specious in the extreme—a conceptual thinker who can't calculate is nothing more than a charlatan, while a calculational physicist who doesn't deeply understand the motivation for the calculation is simply a robot. Furthermore, a hallmark of the enormously gifted physicist— an Ed Witten, say—is the remarkable ability to combine conceptual revolutions with amazing technical skill.

The point of making such distinctions is not to win some bizarre sociological argument on the nature of theoretical physicists, but rather to recognize that if one wants to build an appropriate environment for the practice of this activity, it is essential to understand how these people fit together.

This is hardly revolutionary stuff and is overwhelmingly obvious to anybody who has ever followed a professional sports team. If you find yourself as the general manager of, say, a basketball team, the fundamental aspect of your job is to critically assess the team and see how it fits together as a unit. It would be nice, of course, to possess a team infinitely skilled at everything, but that will likely never happen. Some will be shot blockers, passers and rebounders, others shooters. Some will be fast, others slow. There will be the dignified, universally respected clubhouse leaders and the energetic, potentially abrasive types. With the possible exception of a few overwhelmingly talented superstars (e.g. Michael Jordan), the best way to succeed is to look at the team as a whole. Simply trying to recruit the best people by finding clones of some star player is little more than a recipe for failure.

So too with physics. Obviously we are not competing directly with other institutions in the way the New York Knicks are competing with the Los Angeles Lakers, but that in no way diminishes the appropriateness of the analogy. My job was to create the best possible environment for fundamental physics research in keeping with the unique character and orientation of PI.

In keeping with my anti-despotic tendencies, I had naively assumed (indeed, hoped) that once a few key people had been brought to the institute, recruitment would largely continue without much active involvement from me. That is the way things are typically done in universities, with appropriate search committees selected from the existing faculty. I soon realized, however, that this simply wasn't going to work out very well for us. Unlike a standard university, we had the flexibility to do things rather differently—hire five people simultaneously, say, or hire none at all.

Intelligent recruitment required a steely-eyed objectivity of the strengths and weaknesses of our situation in order to assess what was needed and how, concretely, to achieve it. Most researchers, mired in their own worldview, found it very difficult to travel far down this road. If left to most of them, we would simply plod along in a fairly regular way iterating what we had started (i.e. themselves)—hardly the sort of transformative impact I had in mind.

And then there are the tactics of recruitment itself. Establishing who would be an ideal recruit is a necessary aspect of the game, of course, but hardly sufficient. Most desirable people tend to be recognized as such and are thus simultaneously fielding several offers or are treated quite well by their current institution. It falls to someone, then, to speak for the organization and try to convince them of why they should come here. It soon became abundantly clear to me that

182 · FIRST PRINCIPLES

this was simply not something I could delegate. The task requires, once again, an ability to be starkly objective: to get inside hearts and heads and understand what we can possibly offer that might be sufficiently attractive. It was not just a question of finding the right propaganda—these people are clever and will not be placated by something they perceive is a ploy. One has to genuinely understand their needs and determine how, if possible, they can be met. Such an exchange naturally means developing a real personal relationship with them: just as they have to be convinced that we can offer them something appropriately attractive, I have to be convinced their needs are reasonable. There are always some, of course, who are not bargaining in good faith—they may be testing the waters halfheartedly, or trying to get an offer to increase the likelihood of getting what they really want somewhere else. But such cases tend not to happen as often as people might suspect. I know things are moving in the right direction when I feel I have personally embraced their cause; when I begin to feel more like an advocate than the administrator on the other side of the table. Often, this means that I develop a real friendship with them—which helps.

Of course, most of them don't come anyway, for one reason or another. Jim Hartle, a former director of Santa Barbara's Institute for Theoretical Physics and an original member of PI's Scientific Advisory Committee, once comforted me by relaying stories of how difficult it had been to recruit eminent faculty to ITP. "It's awfully tough," he concluded. "But I learned that if your success rate is too high, then you probably aren't aiming high enough." It was a very useful perspective from somebody who certainly knew the score.

The important thing, of course, is not to panic but rather do the best one can to identify and entice the highest quality people imaginable. They either will be sufficiently attracted by the place or they won't; there's no use overreacting or looking desperate. But most academics are professional worriers, and as an elite research institute where the majority of the faculty is relieved from the grounding influence of regular teaching responsibilities, we take worrying to unprecedented heights.

Some people here worry we are hiring too slowly, others that we are hiring too quickly. They worried the new building would be too large, and now that it's built they worry we will outgrow it too soon. They worry that some research areas are becoming too dominant at the expense of others, and that we aren't sufficiently leveraging our existing strengths. We hold too many workshops; we don't hold enough workshops. We have too many graduate students; we don't have enough graduate students. We host too many visitors; we don't host enough. And so on.

Even when there are legitimate concerns, there are times when their unholy amalgamation of high anxiety, blatant self-interest and often unbounded self-assuredness can make for a particularly toxic combination, resulting in a sense of strategic ineptitude of almost mythic proportions.

It can sometimes be rather infuriating. And yet, it is entirely to be expected. Elite intellectuals are in many ways similar to elite athletes: they can sometimes be high maintenance because almost everything they do is focused squarely around their work. Chat with them about any number of diverse topics and they will strike you as perfectly pleasant and benign, perhaps even a bit reticent to have an opinion (well, some of them, anyway), but tread on their domain—challenge an aspect of their work or, worse still, do something they feel might conceivably jeopardize their ability to successfully pursue their work, and they will suddenly turn into raging infernos of dissent. They are not well balanced by definition—success in research, by whatever metric one wishes to define it, trumps all. It is easy to ridicule them for their inability to take a broad overall perspective, but that's hardly the point. It's essential to recognize that their narrow and overriding focus on their research is in many ways necessary for their success. While there are a few exceptions, most scientists I know find it close to impossible to combine productive research with any sort of regular routine, requiring vast blocks of uncharted time (a sense of de facto infinite time) to fully immerse themselves in a problem and grapple with all of the nuances. Thinking deeply about a problem means walking with it, reading with it, sleeping with it, never having it out of your mind as you munch away on your lunch or attend some seminar, always remaining prepared to dash off somewhere to perform some new calculation to check out some new idea or insight, which seemingly anything can trigger.

Some people make progress through discussion, others prefer private reflection, but the core issue is that everyone understands and respects the process. It is how research is done. It is what we are all about.

And so, when researchers complain that attending a monthly two-hour administrative meeting forces them out of their ruminative routine and effectively ruins their day, I don't get angry and call them spoiled babies: I know full well where they're coming from. When scientists disappear for days on end or don't answer their e-mail for a week, I understand completely. They are working.

Just don't let them run the place.

CHAPTER TWELVE

The 3 Percent Solution

Why outreach? Why should a new foundational physics institute with aspirations of significant international impact occupy itself with an entirely separate mandate of comprehensive programs for students, teachers and the general public? However laudable in theory, surely in practice outreach will prove an unwanted distraction, an added complication that will dangerously distract us from our efforts of achieving our primary goal of scientific excellence, won't it?

Well, no it won't. I don't think so. Quite the contrary.

The standard response I like to give when somebody asks me why the institute is so committed to outreach is that it is a core mandate of Perimeter, proudly enshrined in our mission statement for all to see. This works for a surprisingly large number of cases, but doesn't, of course, answer the question at all, which is why is it in your mission statement? This ability to summarily draw a line under a key issue and prevent further questioning is a powerful feature of mission statements and one I have come to much appreciate over the years. As it happens, I was opposed to the whole mission statement idea at first, assuming it was just another piece of superfluous corporate fluff, but was quickly convinced otherwise when prodded by the eminent University of Chicago cosmologist

Michael Turner. "You really should have a mission statement," Turner told me during an early visit to the institute. "They're wonderfully useful." If Tony Robbins advises me to do something, I'll look searchingly for the exits. If Mike Turner suggests how I can improve my physics institute, on the other hand, I'll take it pretty seriously indeed.

And so I wrote a mission statement. And he was right, of course, it did help enormously in a variety of different ways. But still the question remains to the astute observer: why outreach?

So here's the real story.

Outreach is the key to the entire institute—it is the silver bullet, the coup de grâce, the fundamental distinguishing characteristic of our little enterprise. Outreach represents a magnificent mélange of disparate factors, from enlightened self-interest to rampaging idealism. Outreach—more specifically, the mutually reinforcing combination of outreach and research—is an integral aspect of what makes Perimeter special, what truly makes us important.

Outreach captivates politicians and policymakers across the land, providing a tangible bang for the buck that some isolated home for eggheads in the woods never would and thereby goes a considerable distance to increasing the chances of continued public support; outreach provides clear vehicles for future fundraising for the institute from both the corporate and personal philanthropic sectors. More generally, outreach provides the opportunity to promote the institute by ensuring that the public profile of Perimeter is naturally associated with educational programs for teachers and students and webcasts for the general public. Not for us the championing of our researchers or their research in a manifestly self-promotional cold-fusion-like way. Not for us any official proclamations of our magnificence or the shortcomings of other competing institutions. Any science coming out of the institute must stand by itself and get recognized, or not, by the proper scientific channels.

True, some of our faculty have, from time to time, written books or generally held forth on a wide range of issues on which they have strong views. Sometimes these views are controversial, occasionally deliberately so. As a research institution proudly founded on the principles of freedom of speech, we unhesitatingly support each faculty member's right to do such a thing. But we do not promote them or their works through the institute. Any formal promotion of the institute happens strictly through our outreach programs.

This might seem all very tactical. Is this, then, all that is going on? Cleverly using outreach as a front to both raise money and simultaneously focus the public image of the institute so as not to be dominated by the occasionally megalomaniacal tendencies of some of our star researchers? Of course not. One must never confuse the means with the ends. The remarkable aspect of outreach, broadly construed, is that the means and the ends are strikingly aligned, often interchangeably. As has been mentioned several times already, Perimeter Institute was founded on a desire to make a difference, to make an impact in a world largely uncaring and unappreciative of the importance—culturally, intellectually, technologically and economically—of fundamental scientific research. It was driven by the largesse of an engineer and the passion of a physicist to create something new, something significant, something that could address this issue head on.

Sure, the previously mentioned sociological issues were of some concern—not enough tolerance for diverse approaches to foundational issues, not enough recognition of which assumptions were being made and for what reasons, not enough rigour in recognizing which foundational issues had really been fully addressed. Put in perspective, this was a completely understandable development: in an age when empirical verification of one's theories is exceptionally hard to come by— in the absence of the opportunity to walk into a lab and determine what is wrong and what is right—it was inevitable that sociological factors of fashion and personality would begin to play an increasing role in determining what people should be working on and how they should be evaluated. So there was a strong motivation to create a place where different approaches to foundational issues were countenanced, not only to create a portfolio approach to increase the likelihood of a fundamental breakthrough that could bring some exaggerated fanfare, but more significantly to create a climate where researchers weren't all smugly preaching to the converted, where basic assumptions of their approaches could be probed and tested, questioned anew. All this has been stressed several times throughout these pages. And these sociological factors, however important, are still small beer in the bigger picture.

The real problem, the elephant in the room, is that the vast majority of the world's population is not only scientifically illiterate, but worse still, scientifically indifferent. Much has been made of the failures of the American education system at the primary and secondary levels, but the sad truth is that its incompetence is hardly unique. Global efforts at science education are, by and large, notoriously poor, leaving successive generations of young people everywhere uninformed, uninspired, unaware of some of the most profoundly exciting mysteries of the world around us and oblivious to the intellectual bedrock upon which our entire modern technological society rests.

The practical consequences of this educational failing are little short of disastrous, with vital public policy decisions regarding everything from global warming to nuclear power being made by people who are largely bereft of any clear understanding of the way science actually works, and then communicated to an intimidated and befuddled public through an uncritical media self-servingly oriented towards provocative sound bites. Meanwhile, the chattering classes replete with lawyers and MBAs continue to sententiously hold forth on the importance of innovation and the knowledge economy before zooming off to the golf course in their SUVs, unable to find the clubhouse without GPS assistance. This is the curious state of our world today, and it seems obvious to me that wading through the miasma of hypocrisy and ignorance that lie at the root of this mess is a pressing issue of societal concern far more deserving of our time and attention than a public debate on the details of the string landscape and the relevance and merits of the weak anthropic principle. It is pretty hard to talk intelligently about either string theory or the anthropic principle if one can't multiply.

There is little that is more irksome to me than listening to an enraged scientist dismiss competing research avenues as "a waste of taxpayers' money" in his quest to buttress his own cause. The problem, of course, is not that scientific granting agencies are poorly allocating resources, but that they have, by and large, drastically insufficient resources to begin with, while the vast majority of the populace simply doesn't care. Damning public screeds that accuse the academic community of too much tolerance for competing scientific approaches, or, alternatively, insufficient flexibility to break free from the thrall of a stifling conservatism, may work well at promoting the public image of the author, but on the whole are strikingly counterproductive to the overall effort, as their principal effect is merely to further alienate large tracts of the general public who become convinced that any additional resources given to science would only result in further internal squabbling.

As public attention becomes focused on the salacious human drama of the scientific personalities in question, however, keenly invoking some sort of large-scale societal *schadenfreude* in those who might otherwise feel intimidated by the power of science (you see? However smart these guys think they are, there's no fundamental difference between science and politics!), the rampant ignorance of basic rational principles continues.

Some time ago, I had the opportunity to have lunch with Ed Greenspon, the editor-in-chief of *The Globe and Mail*, and John Stackhouse, the paper's business editor. We spent the majority of the meeting pleasantly chatting about recent progress of the institute and general developments in the region. I was happy to give the standard update because I have this occasional propensity (you might have noticed) to break out into sudden bursts of pedantry, and I sensed that Greenspon would hardly appreciate being bombarded by yet another self-proclaimed expert telling him how to run his paper. Towards the end of the meal, however, he leaned over to me and asked me what I thought of the *Globe* generally and what I would do to change it if I had the chance.

Well. I hesitated for a bit, proffering a few encouraging comments for the sake of balance before erupting with a laundry list of various improvements, culminating with: "why the hell do you have horoscopes in your paper? Don't you see that it's a bloody embarrassment for an allegedly sophisticated publication to promote this kind of idiocy in the twenty-first century? Take them out!"

Doubtless unprepared for my attack, he muttered something about not really paying too much attention to the leisure page and staggered off to the washroom, as Stackhouse's laughter rang throughout the bistro.

Was I overreacting? Not too many reputable people take astrology seriously these days (particularly now that Ronald and Nancy Reagan are long gone from the White House). In a world understandably preoccupied with religious fundamentalism and suicide bombers, surely the prospect of stemming the pernicious astrological menace is not high on the list. Why am I getting so worked up about a harmless bit of fun, a frivolous and irreverent indulgence?

Because I don't, in fact, believe it's harmless. I'm convinced that, at some level, our willingness to give any sort of official recognition or platform to astrology, with its inane notions of how Pluto affects our virility, subtly undermines the intellectual foundations of our society and jeopardizes the hard-won victories of previous centuries that need to be actively reinforced and recognized, generation after generation.

Because I believe that our willingness to countenance woolly-mindedness out of some misguided sense of tolerance and diversity (two concepts, it should be stressed, I believe in particularly strongly when appropriately defined) is precisely the sort of egregiously muddled thinking that leads so many journalists to deny overwhelming scientific consensus on pivotal issues such as global warming in a delusional quest to present "fair and balanced reporting" of "the other side of the story" with potentially perilous consequences.

Because, as it happens, I am sincerely convinced that if we are to successfully defend our society from the likes of religious fundamentalists and suicide bombers, we must clearly and forcibly articulate our allegiance to Enlightenment principles of scientific rationalism and liberal tolerance that separate us from the abyss of fanaticism and irrationality.

And because if we are to ultimately progress as a civilization, if we are ever going to wean ourselves from burning muck from the ground to power our air conditioners, if we are ever going to feed the world and cure our diseases, it is going to happen through science.

So this stuff matters.

The good news is that science is not just good for us; it is also riddled with deeply fascinating and compelling stories, mysteries and wonder. This is not in any way strictly necessary. One can certainly imagine a world ruled by rather boring laws of nature: no vacuum fluctuations, no Big Bang, no black holes, no dark energy, no dark matter, no evolution, no complex systems, maybe even no people—hence no human genome, no neurophysiology, no anatomy and so forth. Thankfully, we don't live in this world. We live in a world where, regardless of our remarkable accomplishments, we are still aeons from penetrating so many of the outstanding mysteries we can now identify, let alone the ones yet to be unveiled. There is still so much to do, so much to discover, so much to learn.

How, given all of this, can science be such a tough sell? Why is enrollment dropping for undergraduate physics courses throughout the developed world? Why is it increasingly difficult to convince high-school students to take advanced mathematics despite our increasingly high-tech age?

As previously mentioned, I started thinking seriously about these issues back in 2000, trying to imagine what a new theoretical physics institute might be able to do to concretely address them. Once again I reflected upon the counterexamples I knew of public indifference to science. Roger Penrose's provocative treatise, *The Emperor's New Mind*, had been a veritable publishing sensation. Carl Sagan's luminous defense of science, *The Demon-Haunted World*, was a *New York Times* bestseller, while Stephen Hawking's *A Brief History of Time* had become nothing less than one of the most popular books in recent memory worldwide.

What was going on? Surely this was some objective support for the notion that all was not darkness and *Survivor* episodes? It wasn't clear how many people were actually reading *A Brief History of Time*, let alone understanding it, but it was uncontestable that people were buying it. Which meant that at the very least millions of people recognized the subject matter was in principle interesting—something worth being aware of, if at all possible. Millions of people. This was encouraging.

The particular advantage of a book, I concluded, is that it is a pretty unintimidating, nonjudgemental way of getting access to information. Take a course in something and sooner or later you're forced to take a test. Attend a seminar and eventually you have to give a presentation, or at least ask a question. But a book—well, that could be patiently perused in the privacy of a living room, allowing the motivated reader to gently dip her toe again and again into the river of knowledge until sufficiently satisfied or exasperated without anyone else being the wiser. For a general populace riddled with significant numbers of otherwise successful people who still bore the roughly healed scars of incomprehensible high-school physics classes, this non-confrontational method of engagement was key.

How, I asked myself, could we tap into this? Perhaps the institute should offer regular lectures on a variety of interesting topics. Not annual or semiannual lectures, which would be too far apart to develop a sense of coherence, but rather monthly lectures. The goal would be to rigorously build up a certain clientele, to carefully nurture a core audience of the same sort of people who had bought, or might later buy, *A Brief History of Time*.

When I first moved to Waterloo, I remember being particularly struck by the enormous level of local pride people seemed to display at the slightest provocation; they were constantly holding forth on the bounteous magnificence of

Waterloo: the universities, the lifestyle, the standard of living, the appropriateness of raising a family here and so forth. I had never really lived in a small town before and I must confess that I found all this local triumphalism a bit hard to take seriously. At first I actually thought people were putting me on: testing out the new guy. But eventually it became obvious that they were completely serious, and I started looking at things quite differently, recognizing that this phenomenon of local pride was a precious resource that could work to our mutual advantage. If we could give them some mechanism with which to interact concretely with us, if we could give them something to be justifiably proud of, they might respond in an overpoweringly positive way. The public lectures were the test case.

We kicked off matters with an inaugural lecture by Roger Penrose in October 2001, coinciding with Roger's first visit to PI and our second Scientific Advisory Committee meeting. The lecture was met with an overwhelming response of some 700 people, but that was hardly ironclad proof we were on the right road. Roger is nothing less than a public phenomenon, attracting hordes of people wherever he goes and whatever he speaks on.

The following fall, I launched the monthly public lecture series with a collection of diverse, if definitely mortal, speakers, intending to transfer it to our new, 210-seat lecture theatre then under construction. By the third lecture, the public response had forced us from our original venue into a 400-seat community centre. One year later, we were forced to move to a still bigger space, this time to a local high-school theatre with a capacity for 600, where we remain to this day, consistently filling the hall.

Doubtless there are those who will say that we continually draw so many people to our monthly lecture series because there is a paucity of other things to do in Waterloo on a

Wednesday night. Well, perhaps—it is unquestionably true that the competition for entertainment is hardly the same in Waterloo as it would be in Chicago or London. But it's worth remembering that these are typically the very same people who glibly informed me that there would simply be no way we could attract sufficient numbers of people for monthly talks on science and society in a town the size of Waterloo—that sheer demographics would limit us to a maximum of fifteen to twenty stragglers each month, the majority of whom could well be certifiably insane. An audience of 600 people per night is a pretty powerful endorsement that we must be doing something right. And most of them seem pretty sane too.

The success of the public lecture series is a concrete example of the mutual reinforcement of the outreach and research agendas that uniquely characterize Perimeter Institute. Because we are a fully functioning research institution in foundational physics, we have the opportunity to attract the likes of Roger Penrose, Ed Witten, Paul Steinhardt, Jim Hartle, Artur Ekert, Frank Wilczek, Lenny Susskind, Lisa Randall and countless others to participate in our outreach programs and provide our audience with nothing less than the highest quality international scientists. But it works the other way as well: most scientists are deeply impressed by our determination to take such an active role in promoting science to the general public. This enthusiasm goes well beyond the aforementioned international superstars and resonates strongly with everyone associated with the institute, from graduate students to senior faculty. At their core, most scientists are idealists: they do what they do because they're completely convinced it is the most fundamentally captivating thing a human being can spend her life doing. The opportunity to be associated with a place that is determined to share that infectious enthusiasm with the wider world and seek new ways of meaningfully contributing to the advancement of science in the public consciousness is invariably appealing, and for many is a large part of the positive atmosphere at PI.

Of course, a public lecture series in itself will only go so far. Significant long-term impact can only really come through focusing on younger people, particularly students. A quick visit to any high school will immediately reveal that most students are almost wholly ignorant of the motivations, background and general orientation of a professional scientist. It is an irony of monumental proportions that so many bright and dynamic young people graduating from high school are steered towards creative careers in law, business and the arts, convinced that mathematics is nothing more than mindless arithmetic, aptitude in physics is equal to memorizing the right formula and science is generally a tedious, algorithmic medium for unimaginative types where all answers to core questions can be found at the back of the book.

These conclusions, however laughably inaccurate to those with more advanced knowledge of the field, are hardly unreasonable ones to draw based on a typical high-school experience. If one's primary interaction with physics and mathematics consisted of calculating projectile trajectories or grinding through a series of factoring problems, it would be easy to see how the elegance of physical law or the creativity of the mathematical experience might seem like rather ridiculously overblown sentiments.

At some point, it is essential to come clean with kids. Yes, they should be told, much of the stuff you're stuck doing actually is boring. Yes, you need to learn how to calculate and understand the principles of Newtonian dynamics before you can move on to tackling quantum computing and dark matter. The problem is that all too often kids never even catch a glimpse of the fascinating end product of all of their labours, which naturally leaves many feeling rather unenthused and uninspired by the entire exercise. It is like spending several years assembling a car without ever realizing that the whole point is to get in and drive the thing somewhere.

It's not, of course, that this information is being deliberately withheld from the students, but rather that most teachers do not have sufficient knowledge or perspective to instill these concepts in their kids. In a world where so many teachers, themselves intimidated by science and mathematics, are pressed into a role of communicating this information to young minds, is it any wonder that the majority of students come away from the experience without any clear understanding of or appreciation for the elegance and impact of the material?

Most scientists I know can directly point to one or two pivotal experiences with high-school teachers that made them appreciate the wonder and mystery of science and launched them on their professional careers. This is the good news: that no matter how inadequate the system is generally, there always seem to exist a small, dedicated minority of teachers who rise to prominence and extend considerable influence over their students. Unfortunately, I also regularly encounter considerable evidence in the other direction: intelligent, capable adults who approach me after a public lecture or other institute event and breathlessly gush over their newfound excitement for matters scientific, loudly lamenting the inadequacy of their high-school experience that never gave them an inkling of these wonders.

I am hardly the first person to have noticed these structural deficiencies in the teaching of science and mathematics, but I once again found myself in the rather exceptional position of actually having the opportunity to do something about it. In early 2001, I hired Richard Epp, a broad contemplative physicist I knew with a strong passion for science education, as

Perimeter's outreach director. Together we developed a variety of programs for students and teachers ranging from in-school discussions on current research topics to intense summer camps for elite high-school students to advanced pedagogical workshops for physics teachers. Richard began to develop strong links with the regional educational community and wrote detailed essays on modern physics for a lay audience that we put on our website, together with links to numerous other science outreach centres.

Once again it was particularly gratifying to see the response of our research staff to our outreach efforts. Perimeter scientists eagerly volunteered to give pedagogical lectures to the summer students and keynote talks to the teachers, delighted at the opportunity to have a tangible impact on the next generation of scientists. For their part, the students and teachers were tremendously excited: here they were, talking to front-line researchers about the trials and triumphs of their field, right in the heart of a fully functioning research institution. Five years later, although Richard has moved on to a faculty position and been replaced by Damian Pope, the programs have now tripled in scope, with significant international participation for both students and teachers.

I recognize that for many the phrase "summer physics camp" might seem more like a euphemism for a penal colony than a source of frantic excitement, but such an unfortunate state of affairs is effectively nothing more than a reflection of our profound lack of appreciation of science combined with our rather idiosyncratic taste for enjoyment. In my neighbourhood, the frequent sight of youngsters loading hockey duffle bags into minivans on a steamy August morning to merrily trek off to summer power skating class, which personally strikes me as a surefire sign of some serious mental deficiency, is near universally regarded as part and parcel of a happy Canadian childhood.

One way to concretely circumvent the negative press that seems to saddle scientific inquiry is to explicitly reject its popular image as a dry, sterile activity pursued by social misfits. I've never quite understood where this stereotype came from in the first place (although I tend to blame the Romantics), but sadly realize that these sorts of things can certainly become self-actualizing and self-reinforcing. If the widespread popular perception is that only social misfits pursue science, then there's a reasonably high likelihood that anyone with competent social skills will feel inexorably drawn away from such a stigmatized situation. Such forces are, I believe, quite real, resulting in a myriad number of effects, one being the strikingly low number of women in fields such as physics. Combatting such pervasive images of the maladjusted scientist is also an essential part of any effective outreach program. In 2005, we realized that the International Year of Physics, commemorating the one hundredth anniversary of Albert Einstein's *annus mirabilis* in 1905, gave us a golden opportunity to do precisely that.

Einstein is a monumentally iconic figure, recognized the world over not only as the acme of intellectual achievement, but also as a paragon of human sensibility and wisdom. Who better to serve as a flagrant counterexample to the geeky robotic scientist than Uncle Al, whose folksy quotations on the shortsightedness of human strivings are fixtures on wall calendars everywhere? Einstein also highlights another curious fact: while the entire planet recognizes his face, and a large percentage of people would be able to rattle off the equation $E = mc^2$, perhaps even with the correct identification of what the letters represent, only a tiny proportion would be able to relate any genuine understanding of what the equation really means, or any real sense of the man's scientific ideas and accomplishments. Here, then, was a man universally revered for both his humanity and profundity, a man who, we were told, transformed our very understanding of space and time, yet still virtually nobody appreciates or comprehends what he really accomplished. Curious, that. Still, there is little doubt that there is widespread admiration, widespread awe, widespread respect.

And yet.

Imagine your child were to be assessed by some special team of juvenile psychologists who breathlessly phoned you in the middle of the night to relate that she had exhibited clear signs of superhuman intelligence. "Not since Einstein," the chief psychologist exclaims, "have we seen such intellectual precocity, such startling insight, such capacity for knowledge and wisdom." And as you burst with pride, I'm curious to know what this news would mean, in practice. Would you think to yourself, "Wouldn't it be wonderful if my exceptionally talented daughter were a theoretical physicist and followed in the great Einstein's footsteps?" And if so, why aren't you thinking about her right now? Perhaps she actually can.

In 2005, the world was celebrating Einstein. As a theoretical physics institute with a strong outreach mandate, it was obvious that we should do something, too, but it took us some time to come up with what, specifically, that should be. After considerable reflection, we devised EinsteinFest, a twenty-four–day festival of concerts, lectures, performances and exhibits that contained separate programs on Einstein's science and personal life, along with his ongoing legacy, consciously leveraging, once again, our abilities and experience as a fully functioning scientific research institution. To further diversify the program and make it considerably more accessible to a wider public, we also added a special feature on *The Times* that put Einstein's miracle year in the appropriate historical context. There were exhibits of 1905 cars and cameras; sculptures from Jacques Lipchitz and Pablo Picasso; lectures on the 1905 state of psychology, mathematics and philosophy; a silent film festival, concerts on the birth of jazz and classical music performances featuring particular favourites of Einstein. We had in-depth lectures by scientific historians on each of the three extraordinary papers Einstein developed in that miracle year, with a special introduction for children and families. We staged Steve Martin's play, *Picasso at the Lapin Agile*, about a fictitious meeting between Picasso and Einstein in 1905. On the final weekend we held lectures by scientific luminaries Paul Steinhardt, Gary Horowitz and Artur Ekert on their individual perspective of Einstein's legacy in contemporary physics.

It was a unique opportunity to take the bull by the horns and put on a highly stimulating program with wide public appeal while simultaneously leveraging our unique scientific expertise. Michael Duschenes, the PI administrator who had coordinated the entire thing, knocked it completely out of the park. American Express stepped in as our lead sponsor, and attendance for the twenty-four days exceeded 28,000. It was an unqualified success. In an age when so many people were mouthing trite platitudes about the intersection of science and art, while hauling out muddled amalgamations of C. P. Snow and Deepak Chopra, we tangibly demonstrated that a high-level festival celebrating science and culture could be coherent, intellectually substantive and popular.

The major media, meanwhile, almost completely ignored us.

At first this was mystifying to me, but eventually I understood: they simply didn't know where to put us. Convinced, despite my explicit protestations to the contrary, that anything emanating out of a theoretical physics institute must inherently be a science story, editors and producers quickly directed us to the standard cadre of science journalists who were naturally uninterested in anything other than the latest scientific result or controversy. If we had held the festival in an opera house, it might well have been covered by a bevy of arts reporters, but given that we were a scientific institution it seemed the only way we could have attracted public attention was if we had announced that we had come up with a theory of everything that week.

As if developing an array of diverse, high-level programs and materials while combating false negative stereotypes weren't enough of a challenge, it seemed we were forced to spend considerable effort on educating the media as well. Still, a success was a success—and attendance of 28,000 for a festival largely bereft of any substantial national or international media coverage was a heartening display of enthusiasm and a welcome endorsement of our efforts, despite any other disappointments.

Our outreach programs for teachers, students and the general public have only begun to scratch the surface of what we can do. Perhaps the most notable thing about outreach is that there is so much to do—so much that is of value, so much that isn't being done, so many worthwhile avenues to explore that would have considerable impact—that it is sometimes quite difficult to prioritize and focus one's time, effort and resources on the appropriate measures.

In order to achieve our core outreach goals, to substantially contribute to a significantly increased societal recognition of the importance of science and scientific reasoning, we realize that we need to provide a balanced spectrum of programs and activities geared to a wide range of individuals. Some programs, such as our summer school, would naturally only apply to elite students, bound to become scientists anyway. Hopefully we can spur them on to even greater heights, provide them with some additional insight or motivation; but realistically it is unlikely that we are effectively doing much more than our part in assisting them on their bright trajectory. This is important, of course, but not, in itself, sufficient.

It is essential to find ways of engaging the students who are not currently motivated, who have not had the good fortune of being stimulated by an excellent teacher or knowledgeable and committed parent. We have to find a way of somehow inspiring and assisting the under-confident teacher who feels out of his depth and incapable of suitably motivating his students. And we have to discover a way to do all of this that is truly scalable and international. As stressed earlier, the problems with science education and awareness are widespread and hardly limited to any one country. Fortunately, science is also nationally blind, suggesting that any effective measure at redress might well be transportable. In my view, an obvious priority for Perimeter to develop substantial impact is through the development of compelling educational materials, simultaneously invoking our scientific expertise and international network of eminent researchers in the process. When one looks at the positive effect of efforts such as Brian Greene's *The Elegant Universe*, it becomes clear that this is an essential way to go.

What we are talking about here is hardly utopia. If we were able to contribute a small adjustment in students' perspective of science today, the results would be little less than transformative. Let us imagine that we could somehow divert a tiny percentage—say 3 percent—of the world's non-science university-bound students into at least a first degree in science. Just 3 percent. That's not too much to ask. Perhaps there would be 3 percent fewer lawyers and accountants; 3 percent fewer MBAS and financial planners. Would it really matter? Would we even notice?

Now imagine 3 percent more science-savvy citizens, 3 percent more young people who are scientifically literate, scientifically aware. They won't all become professional scientists, of course—some will start companies or become teachers or journalists. A few more, sadly, will inevitably return to the dark side and try their hand at law or politics—perhaps both. But each of them would be far better off for the experience; each of them would be better placed to enrich society after having drunk deep from the cup of scientific knowledge. Each of them would have a deep appreciation for the values, process, culture and rigour of science.

Three percent would make a difference. Three percent would change the world.

And that, dear reader, is why we do outreach at Perimeter Institute.

CHAPTER THIRTEEN

My Life as an Arms Dealer

An old high-school friend of mine, who had the good sense to leave academe and make his fortune in venture capital, once wryly remarked to me during a dinner peppered with my mournful lamentations on the horrors of Ottawa that I could take comfort from the fact that my intensive government relations experience had prepared me for a future career as an arms dealer. Throughout my constant treks to the nation's capital to plead my case before countless politicians and bureaucrats, I would often replay his words in my mind with a grim sort of consolation.

As unprepared and unmotivated as I might have been to lead a physics institute, I was a tenacious expert compared to the arena of government lobbying, a field where my ignorance was only eclipsed by my general disgust at the entire exercise. At least I knew something about physics and had strong views of its overall merits; grappling with the inner workings of government, on the other hand, had all the appeal of becoming foreman at the local sausage factory.

To make matters even worse, I started off on very much the wrong foot. The appropriate way to involve government as a partner in a new initiative, I quickly learned, is to leverage their support up front, before any announcement. The tried and true approach is to go to key decision-makers and inform them that you have diligently assembled an impressive amount of private funding for an exciting, highly meritorious venture pivotal to the nation's interest, but sadly these private commitments are contingent on matching governmental support. This not only compels government officials to give the matter some urgency, it also dangles in front of them the tantalizing opportunity to take credit for the formation of a shiny new entity (governments having a natural preference for new initiatives, of course, rather than merely funding existing entities that may be products of previous regimes) with all of the concomitant photo-ops and other tangible evidence of their visionary inclinations.

We, on the other hand, didn't proceed this way at all, electing instead to firmly set the agenda ourselves and bask alone in the glow of our unprecedented $120 million donation before trying to cajole the public sector to follow our noble lead. The obvious question, "Why are you coming to us now?" trailed after me everywhere I went in Ottawa, like a bad smell.

It was a particularly hard question because I wasn't really sure of the answer. The truth was that just by establishing an endowment we had moved a considerable distance away from Mike's original inclinations: at first he had wanted to spend all the money in thirty years. The problem with this idea was that not only did it deny the opportunity for research breakthroughs in the very long term, it significantly misunderstood a central aspect of the academic mindset: any thirty-year program would have real difficulties in recruiting excellent people by the time year twenty-five rolled around. In fact, with academics being the hyper-conservative beasts they are, this argument could be (and doubtless would be) logically pushed back from year twenty-five to year twenty to year fifteen and so on, so that any self-proclaimed thirty-year program would have significant difficulty in attracting top quality faculty right at the outset. To a research community that was inextricably wedded to the mindset of tenure and academic conservatism, a new, unproven institute with corporate roots was scary enough, but a time-limited initiative that held a whiff of some skunk-works special-ops type of scenario was absolutely beyond the pale.

Mike, unsurprisingly, simply wanted to spend his money. From his vantage point, that really was the whole idea. And so those early conversations around the boardroom table had an undeniably Kafkaesque lilt to them, with Mike avowing his determination to spend every penny of his $100 million and the rest of us anxious to talk him out of it, determined to build an endowment instead. Here was a guy who found himself richer than Croesus and despite his best efforts, was constantly denied the satisfaction of tangibly spending his money. It was all quite amusing, really.

But the endowment decision was the easy one. After that, we had to decide whether we should try to attract government support to our cause. There was much concern about attached strings and so forth; nobody wanted to be in a situation where government was dictating what we were doing and how, or bogging us down in a mire of bureaucracy. Even at that early stage, it was clear to all of us that our singular strength, our overwhelming competitive advantage, was the flexibility independence brought. Curtailing this flexibility for additional government funding would be a dubious victory indeed—best not to have the money at all than get it under constraining circumstances.

But still, why not investigate what might be available? The federal government does fund basic research and by not funding us, what sort of statement would that make to the outside world? Conversely, if we could get government support, wouldn't that be an essential step in proving our worthiness to the international scientific community?

And so we resolved to explore the situation, which effectively meant that board members passed finely worded resolutions about the objective merits of securing government funding, while I was left to trek up to the nation's capital, cap in hand, without a clue as to how to proceed.

In this increasingly gadget-dominated world, it is easy to forget that back in the summer of 2000, neither BlackBerry nor its top executives were household names. Most of the senior officials had heard of Research In Motion, and the more tech-proficient of those carried the early black, half-moon BlackBerrys with their ribbons of text and distinctively raised keys (it was that model that actually looked like a blackberry), but by and large the company and its devices were seen simply as curiosities, not as proto-global players. Mike himself had no political profile to speak of and no direct contacts, while my own situation was considerably worse—not only did I not know anyone, but the very idea of the institute was still a rather closely guarded secret (other than my conversations with some 200 academics around the world).

One of the good things about Canada, however, is that in many ways it's still a fairly small country and it doesn't take a great deal of time to learn who the people of influence are. The birth of my Ottawa lobbyist career can be traced back with some precision: it was launched one early August night in 2000 at an intimate dinner convened by Doug Wright and his longtime friend Paul Dufour, then working as the policy advisor in the office of the Secretary of State for Science and Technology (a junior ministry since discontinued). It was a relatively small affair, with only about eight attendees, including David Strangway, president of the Canada Foundation for

Innovation (CFI), Tom Brzustowski, president of the National Science and Engineering Research Council (NSERC) and Arthur Carty, president of the National Research Council (NRC).

I spent the evening in lighthearted banter and relaxed conversation, trying to establish who were the Ottawa movers and shakers we would have to convince to get government support for the institute. At the end of the dinner, I had a list of six names. Three were the obvious suspects: the nation's top politicians—Prime Minister Jean Chrétien, Finance Minister Paul Martin and Industry Minister John Manley. I had no clue as to how we might get to them. Three more—Chrétien's senior policy advisor, Eddie Goldenberg, Deputy Industry Minister Peter Harder and Deputy Finance Minister Kevin Lynch—I had never heard of. Over time I would learn that they were perhaps the most important.

Three weeks later I was back in Ottawa to meet with Peter Harder. Looking back on it today, I see this as little short of astounding and an obvious demonstration of Peter's curiosity, if not interest, but at the time I remember thinking the meeting did not go very well at all. Rather than deluge me with personal assurances to assist in getting us public support, Harder instead quietly probed me with a number of awkward questions: How was PI going to integrate with the surrounding universities? What were we providing that didn't already exist? How could we ensure we would be able to achieve excellence?

I left the meeting with a clear realization that this lobbying business was going to be much harder than I had thought, together with a dull appreciation of some of the issues that needed to be addressed. Under Peter's watch (and doubtless strongly influenced by him), the Chrétien government had recently initiated a string of highly successful programs that demonstrated a strong national commitment to research—

2,000 endowed university research chairs, a well funded national research infrastructure program (the Canada Foundation for Innovation), enhanced scholarships for university students, increased funding to the granting councils and so forth—and here I was coming along and saying that I too wanted public money for my thing, without any clear demonstration that it fit into the research infrastructure the government was painstakingly building. Indeed, there were obvious concerns that, as an independent organization with no tangible links to the surrounding academic community, the existence of PI might even somehow undermine the government's current programs.

Undaunted, I pushed forward and had my first meeting with Eddie Goldenberg a few weeks later. Goldenberg, a stalwart strategist and advisor to Jean Chrétien throughout his long tenure as prime minister, is a frenetic, passionate and engaging fellow who uniquely managed to combine a flair for both political and policy aspects of the job. His flagrant competency bred a fair amount of jealousy from all sides, as is often the case, and he was sometimes referred to, not without some bitterness in some quarters, as "the king of Canada." While doubtless overstating the case, it was undeniable that he wielded considerable power, and it was quickly obvious that it was paramount to have him engaged on our behalf if we were going to make any progress at all on the government relations front.

When I sketched out our ambitions, Eddie was unhesitatingly enthusiastic. He was overwhelmed at Mike's largesse and captivated by the notion that we had the possibility of creating something that could play a cutting-edge role in the world of global scholarship. "This is exactly the sort of thing," he said exuberantly, "that I got into public service for!" Well, this was certainly a much better reception than I got from Peter Harder, who insisted on getting bogged down with all those tedious details like what we were actually going to do. Things were definitely looking up. After a few more minutes of mutual admiration, I asked Eddie what I should do to move our case along at the federal level. "See Peter Harder," he replied instantly. A tarnished end to an otherwise perfect meeting.

Next up was Kevin Lynch, the deputy finance minister. I managed to procure a meeting between Kevin, another of his staff and two board members (Doug and Ken) later that fall. We met in a boardroom in the Department of Finance at 7 A.M., watching the Ottawa sunrise over coffee and muffins. It started off extremely pleasantly: Kevin bounded into the room, evidently filled with good cheer. "That's just wonderful what Mike has done!" he exclaimed. "Simply wonderful." We all nodded and expressed our joint enthusiasm for the wonders of philanthropy, while I expounded on the structure of the institute, the type of research we would pursue and so on. It went on like this for quite some time, with everyone saying something unequivocally positive about how exciting everything was, when it began to dawn on all three of us that Kevin had no idea that we were actually asking the government for money.

This was awkward. No wonder the fellow was in such a good mood: here he was at 7 A.M., starting his day off with a bona fide good news story of enlightened Canadian philanthropy where for once nobody was asking him to do anything at all. Except, of course, we were actually asking for quite a bit, but he didn't know it.

I had met with the staff member some weeks earlier, as it happened, but somehow the message hadn't been conveyed up to the deputy and now we were all sitting in this lovely breakfast meeting demonstrating our enthusiasm, while the clock was ticking.

"Well," concluded Kevin with another smile. "It was great to see all of you here. Thanks so much for giving me a personal report."

I looked at Ken. He looked at Doug. Doug looked at me. I looked at the ground.

"Yes…" I began and then faltered.

"You see," Doug continued adroitly, "we wanted to tell you that we do have a request for matching funding from the government."

Suddenly, Kevin's encouraging grin evaporated and his eyes narrowed into icy, bureaucratic detachment. So much for his rare opportunity to fully relax and simply enjoy a wholesome good news story.

"That will need some deliberation, of course," he replied, outwardly phlegmatic but plainly seething inside. The unfortunate staff member that had let him be blindsided in his first meeting of the day had now retreated towards the window and I could feel the heat of Kevin's gaze on his back. Jumping seemed like a reasonable option at that point, I thought to myself, except that the windows were glazed shut. Maybe Kevin would just throw him through anyway.

So the good news was that I had managed to see Goldenberg, Harder and Lynch. The bad news was that we had a long way to go.

Still, I was learning. It was important, for instance, to create information booklets about the institute both to prepare staff in advance and to leave behind after meetings. People, I was told, will take you more seriously if you have "literature" with you. When I first heard somebody refer to it this way, I remember being confused, wondering why on earth I should contemplate leaving a copy of Dostoevsky behind after a meeting. Eventually, of course, it became clear that this was just corporate-speak for promotional material.

And so I began to write, delighted in the prospect that I could now honestly tell my friends I was being paid to compose literature. I crafted a series of booklets I affectionately referred to as bumf books—"bumf" being slang for propaganda that I had unthinkingly absorbed somewhere and later learned was directly related, etymologically, to the British contraction of "bum fodder." Yet another oblique benefit of a general education.

The bumf books were a strange mixture of high flown claims of our bold ambitions for global domination together with judiciously selected quotes from the government's own propaganda in a desperate attempt to detail precisely how and why we were completely in line with what they had thought of all along. The industry minister had spoken of the importance of basic research? We were all about basic research! The prime minister had trumpeted the merits of private-public sector partnerships? If the government would only support us, we would be the poster children of public-private partnerships! And so on. It was all fairly clever, but I wasn't entirely certain it wasn't just self-indulgent. Somehow we had to get some sort of traction within the system.

I began meeting separately with Tom Brzustowski and David Strangway, the heads of NSERC and CFI respectively, to ask for their advice. Brzustowski was most supportive, but had no clear mechanism for supporting us via NSERC. Strangway, meanwhile, recognized that CFI might play a role.

The Canada Foundation for Innovation was a new federal agency that had been established to distribute much needed research infrastructure funds to upgrade and expand projects throughout the country. It was rigorously arm's-length and apolitical, relying on strict peer-review practices to evaluate requests for support. So far, so good. But CFI was an infrastructure fund that was established to support laboratory facilities and equipment. As a theoretical institute, we naturally didn't have any such things to support. On the other hand, we were constructing a brand new building, which was likely going to be pretty costly. It was worth a shot.

The path was fraught with obstacles. In the first place, as a new, independent institution, we didn't even have the requisite status to apply to CFI and first had to submit a formal request just to be deemed eligible to submit an application. Then there were CFI's internal policies. While the notion of using an infrastructure fund to support a building for theoretical physics might seem reasonable, it was frequently at odds with aspects of CFI's own guidelines. In an understandable effort to ensure that the funds went to the equipment rather than to fancy accoutrements associated with the building that stored them, CFI was only prepared to offer basic support for the plainest, cheapest sorts of buildings. Surely an argument would have to be made that we were exceptional.

Fortunately for me, I was by now quite undeterred by such a requirement. Everywhere I went, I was told that we were different. "I'd love to help you, Howard," came the earnest reply from all quarters, "but we simply don't have a program for you. You guys are different. It would establish a precedent, you see."

Bureaucrats are naturally terrified of setting precedents or engaging in apparent one-offs that all other supplicants would quickly use to try to leverage support for their own projects. But I was no bureaucrat, and it was clear that the way forward for me was to turn things on their head. I would embrace our uniqueness. I would trumpet it from the rooftops. Yes, we were exceptional. Yes, we were a precedent. And yes, the nation would be a damned sight better off if we had a bevy more of such precedents.

It was the only reasonable strategy we could take. I could hardly pretend that we were an experimental institute or that our building was going to be a big featureless box for blackboards—God knows there are enough of those scattered throughout the world of theoretical physics already.

So I sat down to write the grant application. The fact that I had no previous experience writing grant applications was a minor irritant, but hardly a big deal. I was now a physics lobbyist who had by this stage already penned thousands of words of propaganda explaining to all and sundry why we were so eminently worthy of near universal public support. I knew the drill.

It was no use pretending we hadn't bothered to familiarize ourselves with the CFI guidelines; the only thing to do was to respectfully submit that, although their policies were perfectly reasonable, they simply shouldn't apply to us. After all, we were different (as you may recall). For most researchers, paying lots of money for an expensive building to conduct their experiments is largely a misappropriation of resources, but for us, you see, the development of a suitably attractive building to win over and retain the highest quality international minds was an integral aspect of the entire project. It wasn't that, being theorists, we didn't have a laboratory. That was a naive, simplistic way to regard the situation. The proper way to look at things was to recognize that, in an essential sense, the building was the laboratory, and thus should be recognized (and funded) as such!

The evident genius of this argument aside, it is far from clear to me that the good folks at CFI didn't just recognize an interesting project when they saw one, demonstrating an admirable flexibility to overlook standard policy constraints when circumstances warranted. But whatever the internal mechanics of the process, we were successfully awarded a CFI grant of $5.6 million which was matched by the Ontario government, as was the current custom. Suddenly we had not only garnered $11.2 million in public monies to Perimeter, we had, even more importantly, demonstrated that the institute could compete in an open, peer-review competition with other projects. For the first time, I could add objective appraisals of our worth to our own luminous self-serving bumf.

I was also starting to learn that in order to make any significant headway in Ottawa, we needed to have champions—people on the inside of the system who were willing to actively support us. Ideally, the perfect champion of this project would have been the industry minister. In Canada, the Ministry of Industry is a huge, catchall portfolio, encompassing everything from the promotion of aboriginal businesses to corporate governance, regional development to e-commerce. Not to mention all the major granting councils and the entire university research infrastructure. Getting the attention of the industry minister for our project would be pretty difficult, but life was made doubly complicated for us since at this time industry ministers were cycling through the portfolio faster than draft picks in a fantasy baseball league (John Manley, Brian Tobin, Allan Rock). Mike and I saw all of them, and all were pretty positive as far as it went, but it seemed that every time we had something new to tell them we were talking to a different guy. It became clear that the champion would have to come from within the bureaucracy. I set my sights on Peter Harder.

Now this might seem odd given that of all the people I met during my initial Ottawa forays, Harder was perhaps the most skeptical. The fact that I like a challenge doubtless had something to do with it, but I couldn't shake the fact that Harder, for all of his toughness, was essentially, uncomfortably right: I had to make the appropriate case. I thought back to what he had said during our meeting, developing my own mental checklist. He had mentioned that we had to find a way to resonate with the government's mandate, and so off I ran to find all sorts of quotes from senior government officials on the importance of developing meaningful private-public partnerships and provocatively inscribed them in my bumf book. Check. He had talked about how PI must find a way to integrate into the Canadian research infrastructure. And so we got CFI funding. Check again. But he had also mentioned that we needed to find a way of getting support from the Canadian academic establishment. No check there at all. Worse, no clear sense of what to do.

I racked my brains to find out what that would take. The truth was that most of the surrounding universities were either indifferent to us or actively hostile, sensing a threat. Either way, strong endorsements of support seemed a long way from forthcoming. At that point, UW's David Johnston had been the only senior university official to show any support whatsoever for our cause. Once David came to terms with the fact that PI was not going to be created within the bosom of UW, he sat me down in his office and presented me with a sheet of paper that he had just drawn up.

"I thought that it was time that we drew up an MOU between UW and PI," he declared.

"Ah," I replied airily, taking the offered sheet and burying my head in it studiously. I had no idea what an MOU was.

An MOU, I soon learned, was a memorandum of understanding. I read the document carefully twice. It didn't seem to include anything other than some vague, high-minded intentions of how we might, should we be so inclined, possibly explore ways of mutual collaboration. There was nothing binding, nothing detailed. So far as I could understand it, there was really no point to the whole thing at all.

Still, David seemed quite keen on the whole business.
"This is," he explained patiently, "fairly standard practice."
"Okay," I shrugged, and signed it.

Several months later, as I pondered how I might be able to tangibly demonstrate to Peter Harder how we were welcomed with open arms by the Canadian academic establishment, I thought again of these mysterious MOUs. Perhaps I could get more. I could print off different MOUs for every major university in the country and get them signed. The fact that the MOUs didn't really say anything at all or commit us to any particular line of action was perfect: tangible evidence of support with no commitment whatsoever. Who could possibly object to that?

Soon I was fully absorbed in the MOU game, travelling here and there and getting all sorts of signatures from academic administrators from coast to coast. While to a large extent the whole business was comically superficial, producing signed copies of meaningless documents that essentially detailed how we were committed to doing something together so long as we still wanted to do so, I later came to appreciate that there was nonetheless some real overall merit to the exercise as it gave me a pretext to personally meet with academic leaders across the country to explain what PI was all about and listen to their respective concerns. Perhaps this is what Harder had really wanted in the first place. At any rate, after a few months of this, I had produced almost thirty different MOUs from virtually every significant academic institution in the country. The only holdout was University of Toronto. It wasn't that University of Toronto was opposed to the principal of MOUs—not at all. In fact, all the relevant people there assured me that the University of Toronto had had extensive experience in the development of MOUs. No, the problem was that officials at U of T didn't like the form of this particular MOU I was suggesting. They had their own MOU policy, you see, and were adamant that they rewrite the MOU to their specification.

"Fine," I responded merrily. "I'm sure we can find common ground. Send me a copy when you're finished and I'll look it over."

As far as I was concerned, so long as the MOU didn't diverge from my fundamental principal of saying absolutely nothing in particular, it didn't make the slightest difference to me what the words were.

Six months later, they still hadn't responded. I probably would have forgotten about the whole thing, except that the lack of involvement of the mighty University of Toronto was sometimes pointed out to me by anxious bureaucrats scanning the list of signed MOUs in our bumf book.

"Where's U of T?" they would ask with evident concern. "Why haven't they signed an MOU?"

"It's a legal matter," I replied solemnly—which was, I suppose, technically accurate, but nonetheless far too grandiose for what I imagined was actually going on.

After nine months of pondering, I finally received the "amended" MOU from the University of Toronto, with three signed copies. Only one word, I noticed, had been changed from our suggested template. I signed them back immediately.

Meanwhile, my political education continued apace. I was regularly travelling to Ottawa and meeting with whomever I could. Finance, Industry, NSERC, the Prime Minister's Office, bureaucrats, politicians, political aides, whoever. I was having reasonable success in procuring meetings and getting a general lay of the land, but after some time it began to dawn on me that there was a strong likelihood I wasn't getting anywhere.

On one occasion I had procured a meeting with David Watters, then an associate deputy minister in the Department of Finance. I had met with David some months before and found him a most sympathetic and straightforward fellow. Better still, I discovered that he was a closet physicist who seemed to have read every lay physics book he could get his hands on and was thus very supportive of our efforts to get government support and recognition for our noble cause. This meeting, however, was scheduled to be a more formal affair with David, another bureaucrat at Finance and two of their counterparts at Industry Canada. It seemed like things were reaching some kind of focal point.

I phoned Paul Dufour to ask his views on how to proceed. Ever since that first dinner that Doug Wright and Paul had put together, I had used Paul as a sounding board and tutor, trying to get a handle on the strange political world I suddenly found myself in.

"I've got a meeting with Watters and some Industry guys," I told him. "What do you think is going to be on the agenda?"

"What do you mean?" he shot back.

"The agenda? How is it going to go?"

"How is it going to go? Look, Howard, who asked for the meeting?"

"I don't know. I guess I did." I was forever calling people and requesting meetings. That seemed to be all I was doing those days.

"Then it's your meeting."

"Come again?"

"It's your meeting," he explained, with deliberate patience. "If you asked for the meeting, then it's your meeting. You set the agenda."

"I do?"

"Yup."

"Why didn't you tell me this before?"

"I thought you knew. Everybody knows that."

"I didn't!"

"Evidently."

I began to think quickly.

"Can I invite someone else to my meeting?" I asked.

"You can try," he replied. "Give it a shot."

So I invited Tom Brzustowski, the President of NSERC, to the meeting. Tom had been a stalwart supporter of PI from the beginning and was keen to do what he could to demonstrate his endorsement of our project. In all of our official documentation, we had specifically requested that any additional federal monies we might receive should flow, if possible, directly through NSERC. From our perspective it was natural to get the relevant granting council integrally involved. In addition to immediately giving us more credibility in the academic world, it would also firmly establish us within the NSERC structure for eventual reviews and assessments. The prospect of PI receiving federal monies independent of NSERC would necessarily reflect poorly on the optics, giving the appearance of being a politically-motivated one-off.

Brzustowski, of course, had a direct interest in PI's success: the more money that flowed through NSERC, the more relevant NSERC became. But for Tom, it was much more than that. He recognized well that an opportunity like PI, where huge sums of private money were being directed, as philanthropy, towards scientific research, was a groundbreaking precedent that should be encouraged as strongly as possible and he was determined to bring whatever influence he could to bear on the situation to make others realize it as well.

Such sentiments were not, refreshingly, all that unusual, particularly among those in senior positions in the bureaucracy. Mixed in with the expected majority of hidebound stupidity lies a strikingly large number of people in government who are remarkably capable, dedicated people. They are the idealists, and could easily make two or three times their current salary in the private sector, but instead opt for gritting their teeth as they hack their way through the bureaucratic labyrinth to eke out whatever small victories they can to make a difference. You may laugh at this seemingly perverse characterization of the government official as a forward thinking defender of the realm, but I can assure you it is true: I have seen enough of them with my own eyes.

It turns out that the meeting with Tom, David Watters and others was not the most successful of gatherings, but it was interesting. I'm not sure whether or not he was having a particularly bad day or it was all some sort of elaborate role-playing exercise, but the meeting largely consisted of Watters ripping into his Industry counterparts, vehemently expressing frustration at the apparent lack of concrete progress, one way or the other, on our file. It was a bit like walking into a family feud, and I spent most of the time looking under the table to hide my embarrassment at being there. So much for it being my meeting.

Our CFI grant was announced in January 2002 and I was now ready to once again confront the dreaded Peter Harder and make him our champion. I procured a meeting with him for February and, spurring myself onwards with internal chants of "My meeting! My meeting!" like some demented, steroid-riddled technocrat, I respectfully asked his assistant if I could bring Tom Brzustowski, David Johnston and Mike Lazaridis to the meeting. He wanted integration with the government? I'd show him integration. I've got a CFI grant in my hand and the president of NSERC in the flesh singing our praises. He wanted cooperation with Canadian universities? I'd give him a mittful of MOUs and the president of the University of Waterloo beside me at the table. For good measure, I'd ensure that Mike would be there too, the living proof of the "private" in the whole "private-public partnership."

It worked. After listening to Mike and the others speak, Harder looked up and said quietly: "The last time I met with Howard, I told him he needed to do a few things, and it looks to me like he's done them. Let's see how we can move this forward."

It wasn't exactly easy from that point forward, but momentum was definitely starting to build. When Kevin Lynch, the deputy finance minister whom we had inadvertently blindsided a year and a half earlier, was passing through town to see Jim Balsillie's new project (the Centre for International Governance Innovation), he made a stop at Perimeter as well. At that point we had started research operations in the old post office building and when Kevin came by and saw Perimeter in action, he looked genuinely excited and engaged, chatting for long periods of time with researchers about their work and their experience at the institute. It made me appreciate more than ever that for top civil servants, working diligently to establish meaningful, responsible programs in the public's interest and being forced to wade through a daily dose of political machinations, mind-numbing meetings and countless requests for funding for their troubles, such genuine, spontaneous interaction with flesh and blood researchers was little short of an unmitigated joy.

Meanwhile, the groundwork for funding PI was nearing completion. A framework for supporting the institute—$5 million per year for five years through NSERC—had been created. Eddie Goldenberg in the Prime Minister's Office was strongly supportive and had briefed Prime Minister Chrétien about it, who, we were told, looked quite favourably upon the idea. All we needed now was a closeout meeting between Mike and the prime minister. We were almost home.

Meanwhile, Mike's star was beginning to shine much stronger. BlackBerry had steadily become a well-known commodity throughout key government and finance circles in North America. Through his public donation of $100 million to Perimeter, Mike was increasingly recognized throughout the country as a spokesperson for science and research and *The Globe and Mail* would select him as its inaugural "Nation-Builder of the Year" in 2002. Consequently, the number of private interest groups trying to get his attention, support and influence began to multiply drastically, with many trying to get to Mike through me.

Early in 2002, I had been approached by a group of people led by former Ontario Premier Bob Rae concerning ITER, an international fusion experimental collaboration dedicated to constructing the next generation of tokamaks (magnetic confinement reactors). Rae and his ITER Canada colleagues were involved in lobbying government for support for locating the experiment in Canada at an existing fission reactor site just outside of Toronto, and they wanted additional support from Mike to help them make their case. Mike, who never met a science project he didn't like, was unsurprisingly enthusiastic, quickly convinced that Canada should become the focal point of this huge international engineering effort rather than muddling along in its usual benign fashion, fixated on the likes of hockey and beer. However, a few investigatory phone calls shed a little more light on the situation. It seemed that the ITER Canada group had approached Prime Minister Chrétien in 2001 asking for his support. When the wily politician immediately asked them how much it would cost, he was frankly assured that no hard costs were envisioned, they simply needed the Government of Canada's official sanction to carry the day. One year later, things had become more complicated. Other countries, principally, France and Japan, had mounted bids and the competition for citing the facility was heating up. Executives at ITER Canada now found themselves in the unenviable position of having to go back to the prime minister and explain that, despite their initial claims, they now needed a commitment of $1 billion from the Canadian government to make a competitive bid against the French and Japanese. Chrétien was decidedly unimpressed at this latest turn of events, as was his senior bureaucrat, Mel Cappe, the Clerk of the Privy Council.

Meanwhile, in March 2002, our local member of Parliament, Andrew Telegdi, had managed to arrange our closeout meeting with the prime minister. It was common procedure for the local MP to procure a meeting with the relevant cabinet minister and Andrew had done his job admirably throughout with his customary determination, lining up meetings for Mike and myself with Finance Minister Paul Martin as well as each of the cascade of industry ministers (Manley, Tobin, Rock). Now the stage was set for Andrew to arrange a meeting between the prime minister himself and a star philanthropist and entrepreneur from his riding. For a backbencher like Andrew, such a meeting was about as close to political nirvana as it gets and he could barely contain himself, jumping this way and that as we rode together in the courtesy bus on Parliament Hill to the meeting. I tried to ignore him.

It all began reasonably enough. There were six of us in the room: the prime minister, his executive assistant Bruce Hartley, Mel Cappe, Andrew, Mike and me. Mike opened up his briefcase and showed Chrétien all the latest BlackBerrys that were soon to hit the shelves. This was very much according to the usual script we had developed: leveraging Mike's tangible success as an industry leader in a progressive, highly competitive domain, while at the same time stimulating the likely meeting-saturated politician by a concrete, futuristic device that was a showcase of Canadian technology. My role throughout these political meetings was to try to say as little as possible: I was the quiet resource who would only proffer comments whenever factual material about the institute was needed to support the discussion or judiciously insert a well-chosen remark if it seemed that the conversation needed to be gently steered in another direction.

Chrétien looked at the devices for some time and began to ask Mike some questions. He passed on a BlackBerry to Mel Cappe. Everyone seemed to relax. Then Mike began to segue towards PI and the importance of balancing applied research, such as the BlackBerry, by basic research, such as Perimeter. It was all very much in keeping with the script and Chrétien was engaged. Mel Cappe was smiling. It seemed almost too good to be true.

And it was.

Telegdi, unable to contain himself any longer on the sidelines, perked up.

"Mike believes that basic research is extremely important!" he cried. "It's not just Perimeter; he also supports ITER!"

Chrétien's face clouded over immediately.

"ITER!" he fumed. "Those goddamned bastards just came back to me with a request for a billion dollars! A billion dollars! After telling me that it would cost nothing!" Cappe nodded emphatically.

I looked at Telegdi with hatred in my eyes. "Yes, well," I interjected breezily, "this is not about ITER. What we're talking about is theoretical physics. Very cheap. And let's not forget that Mike gave $100 million of his own money to start Perimeter."

Chrétien looked back up at Mike with evident respect. "Yes," he began, "I heard that. Very impressive. The three of us should have dinner at some point—you, me and my brother

Michel. He's always bugging me to support science. I tell him that there are no votes in it—nobody cares about science—but I do it anyway. He's right."

I breathed a sigh of relief. Things seemed to be getting back on track. Mike began to expound on the limitless benefits of science and how many mysteries remain unsolved, and we were gradually making our way back to the promised land of fundamental theoretical physics. And then, like a creature from a B-movie horror flick, Andrew rose again.

"Show him the new BlackBerry, Mike!" Telegdi interrupted. "It has a phone!"

"I have a phone," the prime minister replied curtly. Evidently, I'm not the only one who wanted Andrew out of the room.

Then Mel Cappe stood up.

"I'm sorry," he announced without the slightest regret. "We have another meeting." And out of the office we went.

Andrew, blissfully ignorant of what had just transpired, enthused, "I thought that went very well," as the three of us rode back in the parliamentary courtesy bus. I stood quietly in the corner, rhythmically clenching and unclenching my fists.

Yet all was not lost. I desperately replayed the meeting back in my head over and over and settled on the prime minister's musings about another possible get-together with Mike and his brother Michel. It was not much, but it was all I had. I worked frantically with Mike's assistant, Michel Chrétien, Bruce Hartley and Eddie Goldenberg to set up a follow-up meeting. We organized a lunch for early May before Michel, citing other commitments, gracefully withdrew. The stage was set for Mike to meet privately with the prime minister at his home at 24 Sussex Drive.

I went with Mike to Ottawa in his jet and we discussed strategy, as usual. Chrétien was obviously impressed by Mike's personal commitment to the enterprise, and so nothing terribly fancy should be in order; he should just be himself. Recalling the prime minister's previous lamentation that scientific funding never helped him at the ballot box, we agreed to offer him the possibility of a photo-op at a groundbreaking for the new building, should he wish to come to make an announcement himself.

We rode in a limo from the airport to 24 Sussex Drive to drop off Mike for the lunch, and then the driver whisked me to a local Starbucks where I waited, sipping lattes and musing at the strangeness of my Ottawa experiences that resulted in me being ostentatiously taken to a coffee shop. Two hours later, I climbed back into the limo and we picked up Mike from his lunch meeting. He approached the car with a wave and an ear-to-ear grin. It was official.

Of course, that was just the federal part. Once they committed, I had to try to leverage that to further involve the Ontario government as well. This, too, is par for the course. Talk to anyone in Ottawa about support for your wonderful new initiative and the first response is likely "Where is the province on this?" A similar reaction can be guaranteed from the province concerning the status of the federal government.

While the lion's share of my efforts to date had been directed towards the federal government, we had certainly had our dealings with the province as well. Ontario had matched our CFI grant of $5.6 million through its own infrastructure granting council, the Ontario Innovation Trust. Back in 2001, I had also written a successful grant proposal to the Ontario Research and Development Challenge Fund (ORDCF), positioning PI in partnership with UW's incipient Institute for Quantum Computing (IQC). At the time, we were hoping this would be the appropriate vehicle for the province to match the federal award of $25 million, but unfortunately the fund was running out of money at the time (it has subsequently been shut down and morphed into something else) and so we were awarded roughly $6 million for both PI and IQC. The strange thing was that they didn't tell us how to divide the money and somehow it fell to me, as the author of the grant, to make the decision. In an effort to show true partnership with the IQC and, it must be admitted, out of a sense of gratitude and respect for all of David Johnston's efforts, I proposed to split the award down the middle, giving both PI and IQC $3 million. This became the first solid public funding commitment to IQC and with that $3 million plus the Canada Research Chairs given to Raymond Laflamme and Michele Mosca, the Institute for Quantum Computing would be officially established. It wasn't quite the same as giving $100 million of my own money, of course, but it was something: I felt a bit like a philanthropist myself.

Still, the clock was ticking. At this point PI had only managed to get a commitment of $8.6 million from the provincial government, as opposed to the $30.6 million from the feds. With the prime minister coming for the official groundbreaking ceremony, here was our chance to draw attention to ourselves and leverage matters with the province. To the constant provincial queries of "Where were the feds?" we could now confidently reply that they had just committed an extra $25 million and that the prime minister himself was coming to make the announcement. Surely the province didn't want to be sitting on the sidelines as those nasty federal politicians stole all the glory?

Fortunately, such arguments met with a most receptive ear at Queen's Park, largely owing to the fact that our local member of provincial parliament, Elizabeth Witmer, was also deputy premier at the time. I had come to know Elizabeth quite well, regularly informing her of our progress (or lack thereof, as the case may be) in Ottawa as we meandered through the lobby labyrinth. She is the sort of person that gives one genuine hope in the democratic process: an unpretentious, hardworking and exceptionally decent individual with a long record of public service and an often underappreciated knack for quietly getting things done. Recognizing the opportunity at hand, combined with the fact that we had already received substantial independent endorsement from Ontario's own research infrastructure (through the peer-reviewed ORDCF award as well as the matching infrastructure grant for CFI), Elizabeth managed to persuade her cabinet colleagues of the importance of committing an additional $15 million to PI ($5 million per year for three years to begin in 2004) in the 2002 provincial budget.

By June 2002 we had therefore procured a total of more than $54 million in government support to Perimeter Institute, an amount that was forecast to meet virtually all of our spending requirements for the next few years, other than for our share of the new building. In short, we had established a true public-private partnership for an independent research institute, with the public sector effectively supporting the annual operating budget and the private monies directed towards a steadily rising endowment that would allow us to more effectively compete with the major endowed research institutions in the United States and elsewhere.

I was naturally pleased by the end result of our labours, but quickly became disheartened by the general reaction to the announcements. Of course, there was the usual dollop of envy and jealousy caused by those (typically in academe) who felt we had inappropriately circumvented process to help ourselves to a piece of the public pie by utilizing our dark, corporate political contacts and all of that. That much I expected.

No, I was disheartened far more by the majority of the overtly positive responses. Hearty congratulations were offered for our evident ability to somehow penetrate government; but after some time I began to appreciate that these backslapping sentiments had little to do with an endorsement of our cause, but rather were simply a recognition of victory in the great game of extricating money from the public purse. We had won the match, you see, and had therefore earned the prize of public support. It didn't seem to matter to these people whether or not we were actually worth supporting—the only thing that mattered was that we became supported. I suddenly felt overwhelmingly naive. All of the strategies, all of the tactics, all of the propaganda, all of the mountains and mountains of effort had been nothing more than a means to an end, a way of getting the attention of the key decision-makers to convince them of the merits of our case. Of course, one had to deal with egos and political realities and appropriately framing the issue and all of that. But the whole point was that this was something worth doing, something worth supporting and something important for the public sector to be seen to be proudly supporting.

Mike and I wanted PI to be under the rubric of NSERC because, as the national granting council, it was the appropriate nonpartisan government body for us to be associated with. Moreover, I wanted to be in a system where we would be regularly reviewed and held to account. Of course, I was strongly of the view that we deserved public support, but only if we delivered, only if we met our ambitious goals. When asked by government officials whether we thought our funding should be renewed five years later, I told them I didn't know; moreover, I couldn't possibly know. The whole point, you see, was to come back to us in five years or so and assess the situation. If we met our lofty benchmarks and had a clear, attainable vision for the next five years, then absolutely we should be funded. If we didn't, then of course we should be cut off. Obvious, no?

No.

In the world of professional fundraisers, such talk is anathema: naive, deluded and not a little dangerous. The goal for them is simple: get money, as much as possible, as often as possible. If offered a choice between $10 million per year for three years and $30 million today, they would all unhesitatingly opt for the $30 million—a bird in the hand, and all that, not to mention the potential additional revenues from the investment income. Three years from now, they'd say, we can come back and try again for another $30 million. Maybe $50 million.

I can't imagine what it must be like to be in the professional lobbying business, spending one's time cultivating relationships with key people to quietly promote whatever project is willing to hire you. One day you have breakfast with some chief of staff and you find yourself pushing the importance of subsidizing grain farmers. The next day, you are equally adamant that small businesses need an improved tax structure to compete effectively. On another occasion you are a stalwart defender of high environmental standards. How, on earth, can anyone take you seriously? How can you have any effect whatsoever?

But apparently they do. Of course, the good lobbyist offers much more—closely attuned to the political ambitions and impediments of her target audience, her job is to sell her product in such a way that it manifestly supports the relevant political agenda.

This may be helpful to some politicians, and it is doubtless vital to the well-being of scores of lobbyists, consultants and other parasites anxious to suckle the public teat. But, as has often been recognized, it makes for absolutely abysmal public policy. Good public policy is necessarily outside the realm of local political agendas—it serves, by definition, the national interest and thus should be comprehensive, justifiable and largely transparent. Furthermore, while there may be scant evidence as yet to support this claim, I do believe that it is at least possible that good public policy can be politically successful.

When Jean Chrétien claimed there was no political reward for funding science, maybe he was only half right. That is, while it is doubtless true that the general public insufficiently recognized his government's efforts in supporting research and education, perhaps much of the problem was that these accomplishments weren't highlighted sufficiently—there was not enough of a clear sense that they represented an integral aspect of the core priorities of his regime.

Imagine a political party that eschews empty homilies and craven rhetoric, a party that transparently states its core priorities and delineates concrete approaches to address them. The standard consensus among the punditocracy is that this is simply political suicide: any party that comprehensively details such a platform will simply be exposing countless targets for the opposition to attack—indeed, in the 2006 Canadian federal election, the official party platforms were not even released until shortly before election day.

Ah, the 2006 federal election! I remember it well. That was the time that, for a brief shining moment, the papers were full of talk of funding announcements and physics, although certainly not in the way I would have preferred.

The story begins roughly a year earlier, when Mike and I were having one of our regular conversations about how best to continue to involve the federal and provincial governments in PI, IQC and other related efforts. Our government grants were expiring in 2007 and I was naturally concerned about the future. Mike, too, was anxious to ensure that we had sufficient resources to continue to develop at the highest possible level and expressed a willingness to make still another large-scale personal donation if we could simultaneously attract matching funds from the provincial and federal governments. Together we began working on a large funding proposal for both the IQC and PI—one that would safeguard our future opportunity to expand, while robustly growing the endowment.

My discussions with policymakers in Ottawa and Queen's Park found a fairly receptive ear, leading me to become cautiously optimistic. The situation was much different from when we first tried this sort of thing back in 2000: PI was now already funded by both levels of government and so mechanisms were already in place to support us. Moreover, in the intervening years I was very confident that we had established an impressive track record of accomplishment in both research and outreach that would naturally emerge in any objective review. To top it all off, Mike was by now a much admired national figure with access to all the top people in government.

Our timing for this latest quest seemed quite propitious. The Liberal Dalton McGuinty government in Ontario had that year unveiled a new Ministry of Research Innovation (MRI). While announcing new ministries may in itself be somewhat overrated, given that it's fairly standard practice for a new government to rename ministries in its own image, the fact that the premier elected to specifically stress both research and innovation as well as, even more emphatically and unusually, place himself as its minister, boded particularly well for our chances.

In Ottawa, meanwhile, I received a warm reception from Peter Nicholson, then a senior policy advisor to Prime Minister Paul Martin. He assured me that if the Ontario government made this a priority then the federal Liberals, with their natural focus on research and innovation, would look most favourably on the proposal and could well imagine something like this being supported in the spring budget, should the government last that long. Of course, the relevant authorities would have to do their due diligence and rigorously assess both PI and IQC through an impartial review, but if that proved successful, as he imagined it would given our joint burgeoning reputation, then he was quite confident that our proposal would be supported.

Everything seemed to be falling into place. But the federal government didn't last, of course, and an election was called for January 2006.

An added benefit of the success of our previous lobbying expedition was that, by getting endorsed by both the federal Liberals and the provincial Conservatives, we could manifestly trumpet our nonpartisanship. This was, I recognized, highly important—not only for the obvious tactical reasons (given that one never knows who's going to be in power at any given time and it would be disastrous to have one's funding tied to the success of any one political party), but also for the overarching image of public leadership that we consciously sought out: as a new research institution that was claiming to be the poster boy for the next generation of public-private partnerships in the national scientific interest, it was essential that we remain firmly beyond the grimy world of partisan politics. After all, an avowed goal of PI was not only to do world-class scholarship in fundamental physics, but also to concretely affect Canadian public policy, to shine proudly as a beacon that would represent the new Canadian image of research and scholarship to all and sundry. How could we ever have any legitimate impact on the national research picture if we were seen to be anything less than rigorously objective and formally independent from any political party?

Simple, no? You would think so. But Canadian politics was pretty unusual by early 2006. The federal Liberals had been in power for thirteen years straight and many otherwise rational people simply couldn't imagine that they might lose. So when officials from Paul Martin's team tried frantically to reverse their sinking fortunes in the dying days of the campaign by suddenly announcing our requested federal funding to PI and IQC as an election pledge (the intrinsic merits of objective review and due diligence, it seems, can easily be trumped by the prospect of electoral defeat), I was amazed to discover that surrounding university officials and representatives were ecstatic to make the lemming-like drive off the cliff to wed their fortunes with those of the desperate Martinites.

Sacrificing one's high-minded principles to make a Faustian bargain for funding is one thing—hardly laudable, but at least understandable at some level. Sacrificing one's high-minded principles to throw one's lot in with the losing team, thereby significantly jeopardizing future success is little other than sheer madness. By January 2006, however, madness seemed to be the order of the day.

What to do? Here I was, helplessly watching from the sidelines as these modern day Machiavellis seemed intent on toying with the fortunes of my institute, needlessly sacrificing both our principles and our prospects to saddle us with the millstone of a failing political campaign.

So I wrote something.

I wanted to go on record and voice my opposition to this latest bit of electoral tomfoolery, doing my bit to reposition the institute as politically neutral in an attempt to recover some part of the higher ground that we had so pointlessly and needlessly sacrificed. Of course, this would be, I felt, particularly important if the Liberals lost, as all the polls were indicating they would, but would also, in the long run, prove

important to what the institute represented even if they somehow recovered.

I penned a carefully worded piece to send to Paul Wells's
blog. Paul is a reporter for *Maclean's* whom I had come to
know and respect over the last year or so, and it seemed like
a reasonable place to go on record and make a statement. I
pointed out the impressive research and education policies
that past Liberal governments had invoked over the previous
decade and explicitly highlighted my concern at the paucity
of specific research and innovation policies that had emanated
from either the Conservatives or the New Democratic Party.
But I expressed considerable frustration that, in an election
wholly devoid of any discussion of research policy, the
Martinites had reverted to manifestly pork-barrel politics that
cheapened both science and the Liberals' past accomplishments in the process.

This provoked a small firestorm that hardly dominated the
election campaign, but did manage to rise above the noise
somewhat, receiving significant coverage in *The Globe and
Mail* the next day and briefly revived in a weekend op-ed by
Margaret Wente on "Mr. Martin's Very, Very Bad Day" a few
days later.

Suffice it to say, my literary musings weren't terribly well
received by the surrounding community, who saw them, I
think, as some quixotic attempt to grandstand on principle,
like some self-righteous latter-day Cato. What they manifestly failed to understand was that while my principles were
offended, I only felt obligated to write something because
of the sheer inanity of the circumstances. Had the Liberals
been up fifteen points in the polls at the time, I wouldn't
have been much happier at the way things played out, but
you can rest assured that I would have been a good deal qui-
eter about my discomfort.

All's well that ends well, I suppose. The Conservatives won the 2006 election, of course, and over the next year and a half both the Ontario Liberal government and federal Conservative government jointly committed a further $100 million to ensure that Perimeter could continue to expand and meet its vigorous operational goals for another five years. As part of the federal government's review process, the institute was appropriately submitted to a rigorous third-party assessment from the international scientific community, which I'm delighted to report we passed with flying colours.

It's hard to say whether my small attempt to depoliticize research funding in the heat of an election campaign had any effect whatsoever on the eventual bipartisan support that PI received—probably not, I would guess. Still, I do believe it is both important and ultimately productive to reassert one's principles from time to time, if only to ensure that you are not turning into an arms dealer.

CHAPTER FOURTEEN

Something Tangible

Ask any physicist about architecture and you will most likely get a general shrugging of shoulders indicative of a standard reticence to comment on matters far outside their core expertise. But ask the same physicist about the appropriateness of most physics buildings and you will invariably get a torrent of sarcastic comments and wry, bitter laughter, for it is an old adage throughout the community that in a world of ugly, ineffective and largely undesirable structures, physics buildings are almost universally the nadir of architectural achievement. It has gone so far that many experienced physicists I know, when visiting another university campus for the first time, don't even bother asking for directions to the physics building, so convinced are they that they can immediately spot its typically boxy, 1960s style hideousness.

So when I was faced with the prospect of constructing a new building from scratch, it was comforting to know that, in this area at least, the bar was fairly low: I could screw up pretty badly and still end up with a facility that was one of the best of its kind in the world. Of course, the goal was to do considerably better than that, but it was still a relief to know that in this area at least, I was pretty well guaranteed success just by attempting to design a facility that was dedicated to providing the optimal research environment.

Given how simple the basic requirements are for such a place, it's particularly perplexing why so many of them end up being so monumentally lousy. We are hardly talking about sophisticated adaptable facilities for laboratories here, with fireproof materials and special resources to handle toxic chemicals. A building for theoretical physicists is effectively just an office building: a place for people to scribble equations on pads of paper, send e-mail and download papers from the Internet.

There have to be places where people can informally discuss in groups and places for quiet reflection. There should be seminar rooms and lecture theatres as well as a small library to store standard monographs in the field and serve as a respite for those who want an additional quiet space. In recognition of the fact that physicists are human beings, it is also helpful to provide lounges, coffee machines, fitness facilities and a bistro to provide a casual, informal atmosphere that both accommodates them while tacitly recognizing that scientific discussions can happen in a wide variety of settings (particularly over food and coffee). An abundance of natural light is much appreciated, as is a general sense of aesthetics—people tend to enjoy work, and hence work better, in places that they find attractive and engaging. And then there are the obvious things not to do: don't create long, soulless corridors of offices; don't seal off researchers on separate, self-enclosed floors where they won't see each other unless they happen to meet in the elevator; don't, in short, make your precious staff (the whole purpose for your institutional existence, it is worth remembering) feel like tiny cogs in a large, Orwellian machine.

So the basic idea of what to create was pretty obvious. What was rather less obvious was how, precisely, to go about it. What I knew about architecture, even how to go about selecting architects, could be placed within a very small thimble. But I was becoming immune to those sorts of concerns at that point; virtually everything I had done to date had been embarked upon with full knowledge of my flagrant inexperience—adding yet one more thing to the list hardly seemed like that big a deal.

By the spring of 2000, we had selected the site with the dilapidated hockey rink on it and I was ready to go hunting for architects.

I contacted the local heads of the schools of architecture at the University of Toronto, Ryerson University and University of Waterloo and invited them to Waterloo to give me some background on the world of architecture and to design an appropriate selection process for the architects. We walked around the site before moving to a nearby restaurant for lunch. En route, we ambled over some train tracks on the southern edge of the property. Larry Richards, then dean of Toronto's school of architecture, asked me if the tracks were ever in use. Never having seen a train come through in all of my various wanderings, I quickly assured him that they were not. The words were barely out of my mouth before a shrill whistle pierced the air and a small cargo train of sulfuric acid came rumbling past. More credibility issues to overcome.

Richards, Ryerson's Michael Miller and Waterloo's Rick Haldenby drew up a competitive short list of various top architectural firms to compete for the contract, and both Miller and Haldenby agreed to participate in the selection process throughout. We formed a small selection committee of Haldenby, Miller, a few board members and me (Mike participated when he could, but it was understood that he might not be able to spare the time to listen to all of the presentations). The architectural experts designed a two-stage selection process where we would invite six or seven top firms to propose a brief conceptual sketch of their plans for the site. We would pick the top three ideas for the next stage of a more comprehensive proposal, after which we would make the final selection. My only contribution to the list was the name of the British firm that had designed the Newton Institute in Cambridge, England, some ten years earlier. As one of the few other buildings specifically designed with the needs of mathematical researchers in mind, it seemed reasonable to add them to the competition, which we all agreed should be international.

It was quite an interesting process, particularly for someone who had never imagined being in the position of hiring architects for a home renovation, let alone an entire building. For a couple of weeks, we were submitted to a bevy of imaginative, often intriguing pitches by the various principals of major architectural firms, striding into the presentation room with their diagrams, stylish clothes and artistic temperaments. Some seemed suffused with confidence to the point of hubris, waving aside any of our concerns while assuring us that they already had all relevant issues well and truly under control. Others seemed competent but somehow uninspiring, a bit too much like technicians. One or two were frankly unintelligible. One group stood head and shoulders above the rest: the Montreal firm, Saucier and Perrotte Architects. Their proposal incorporated many of the ideas others had remarked upon (maximizing the presence of the surrounding small lake and parkland, capitalizing on the proximity to the centre of town), but was somehow *different*, more thoughtful, more conceptually developed. Gilles Saucier and André Perrotte had obviously given considerable thought to the prospect of designing a building that incorporated both quiet reflection and a public presence, and they cleverly integrated nature throughout with combinations of light, greenery and water.

When it came time to rank the initial presentations, everyone had rated Saucier and Perrotte at the top of the list. This unexpected turn of events was too good not to capitalize on: why bother going on with another more involved round of a selection process if we were already unanimous? A few days later, a week before Christmas of 2000, I phoned Gilles and André and told them that we had decided to cut matters short and award them the contract.

I wrote a brief program of what sort of things we needed to incorporate in the building—both formal (how many offices, how many seminar rooms, size of the lecture theatre, necessity of kitchen and dining facilities) and cultural (natural light, informal interaction areas, lounge areas, coffee machines and so forth). In early 2001 André, Gilles and I travelled to Cambridge, England, to see the Newton Institute and other locales, giving them an opportunity to meet with a large number of scientists to gain a better sense of the community and to expose them to a large cross-section of views on what theorists thought was important about their work space.

Adjacent to the Newton Institute, Cambridge University's new Department of Applied Mathematics and Theoretical Physics complex was just being constructed, giving us clear examples of both what to consider and, perhaps more importantly, what to avoid. It became apparent that a widespread irritant was the excess of automation throughout—in particular, all of the window shades had been outfitted with sensors to detect sunlight so that they would raise or lower themselves automatically. This being England (a point curiously lost on the keen engineers who designed the system), the weather patterns were constantly shifting, producing varying degrees of ambient light. The high-tech window shades responded to these momentary fluctuations by constantly raising and lowering themselves, thereby providing a wholly superfluous frustration to those inside the offices simply trying to concentrate on doing a calculation.

As we neared completion of the final design, I inserted a few more specifics to the program: wood-burning fireplaces and musical acoustics in the lecture theatre, both of which proved somewhat more complicated than I had envisioned. Wood-burning fireplaces, I was assured, would be difficult. Surely gas would make more sense? No, I responded adamantly, it had to be wood. The whole point, I patiently explained, was one of atmosphere (I was actually counting on my heating systems to appropriately warm the building), and wood-burning fireplaces were vastly more pleasing, with their crackling and popping and general authenticity, than sterile gas fireplaces, which could be turned on and off with a light switch. Besides, there would be the added drama of theoretical physicists arguing about the secrets of the universe with red-hot pokers in their hands—talk about atmosphere. One has to work with what one has. In Santa Barbara, there is the beach, sunshine and a perfect climate year round. In Waterloo, it can snow from November to April. There's little point in denying the reality of a Canadian winter—you'd better find a way of dealing with it, and a roaring fire is an obviously attractive way to make it through those long winter nights. As an undergraduate, I had spent much time (arguably too much time, but never mind) in front of the large, crackling fireplaces of University of Toronto's Hart House, a faux-Gothic building that consciously invoked the academic spirit of Oxbridge colleges—an example, to my mind, of something worth copying. And so I demanded real fireplaces. Lots of them (we settled on six).

There were a few other, unique touches I had some fun with. Legend has it that glowering over the entrance to Plato's Academy was the phrase "Let no one ignorant of geometry enter here." Tipping our metaphorical hat to the rigour of the Ancient Greeks while simultaneously invoking our outreach mandate, I contacted a classicist so that I could eventually inscribe a Greek translation of "Let no one uninterested in geometry enter here" over both the north and south doors of the building. It's possible that some willful geometrical ignoramuses could penetrate the facility through another entrance, of course, but they'd have to go to a fair amount of trouble to do so.

The lecture theatre was a different matter altogether. Of course, its primary purpose was as a venue for scientific lectures, conferences and public events, but I soon started seriously thinking about the potential for music. One doesn't get a chance to build a building every day.

The idea of hosting classical music concerts in a research institute is hardly revolutionary—indeed, the curious resonance between the mathematical sciences and music is fairly well documented, and many well-established research locales, from CERN to the Institute for Advanced Study and beyond, hold regular concerts for their staff. But as we started discussing the specifics of our lecture theatre, I began to get another idea: what if we went a step or two beyond, not merely engaging solid local and regional musical talent, but taking advantage of our unique atmosphere (and the surrounding community's strong support and tradition for classical music performance) to establish ourselves as a premier, elite performance facility, where top international recording artists would come. To achieve this, much would be required, not least of which being a focus on acoustics at the outset.

We hired an acoustician and were immediately presented with both good news and bad. The good news was that the envisioned size and shape of our lecture theatre—a small shoebox—was pretty well ideal for music. The bad news was that the two envisioned uses of the space conflicted pretty starkly. The standard way of dealing with a lecture theatre is to deaden the room with absorbing surfaces (carpets, banners, etc.) and then use microphones to control and amplify the sound. With live music, on the other hand, one wants to do quite the opposite: maintain hard surfaces throughout that will suitably reflect the music coming from the stage. Obviously, I was not interested in sacrificing the use of the lecture theatre to hold lectures for the benefit of music, but equally obviously there was no way of fulfilling my dream of bringing Alfred Brendel to Perimeter Institute if the acoustics weren't top notch. In the end, the acousticians designed a system whereby the room was actually designed for music, but by creative use of additional speakers, the audio experience for lectures wouldn't be in the least bit compromised. Or so I was assured. The curious thing about the field of acoustics, I learned, is that for all of the mathematical modelling involved at the front end, there is no real way of knowing how things will work out until one listens.

Meanwhile, the site had revealed additional complications. The location was technically in a municipal park, despite the fact that the gravel parking lot surrounding the listing rink was hardly what one would imagine in a serene park-like setting. Nonetheless, this meant that any development of the site would not only involve a significant amount of interaction from the local parks committees and other city officials, it would also present challenges on how best to integrate with the community while still protecting the required privacy of a research institution. Gilles and André developed a clever solution to this particular issue by creatively using landscaping, contouring the surrounding land with hills and placing a long rectangular reflecting pool on the north side. This pool would not only become a captivating aesthetic feature, reflecting the jagged rows of north research offices from on high, but would also serve an important practical purpose: that of, effectively, a moat subtly demarcating our land from that of the surrounding public park. Meanwhile the original plans to create an Oxbridge-style courtyard inside the building were modified slightly by leaving the entire western side of the building open, thereby allowing maximum passage of sunlight inside the building in the afternoon. The two sides of the building would be connected by three bridges on two different levels, further marrying form and function while fully capitalizing on the surrounding park-like ambience.

Designing a building is not only intrinsically interesting, it has considerable secondary benefits as well. There is nothing quite like the hard constraints of a physical structure to focus the mind on concrete decisions, such as how many faculty to plan for, how many visitors to accommodate and so forth. The act of planning the building had a significant effect on the development of the entire scope of the institute.

My architectural experience also greatly amused my wife, who was otherwise pretty sick of my incessant whining about politicians, board meetings and monomaniacal physicists. I must admit that I am a spectacularly poor husband on the domestic front. I do nothing. Worse, I don't even notice when something has been done. When we first bought our Waterloo suburban home, Irena spent countless hours repainting and modernizing it in a desperate quest to move it from its brown Teutonic oppressiveness into the twenty-first century. She would typically try to finish a project whenever I was travelling somewhere for a week or so, likely because I would just screw it up if I was around when it was happening. It got to the point when I would return, fully aware that something had likely changed, but invariably at a loss as to what, precisely, it was. I usually asked her if she'd had her hair done. So when I made the mistake of confiding to her at some point that I had just spent two days in Montreal discussing the specifics of floor tiles and plumbing in a desperate effort to trim costs, it was hard to mistake the sheer ironic glee in her voice. "Really!" she exclaimed. "How interesting!"

I began to look forward to my regular meetings with Gilles and André. I had never been particularly interested in architecture, but now that I found myself in the position of designing an entire building, I had to admit that it had a certain appeal. I understood immediately that I would never have the right architectural look personally—certainly nothing like Gilles with his chic square glasses and simmering artistic temperament, but it was fun to play along. Ultimately, though, my job was to ensure the functionality of the space. I had always been nervous about the stereotypical architectural tendency to create useless monuments of stunning artistic originality rather than building facilities that actually worked, and I was naturally determined that that didn't occur in our case. In practice, this meant that all of my attention was directed to the inside of the building, leaving the exterior completely in the capable artistic hands of Gilles and André.

It was clear that the south façade would be Gilles's showpiece: this was the public face of the institute, the large side directly facing the city centre that would establish the building firmly in the public's consciousness. Every so often, though, I'd ask Gilles what it would actually look like—mostly because people kept asking me about it and I didn't have a clue as to how to respond. Gilles's eyes would light up when I'd bring up the south façade and he'd jabber on excitedly about its transformative dynamism, magnificent reflexivity and how it would be a transparent metaphor of the scientific spirit. Eventually, I gave up trying to understand what on earth he was talking about and turned my attention back to more pressing issues inside the building.

Still, I was warmly indulged by both Gilles and André, both of whom I grew to like and respect. Of course, I recognized that my comments were welcomed not so much because of my sparkling personality or keen insights, but as a direct result of my vaunted position as "the client." People laughed at my jokes and scurried to incorporate my every whim, or at least pretended to do so, furiously scribbling down every suggestion I made. Then again, they had to: I was paying.

And paying.

When I first told people about our intention to build a brand new facility, I was ruefully informed by each of my more experienced acquaintances that rest assured, like any construction effort, it would be over time and over budget, and that my job was to do everything possible to minimize both. Trying to take the bull by the horns, we hired a cost consultant before we went to tender at the end of 2001 and discovered that the expected total was, indeed, over budget. I met with Gilles and André for intensive cost-cutting meetings to whittle things down to size before resubmitting the plans to the consultants. The projections, infuriatingly, rose. Desperate to put an end to the madness, we elected to go to tender. The price was considerably higher still.

And so to the joys of construction. Everyone who has been involved in even the most basic home renovation knows construction can be a terribly frustrating experience. Fortunately for me, I had had no such experience and therefore had no clear understanding of what I was in for.

Let me begin by elucidating some clear principles: Everybody who is involved in construction is a scoundrel. Nobody tells the truth. Ever. Nothing gets done on time and it's always somebody else's fault. Once you understand these basic principles, all the consequences follow pretty naturally.

Of course, true to form, we had additional complications. I soon discovered that before the hockey rink, our site was actually the city dump. Before that, it was a swamp. There was a reason the old arena was falling down. For the first few months, we drove hundreds of piles into the ground, constantly ringing the air with reverberating metal spikes, much to the annoyance of the locals who were actively pining for the good old days of quiet hockey games with all of the violence contained to the ice surface.

My projections led me to believe that we would outgrow our temporary space in the old post office by 2003 and would need to move into the new building by the fall of that year. Heeding the warnings of my jaded construction-savvy friends, I insisted to all and sundry that our target date for completion should be the spring of 2003, figuring that when the inevitably missed deadlines occurred, we would still be in a position to move in by the fall. Clever, no? This whole construction thing, I said to myself confidently, wasn't all that difficult: it just required careful managing and planning.

Well. We moved in by the fall, which was indeed an accomplishment of sorts. Except that it was the fall of 2004. The truth is that we still might be waiting to move in had I not, out of sheer frustration, planned a grand opening gala for early October of that year and managed to procure the prime minister's attendance to cut the appropriate ribbons. Suffice it to say that the pace of work during September 2004 was impressively frenetic, particularly towards the end of the month.

But we made it (with about six hours to spare) and the opening gala was a large success. We decided, just for the hell of it, to make it a black tie affair, quite possibly the only time in the history of the world that there has been a political black tie physics function. From my perspective, I felt that if I had to be forced to participate in the barbaric ritual of wrapping a cord tightly around my neck, I might as well do it in style. We had full press coverage, a "time capsule" (I remember thinking, as I penned a few phrases unthinkingly in between countless other last-minute tasks, that I should probably spend more time writing the text of something that is destined to be read one hundred years later) and a delightful private concert by Holly Cole, one of my favourites (another perk of being the boss). Prime Minister Paul Martin did indeed drop by to make a speech in the lecture theatre on the importance of innovation, science, scholarship, philanthropy and all of that before cutting the appropriate ribbon (he got the biggest one) with other dignitaries. We had requested that he stay for the dinner as well, entreating him with promises of hobnobbing with Nobel Laureates and other international scientific stars whom we had invited, but he politely demurred—one can have only so much science and innovation in one day, I suppose.

One of the scientific superstars I had cajoled into coming after considerable difficulty (thanks largely to the efforts of PI Associate Cliff Burgess, one of his former students) was Steven Weinberg. Weinberg has always been one of my heroes—a brilliantly incisive physicist who made many seminal contributions to our understanding of the Standard Model (in particular, the unification of the weak nuclear force and electromagnetism, for which he won the Nobel Prize), he is a formidable character of the unabashedly "no bullshit" school of physics and has, to invoke Douglas Adams, a head the size of a planet. When the seating arrangements for the head table were produced, I noticed that I was slated to be next to Weinberg. "NO!" I shouted, horrified, to my unfortunate assistant, who was doubtless shocked by such a negative response to an issue as benign as seating arrangements, which typically had no effect on me. "I will *not* sit next to Steven Weinberg!" I continued. "I know what he's

252 · FIRST PRINCIPLES

going to do. He's going to look me in the eye and ask 'what are you working on?' and I'm going to have to say something intelligent and sufficiently impressive to one of the smartest people alive, which I'm absolutely positive will be completely beyond me right now. I'm MCing the event and I don't need this right now!" So we moved Weinberg across the table and I sat next to Jim Hartle instead—an equally impressive intellect, but far more familiar with my limitations. (The next day I told Weinberg about my anxieties. He laughed and told me that I had done a good job as MC before piercing me with an intense look and asking, "So what are you working on?" I scurried away.)

The dinner was particularly special for me because it provided a unique opportunity to publicly acknowledge the debt we all owed to Mike for making Perimeter possible. After conferring privately with his wife, I decided to name the lecture theatre after him (the Mike Lazaridis Theatre of Ideas) and composed a laudatory plaque detailing his generosity and passion for science. I was most excited about the opportunity of surprising him with this on the opening night.

At the same time, I had dedicated the library to the memory of founding board member George Leibbrandt, the man who had quietly done so much to both support me and bring the institute to fruition. Watching George's family unveil the plaque in his honour was an especially moving moment.

The opening gala was actually a two day affair, beginning with the aforementioned invitation-only, black tie physics schmooze followed the next day by a public open house complete with tours of the building, hands-on physics demonstrations for kids and five successive lectures to the general public by the aforementioned international scientific luminaries: Steven Weinberg, Roger Penrose, Tony Leggett, Jim Hartle and Juan Maldacena.

The University of Waterloo, never one to miss an opportunity for a free ride, quickly sprang into action, requesting the chance to bestow honorary degrees to the lecturers we invited. This, I was told, would necessitate turning our lecture theatre into official UW territory for a few hours the next morning, like a monarch temporarily annexing territory to the realm. I shrugged my shoulders. Whatever. As long as our guests were not put out it made not a whit of difference to me.

In the end, everything went fine, of course. Steven Weinberg stood up and gave a glowing speech on the global importance of Perimeter Institute, understandably confused that he was now temporarily on UW soil.

More than 8,000 members of the general public happily trudged through our building later that day, soaking up the lectures and enthusiastically touring the facilities inside and out. Not for the first time, I was amazed at the power of local pride and how enthusiastically our community was determined to embrace a physics institute, of all things.

This pride would be severely tested several days later, however, when Lisa Rochon, the architecture critic for *The Globe and Mail*, wrote a glowing review of our new building emblazoned with the loud headline "This in a city of exceeding ugliness." After a couple of paragraphs of enthusiastic introduction, Ms Rochon began her third, "Bizarrely, this story comes to you from Waterloo, Ont., a city of surpassing ugliness," before taking a shot at "the strategies of car-dominated planning that have created Waterloo's version of dystopia."

Suffice it to say that this rather strident prose caused significant distress among the good burghers of Waterloo as they scrambled to reconcile their pride in the positive attention shown to their latest building in the national press with the harsh indictment of the entire region. The *Kitchener-Waterloo Record* promptly called to get my views. What did I think of the Rochon piece? Wasn't it awfully unfair? Did we really live in an ugly city? An exceedingly ugly city?

"Well," I replied cautiously, doggedly pushing aside any thoughts of the hideous purple and green neon signs that dominated the strip-mall-riddled town as I contemplated how best to respond productively to this question while not becoming a local pariah, "that's really not for me to say." I was merely grateful that our building was recognized for its unique accomplishments and its contribution to the international architectural scene. Perhaps unsurprisingly, this evasion worked remarkably well. There was no immediate follow-up— "Yes, but what do you actually think of Waterloo? Is there anything to what Rochon says, in your view? How might we improve things around here more generally?"—that one might expect under the circumstances, likely because most people were so taken aback by Rochon's salvo they were unable to countenance that she might actually have a point. Instead, the article was perceived as a cheap shot, like a spontaneous attack on the intellectual acuity of one's kindly old aunt: sure, she was hardly an Einstein, but was that really fair? There weren't many Einsteins around anyway. Leave the poor woman alone.

It was summarily concluded that Rochon's attack must have been personally motivated. Frantic investigations revealed that she had pursued undergraduate studies here: obviously she had been traumatized by some intensely disagreeable personal event that had left her with an irrational bitterness for our community. The mayor publicly invited her to come back to meet him for lunch and a regional tour so that he could gently demonstrate the error of her ways. To the best of my knowledge, she never took him up on it.

Meanwhile, the building went on to gain an increasing amount of recognition. Gilles and André were chosen as the sole Canadian architectural representatives for the 2005

Venice Biennale and prominently featured our new facility in their display. The building won an Ontario Architecture Award, a Quebec Architecture Award (which has always confused me, given that our building is some distance away from Quebec, but never mind) and, ultimately, the Governor General's Award, the highest architectural recognition offered in Canada. In rather typical Canadian fashion, the Governor General herself didn't actually show up at the awards ceremony, which is vaguely disconcerting when one considers that giving out awards and shaking hands is pretty well the sum total of her job description as the Queen's representative.

At any rate, awards are all well and good, but far more important is whether or not the place actually works. By and large, I think it does: most scientists I talk to are decidedly impressed by the place, not only because of its obvious aesthetic and functional features, but because its very presence demonstrates our determination to do whatever we can to create the optimal research experience.

To successfully compete with the best the world has to offer, one has to be both focused and realistic. We can make no credible claim to a proud and glorious intellectual tradition on par with Princeton or Oxford, we hardly have the most idyllic climate and the surrounding environs are, if not exceedingly ugly, seldom identified with the most picturesque parts of the country. No, the only way we can hope to vie with the top places in the world is if we tangibly demonstrate to the global theoretical physics community that we are aggressively determined to use all of our effort and resources to construct the ideal research environment, and the building is naturally a key aspect in that equation.

There are good reasons to feel confident that this approach is working: after all, it's getting to be time to build another one.

CHAPTER FIFTEEN

Reflections on Past and Future

There is only one argument for doing something; the rest are arguments for doing nothing. The argument for doing something is that it is the right thing to do. But then, of course, comes the difficulty making sure that it is right.

—F. M. Cornford, *Microcosmographia Academica*

So what have we really done?

Looking back now, more than seven years since this strange odyssey began, it is worth taking stock. Much of the original plan has been established: the creation of a high-level, internationally recognized physics institute focused on several overlapping areas of foundational physics within a uniquely diverse and tolerant intellectual culture. We are broadly integrated with the surrounding academic community while still vigilantly maintaining our independence and flexibility. We built an award-winning, tailor-made facility, achieved solid government support and developed a comprehensive series of programs and products to promote the wonder and mystery of theoretical physics to the general public. We're off to a good start.

Along the way, of course, we have certainly had our share of surprises.

The Scientific Advisory Committee, originally envisioned as a stodgy collection of conservative academics that would provide a balanced, sober check on the freewheeling innovation of our dynamic research staff, has frequently demonstrated an amusing tendency to be quite the opposite, suggesting innovative ways to capitalize on the institute's unique structural strengths, often inciting surprised reactions from some of our faculty.

The internal sociology, too, has produced a few unexpected developments. For an institute deliberately structured to address the much ballyhooed stereotypes of closed-minded arrogance typically associated with the superstring community, it is rather amusing, and not a little ironic, that our string theorists are frequently regarded as the most tolerant, knowledgeable and open-minded physicists at the institute, firmly committed to the unique culture of Perimeter and determined to establish us as an innovative and dynamic centre of top level scholarship. Of course, the best intentions are meaningless if one can't attract the right people to make things happen. It is one thing to spew fine words about creating a culture of interaction between different approaches to foundational issues in quantum gravity, but without open-minded and mathematically sophisticated scientists on both sides, no such interaction will occur. Similarly, being on the cusp of a new era in foundational cosmology will only revolutionize our understanding of nature if we can continue to recruit the brightest young minds on the planet into the mix.

I will proudly admit that I am particularly inspired by the heavy lifting being done by our dynamic young faculty members. I think it's safe to say that the spirit of the

Institute (both in terms of research and, amusingly enough, administration) is now largely driven by the likes of Freddy Cachazo, Jaume Gomis, Justin Khoury, Daniel Gottesman and Laurent Freidel—names that may not yet register significantly with the general public, but are becoming increasingly respected and influential in the scientific community. That is as it should be. The torch has not just been passed—it is being taken up with increasing fervour by a new generation of physicists anxious to make the Perimeter dream their own.

So, we're off to a good start, I think. But where will we end up? That, of course, is the key question.

The answer, equally obviously, is that I simply don't know.

But I do know it is important to be realistic, to be objective. It is vital not to believe one's own press, to rest contently on one's accomplishments and declare that true excellence has been achieved, the game is over, we have won. Because we haven't. Not by a long shot.

We are, in my view, pretty well precisely where one could have reasonably hoped we would be after the initial few years of research operations. We are poised to achieve real greatness and have managed to attract some genuinely top quality people. We have tried to capitalize on our competitive advantage: our independence, flexibility, resources and unique culture of having the convenience of North America within an immigration-friendly modern social democratic framework. We have successfully picked some reasonable research areas to focus on (such as quantum information theory), which not only had a natural intellectual overlap with other areas, but were also strategic targets of opportunity given the slow response of many established institutions. By moving proactively, we had the chance to recruit top theorists to Waterloo, working in tandem with UW's burgeoning IQC. We have become a powerful global force in quantum gravity research and established a pioneering program in quantum foundations; we have a highly respected and progressive string theory effort and are enthusiastically constructing a dynamic young group of the next generation of theoretical cosmologists, all the while actively turning our sights on particle physics, condensed matter physics and other fundamental areas. Our researchers have produced many excellent, top-cited papers and the institute has hosted several original and productive conferences. We have received an emphatically positive endorsement of all of this, and more, from an objective scientific review committee commissioned by the National Science and Engineering Research Council.

We have raised some eyebrows, we have earned some respect, we have become noticed by the top places. We are on a most interesting trajectory. We are loaded with potential. But we are not yet there.

When Perimeter becomes the natural destination for virtually all the top postdoctoral fellows in the world in the majority of our research areas, we will have arrived. When more of the most prestigious theorists clamour to visit than can be accommodated at any given time, we will have made it. When I travel to Stanford and Princeton and Oxford and there is a distinct sense of fear behind their researchers' current expressions of lively interest and curiosity, then the landscape will have shifted in our favour.

That this is even possible for a Canadian institution, that one can now talk with a straight face about the relative chances of a Waterloo-based theoretical physics institute one day attaining genuine international prominence, is an unquestionably significant accomplishment. But it is not enough. It is not enough to play the game, however intrinsically Canadian that sentiment might be. One should play to win.

Because winning in this context is not some mindless macho game, some childish quest to grab the top spot in the international academic pecking order so as to crow the loudest and beat one's breasts with monomaniacal satisfaction. To win here means gaining the opportunity to lead: to pioneer new and effective approaches to understanding nature's profoundest secrets; to drive the scientific culture forward rather than carping from the sidelines; to galvanize both government and international public opinion towards a renewed appreciation for science and scientific principles; to assume a genuine position of global leadership.

There is so much to do. I am pleased, for example, that we have already managed to create a top international group of researchers in quantum foundations, making PI perhaps the worldwide leader in this often overlooked endeavour. But it is not enough. Ultimately, where will our postdocs go after their tenure at PI? It is one thing to start a group in an institute, and quite another to change the prevailing culture in any substantive way.

Typically, discussions along these lines among quantum foundations-friendly researchers generate into general bemoaning of underfunding, lack of resources, petty hostility from "orthodox" members of the physics establishment and so forth. Much of this, I feel, is an inappropriate response. If the goal is to somehow redress a key scientific omission, to dedicate resources towards an essential topic in theoretical physics that has been erroneously ignored for a combination of reasons ranging from complexity to confusion to a false sense of intractability, then we must do much more than wag our finger at the prevailing orthodoxy, hem and haw about the intrinsic difficulties of suitably defining our terms and snidely accuse our detractors of closed mindedness. The essential argument to be made is not simply that this area is underfunded (which is certainly true for a wide spectrum of activities, most of which I would be personally horrified to see funded), but rather that it is intrinsically worth supporting. We must make the case.

To this end, I recently developed a somewhat (but only somewhat) tongue-in-cheek notion, the Wilczek test. I pictured myself sitting across the table from Frank Wilczek while he was making skeptical comments about the value of the institute's various efforts in quantum foundations. Rather than launching a counterattack, accusing Frank of being anti-philosophical, dogmatic and so forth (which, as it happens, he most definitely is not), the onus is on us to mount a clear and substantive response, justifying our support while clarifying what, precisely, we are supporting: What were the current open problems in the field? What are the active avenues of research to address these issues? What were some concrete past accomplishments? How, specifically, has the field impacted other areas of physics?

Mounting such a spirited, thoughtful defense requires considerable self-reflection and rigour in and of itself. Understanding the skepticism that surrounds a field of study plagued by considerable vagueness and lack of definition is hardly unreasonable and demands an honest, comprehensive response if one wishes to be taken seriously. Perimeter's great opportunity is not simply that it supports foundations, but that it does so squarely within the broader context of a fully-fledged theoretical physics institute that allows for (nay, demands) regular, critical exchange with its various practitioners.

To pass the Wilczek test, then, does not necessarily involve converting the skeptics to one's cause, but rather making the effort to present a serious case that could, in principle, do so. And if it can be somehow determined that this cannot be done, then it hardly seems worth supporting the entire enterprise. That too, would be a form of progress.

All of this is precisely the sort of thing I am referring to when I talk of taking a leadership role and doing our part to positively affect the future of physics. From quantum foundations to quantum computing, cosmological conundrums to whatever weirdness the Large Hadron Collider (LHC)—the world's largest high-energy particle collider—throws at us in the years ahead, there is so much to do, so much to understand, so much to solve. And we have a glorious opportunity to be right in the thick of it.

Government officials everywhere like to measure things through the filter of competition. In their zeal to embrace the market, I think they often miss the point, particularly when it comes to science. Who cares if the ultimate scientific breakthrough happens in Singapore or Santa Barbara, Warsaw or Waterloo? The essential thing is to use one's best efforts to ensure that it happens somewhere, but in practice a wonderful way to do just that is to make everyone feel appropriately anxious that the other guys are getting ahead of them so that they need to invest ever increasing amounts to catch up. If you are the leader, you can intelligently drive this process forward. But if you are consistently mired in the middle of the pack, you're all too often reduced to irrelevancy.

It's ever so much more fun to lead than to follow.

To Canadian ears, this might seem a glib and immature conclusion. We're talking about serious policy issues here—what difference does it make if these things are fun? But this is, I think, a pivotal part of the problem.

In fact, the whole notion of fun, with its natural connotations of self-indulgent frivolousness, is drastically underappreciated in Canada, with corresponding, shall we say, serious consequences. To have fun is to be creative, to play, to imagine, to dream. To have fun involves not taking yourself so seriously, not worrying so much about what your neighbours are doing, being unafraid to let your hair down, to take a chance. We are not, sadly, a particularly fun people and we pay the price for it.

For all those Canadian bureaucrats and think-tank denizens who are fretting that we're not innovative enough, plowing through policy papers on how we might structure matters to come up with more good ideas or devise algorithms to increase the number of entrepreneurs, here's a suggestion: Get out of your office and get on a plane. Drop in on a company like Google and watch how people talk to each other. Go to any scientific group meeting at a top university or research laboratory and observe how researchers interact. Get invited to a dinner party in London.

What will you notice? People are actually having fun. They are enjoying themselves. They are at play in the theatre of ideas. And they are, ever so naturally, ever so spontaneously, ever so delightfully creating.

I know a bit about this, because the last seven years have been enormously fun for me.

I have chatted with Stephen Hawking, lunched with Carlo Rovelli, dined with Lenny Susskind and laughed with Nima Arkani-Hamed. I have been impressed by Gia Dvali, intimidated by Steven Weinberg, challenged by Frank Wilczek, critiqued by Ed Witten, overwhelmed by Slava Mukhanov, humbled by Juan Maldacena, charmed by Tony Leggett, supported by Paul Steinhardt, prodded by Steve Shenker, ridiculed by Antony Valentini, engaged by Gerard Milburn, assisted by Jorge Pullin, delighted by Artur Ekert, consoled by Jim Hartle, inspired by John Preskill, stimulated by Chris Isham, encouraged by Roger Penrose and questioned by Scott Tremaine.

I have amused myself by interviewing nervous, yellow-tied financial types to manage our endowment a few scant months after having narrowly escaped the soulless world of derivative modelling, and I have listened, quietly enraptured and over-whelmed with emotion, in the darkened back row of our theatre as Emanuel Ax rehearsed a Brahms Ballade for an upcoming evening performance.

I have spoken with enthusiastic high-school students and been profoundly moved by the gratitude of appreciative high-school teachers. I have chatted with historians, jazz musicians and artists and had the marvellous opportunity to invite and meet numerous authors to participate in our outreach pro-grams simply because I was intrigued by what they had written.

I have travelled around the world and met with some of the most impressive intellects alive today.

I built a building with its own bistro and chef.

I've had a blast.

And the truth is that at some level I wouldn't have done any of it if it hadn't been fun, if it hadn't been something I believed in. And neither, needless to say, would Mike, who seemed to be having an equally enjoyable time watching PI develop while he rocketed BlackBerry to international promi-nence. Fun matters.

I sometimes think back to when I was doing my PhD at the University of Waterloo, fervently working away in a cor-ner somewhere to master material that was eluding me, usually without anyone around to answer my many questions. And now here, suddenly, is this institute, this thing I built filled with dozens of people who could give me detailed answers of countless problems without even looking up from their cal-culations. But I don't have time to ponder those sorts of questions anymore.

"Do you work at Perimeter Institute too?" I am asked with increasing frequency these days; and I am always a bit taken aback, like a novelist invited to have dinner with one of his fictional characters. "Perimeter Institute!" I feel like responding, "C'est moi!" But it's not, of course. Not any more. Not for a very long time now.

It is home to ten full-time faculty and eight part-time associates, passionately enthusiastic professional scientists who are intent on establishing the place in the uppermost echelons of international excellence.

It is a natural point of attraction to researchers who picked up and moved to Waterloo from California, from France, from Germany, from Australia—people who started families and bought houses here. Since we began research in 2001 we've attracted fifty postdocs, forty graduate students and more than 700-odd visitors. We've produced more than 700 scientific publications, hosted more than thirty international conferences and held more than 800 in-house seminars.

It is an enterprise assisted by a collection of some of the world's most eminent professional scientists and governed by a board of dedicated volunteers.

It is the recipient of more than $150 million in public funding from provincial, federal and municipal governments and a strong source of community pride.

It is a summer destination for high-school students and science teachers and a burgeoning focal point for science outreach for the general public.

And it is the workplace of many extremely dedicated administrative support staff, proudly determined to do whatever they can to create the optimal research experience for our staff, from IT to the bistro, visitor logistics to conference support.

We even have our own HR department now to handle a wide variety of functions, including the occasional unsolicited request for employment.

Or you can write to me directly.

Epilogue

Or not.

I left my position as executive director of Perimeter Institute in June 2007 after an all-too-abrupt announcement a few weeks earlier. The official reason given for my departure was that contract negotiations broke down, but I think it's fair to say that such a justification hinges on a particularly loose interpretation of the word "negotiations." In any event, based on the veritable deluge of e-mails and phone calls I received shortly after the formal announcement, the scientific community was stunned—not so much by the fact that I was leaving, but rather by the highly unusual and, shall we say, corporate manner in which the decision was so obviously effected.

For that was the rub. The fact that I would one day leave PI confused nobody. I had always maintained I was not interested in doing this for the rest of my life and there were good reasons to see that, having built the place, I would naturally wish to move on to other things. In many ways, the particular time was also not inappropriate: PI had been firmly established in the scientific community (as witnessed by the laudatory, objective NSERC review in the fall of 2006); it had recently garnered sufficient operational funding from government

($100 million) to last for the next five years; and had lately adopted a tenure policy to attract and retain internationally established senior faculty. Had things been done in the usual, reasonable way for academic institutions—had I announced that I was leaving in a year or so after devoting the lion's share of the interim period to rigorously search for a successor with other key members of the institute—nobody would have batted an eye, and the scientific community would have accepted the situation as what it would have been: a genuine opportunity for finding the right person to take the institute to the next level.

Unfortunately, that was not the case.

And so the research community, both inside PI and out, was left completely mystified as to what happened. My contract was not renewed, but the board had expressed nothing but unbounded satisfaction with the direction of the institute and my leadership, explicitly denying that this move had anything whatsoever to do with my vision of PI's future progress.

Odd. Perhaps I just suddenly up and left, then, wooed away by an offer I couldn't refuse?

No, that didn't seem to be the case, either; and after some time it became clear to the research staff that I never had any intention of suddenly walking away in such an abrupt fashion, which I naturally understood would be highly deleterious to the institute and its standing in the international scientific community. So what on earth had happened?

What happened, so far as I can determine, is the book you hold in your very hands. Bizarre as it may seem, it appears that a major preoccupation of the institute's board of directors for the first six months of 2007 was what to do about this pernicious book, followed closely, presumably, by how to get rid of its author who had the brazen temerity to once again bring the dark story forward publicly.

A good question to ask the author of any book—and one that, in my humble opinion, is not asked nearly often enough—is simply why write? What are you trying to achieve by publication? What message are you so insistent on broadcasting and who is your audience?

In this particular case, the answer is both simple and frighteningly mundane. Over the years I have given countless speeches and lectures and written hundreds of articles and commentaries explaining what the institute is, why it was created, what it hoped to accomplish and why I was convinced it was so deserving of widespread support. This is all par for the course: recruiting scientists necessarily involves a careful articulation of what you stand for and what you hope to accomplish; soliciting funding requires the same, albeit presented in a rather different manner as does, in yet a third way, the prospect of galvanizing public support for both our scientific and outreach agenda.

Under the circumstances, I naturally feel quite apologetic for the contents of this manuscript. While it is certainly true that I could have included some more colourful and contentious anecdotes from a variety of quarters—potential conflicts of interest, questionably mixed agendas, the odd unsolicited suggestion to concentrate on rather dubious areas of scientific inquiry—I naturally went some distance to refrain from mentioning any of this sort of thing.

In my more whimsical moments of iconoclastic daydreaming, I have often wished that I might one day write something that would be deemed dangerously heretical and

270 · FIRST PRINCIPLES

subversive by the authorities of the day, forthrightly standing in opposition to the philistine hordes by boldly speaking truth to power and all that. But the very idea that this book, with its mild protestations and wilful determination to err on the side of self-deprecation, somehow became my Voltairean moment, my cause célèbre to man the barricades in defense of freedom of expression was, quite frankly, little short of mind-boggling. Hardly what I had in mind, needless to say. Further proof, if any more were needed, that it's always good practice to be very careful what you ask for.

The obvious conclusion to draw from this affair (and one the vast majority of people around me seem to have unhesitatingly assumed) is that the entire imbroglio was some absurd clash of egos, with Mike and myself vying to take credit for building the institute. It is hard to feel that there isn't at least some grain of truth to that interpretation, but I must confess that the whole business is all still, frankly, mystifying to me. It is true that, given my role, I'm naturally convinced Perimeter Institute wouldn't have occurred without me (at least not anywhere near its current shape). It is also overwhelmingly obvious that it wouldn't have occurred without Mike (in any shape).

I hope by now it is clear that the reason my account of the history of the institute is so personal is that, in my view, it is necessarily personal: to understand why things were done it is important to know the motivations, passions and principles of the key players involved. I can't speak for Mike, obviously, but throughout the book, just as throughout the countless other related pieces I have authored on the subject of the history and orientation of Perimeter Institute, I have tried my best to be as accurate and respectful as possible. This is, as it happens, not terribly difficult: Mike Lazaridis launched a remarkable philanthropic foray for basic science, setting a global standard that still resonates around the world. Would that only a tiny fraction of the world's wealthy copy his actions in any number of meritorious avenues and our planet would be a vastly improved place. Three large cheers for him.

I sincerely hope that this whole ridiculous business of personalities is irrelevant. After all, the true test of the success of an institution, the correct evaluation of whether or not one has "made a difference" is integrally related to whether or not the important values and culture of the place can survive beyond the character of its founders and continue to flourish at the highest possible level, embraced by future generations. That is the important question; that is the "legacy." Nothing else matters.

And yet, I am convinced that there are important lessons to be learned from this experience in matters of public policy. How is it possible, I wonder, that a charitable organization essentially running off public funds has no effective oversight of the board of directors? How is it possible that governments can invest in excess of $150 million to a scientific organization without acquiring, or even requesting, a seat on the board? How is it possible that the executive director of such a publicly funded institute could effectively have no recourse to meaningfully interact with the board of directors during a time of crisis?

One hears a lot about board governance these days, but almost all of that concerns corporate boards (Sarbanes-Oxley and all of that). Appropriate regulation of corporate boards is naturally important, and I certainly don't claim a great deal of expertise in this particular area. But I wonder if it isn't at least equally important to ensure that publicly funded nonprofit boards are adequately monitored. The primary goal of corporations is simply to make money—it is hardly surprising then, that the knives only come out when the company totters financially and there is a corresponding motivation to sweep any potential regulatory improprieties under the rug so long as profits are made and the shares are rising. In the not-for-profit sector, on the other hand, the financial incentive is removed, making evaluations of proper procedures and good governance particularly essential to ensure that an organization's fundamental goals are achieved. If the organization is wholly private, any unusual practices are its own affair, so long as no laws are broken. But if the entity in question is demonstrably supported by taxpayers dollars, surely the government has an obligation to do its utmost to consistently ensure that best practices are being followed at all levels. Isn't that what it means to really have a stake in the future of the enterprise?

Such concerns are particularly appropriate not because I believe PI and other similarly meritorious philanthropic initiatives shouldn't be strongly supported by government—as I hope has been made clear by the preceding pages, I am firmly of the view that they should be—but because if the model is to be emulated and improved upon, if worthy private-public partnerships are to be expanded in number and impact (as I would sincerely like them to be), then the onus is on the public sector to do its utmost to ensure that both funding and oversight of such organizations is regular, thorough and as firmly removed from political considerations as possible.

Based on my experiences, I'm convinced that the vast majority of civil servants, consistently striving valiantly to create and enforce fair, productive and responsible mechanisms for the handling of taxpayers' money, would strongly agree with these sentiments. Meanwhile, the political realm struggles with its own pressures and criteria, even when simply trying to demonstrate appropriate leadership and create innovative policies.

It is, of course, a complicated issue. But it is an important one to get right.

Acknowledgements

One seldom gets a chance to stop and recognize so many of those who, by their actions, had an important impact in the development of an idea, and I'm pleased to have the opportunity to take a moment to acknowledge my sincere appreciation to the many people I have met who have made such a positive impression on both Perimeter Institute and me personally:

Ian Affleck, Andy Albrecht, Stephan Alexander, Jan Ambjorn, Nima Arkani-Hamed, Michele Austin, Emanuel Ax, Jonathan Barrett, John Baez, Charles Bennett, John Berlinsky, Dick Bond, Steve Bradwell, Robert Brandenberger, Gilles Brassard, Colleen Brickman, John Brodie, Harvey Brown, Jim Brown, Tom Brzustowski, Jeff Bub, Alex Buchel, Cliff Burgess, Ed Burtynsky, Jeremy Butterfield, Freddy Cachazo, Arthur Carty, Amit Chakma, Edna Cheung, Jean Chrétien, Michel Chrétien, Dan Christensen, Joy Christian, Richard Cleve, Alan Coley, Rob Corless, Don Couch, Bianca Dittrich, George Dixon, David DiVicenzo, Jennifer Dodd, Fay Dowker, Olaf Dreyer, Paul Dufour, Gia Dvali, Paul Eichinger, Artur Ekert, Victor Elias, Herb Epp, Richard Epp, Simon Farbrother, Janet Fesnoux, Dave Fish, Chris Fuchs, Jerome Gauntlett, Jack Gegenberg, Steve Giddings, Eddie Goldenberg, Daniel Gottesman, Debbie Guenther, Sheena Gilks, Rick Haldenby,

David Hanes, Peter Harder, Lucien Hardy, Bill Harper, Jim Hartle, Greg Hillis, Steffan Hofmann, Gary Horowitz, Mike Hudson, Viqar Husain, Ted Jacobson, Cecilia Jarlskog, Clifford Johnson, David Johnston, Catherine Kallin, Nemanja Kaloper, LeeAnne Kane, Gabriel Karl, Sheri Keffer, Adrian Kent, Robin Khortals, Justin Khoury, Igor Klebanov, Ken Knox, Roman Koniuk, David Kribs, Gabor Kunstatter, Raymond Laflamme, Brian Lasher, Hon Lau, Tony Leggett, George Leibbrandt, Matt Leifer, Daneil Lidar, Etera Levine, Hoi-Kwong Lo, Renate Loll, Fred Longstaffe, Mike Luke, Dan Lynch, Kevin Lynch, Richard MacKenzie, Juan Maldacena, Rob Mann, Fotini Markopoulou, David Mateos, John Matlock, John McCormick, Art McDonald, Dalton McGuinty, Gerry McKeon, Tim McTiernan, Catherine Meusburger, Gerard Milburn, Volodya Miransky, John Moffat, Marie-Lucie Morin, Michele Mosca, Slava Mukhanov, Wayne Myrvold, Michael Nielsen, Kathleen Okruhlik, Garnet Ord, Amanda Peet, André Perrote, Itamar Pitowsky, Eric Poisson, Joe Polchinski, Dawn Poll, Damian Pope, Sandu Popescu, Maxim Pospelov, Stefan Pregelj, John Preskill, Laurier Proulx, Jorge Pullin, Claudia de Rahm, Karen Redman, Michael Reisenberger, Greg Romanick, Lisa Romanick, Carlo Rovelli, Moshe Rozali, Gilles Saucier, Simon Saunders, Konstantin Savvidis, Sue Scanlan, Kristen Schleich, John Schwarz, Adel Sedra, Gordon Semenoff, Steve Shenker, Peter Shor, John Sipe, Constantinos Skordis, Simone Speziale, John Stachel, Andrei Starinets, Jacob Stauttener, Joseph Stauttener, Tom Steele, Aephraim Steinberg, Tom Stockie, David Strangway, Leonard Susskind, Danny Terno, Max Tegmark, Barbara Terhal, Thomas Theimann, Andrew Tolley, Peter Tremaine, Michael Turner, Bill Unruh, Ram Valluri, Vlatko Vedral, John Watrous, Steve Weinstein, Karen Wiatowski, Frank Wilczek, Oliver Winkler, Mark Wise,

Elizabeth Witmer, Don Witt, Lynne Wolstencroft, Mark Wyman and Anton Zeilinger.

It has truly been a pleasure working with all of you.

Particular Perimeter appreciation on both the personal and professional front goes out to Michael Duschenes, Laurent and Nathalie Freidel, Jaume and Sheila Gomis, Chris Isham, Rob and Renée Myers, Roger Penrose, Lee Smolin, Paul Steinhardt and Scott Tremaine. This book has had a rather curious history and I am grateful to many people for their support and assistance throughout the last couple of interesting years.

My agent, Linda McKnight, has been nothing less than a jewel. Without her, *First Principles* would most likely never have seen the light of day. Related thanks as well to Michael Levine, who got the ball rolling with Linda and WCA as well as Jordan Fenn and the entire team at Key Porter.

On a personal level, I would like to take a moment to extend my sincere appreciation to Andrew Abouchar, Sasha and Richard Judelson-Kelly, Harriet Millstone, Don McCutchan, my parents, Ron Pushchak, John Spearn, and Antony Valentini, whom I somehow can't bring myself to put in the above 'PI category' and was, amusingly, right all along.

Finally, it seems to be standard practice in many circles to recognize the heroic sacrifices that one's spouse and family has made in putting up with the distracted author during the creation and publication process. This is hardly the sort of scholarly work that would normally warrant such comments, and yet I can't help but feel that they may be more particularly apt in this case. So heartfelt gratitude to Irena, Louis and Emmy for teaching me about what is truly important. Eventually, even I get it.

Index